NAG HAMMADI STUDIES

VOLUME XIV

NAG HAMMADI STUDIES

EDITED BY

MARTIN KRAUSE - JAMES M. ROBINSON
FREDERIK WISSE

IN CONJUNCTION WITH

ALEXANDER BÖHLIG – JEAN DORESSE – SØREN GIVERSEN
HANS JONAS – RODOLPHE KASSER – PAHOR LABIB
GEORGE W. MACRAE – JACQUES-É. MÉNARD – TORGNY SÄVE-SÖDERBERGH
WILLEM CORNELIS VAN UNNIK – R. McL. WILSON
JAN ZANDEE

XIV

VOLUME EDITOR
R. McL. WILSON

LEIDEN
E. J. BRILL
1978

NAG HAMMADI
AND GNOSIS

Papers read at the First International Congress
of Coptology
(Cairo, December 1976)

EDITED BY

R. McL. WILSON

LEIDEN
E. J. BRILL
1978

ISBN 90 04 05760 9

PRINTED IN BELGIUM

CONTENTS

INTRODUCTION

At its meeting in Cairo in December 1970, the International Committee for the publication of the Nag Hammadi Codices envisaged as its primary task the preparation and publication of a complete facsimile edition of these texts, and in the years that followed this aim was energetically pursued. At the date of writing, eight volumes have been published, and others are in active preparation, so that there is every reason to expect that the project will soon be completed. It is hoped that a complete English-language edition will be available by the end of 1977, and plans are also on foot for editions in French and German.

Dr. Pahor Labib's photographic edition of 1956, with the subsequent publication of translations of the texts which it contained, and also the publication of texts from the Codex Jung, had already led by 1970 to an impressive quantity of scholarly publication. The committee therefore anticipated a similar acceleration of research as the result of the publication of the facsimile edition.

A second function which the committee had in view was the furtherance of Coptic studies in general, and as the facsimile edition neared its completion steps were taken to fulfil this second project. In December 1976 the First International Congress of Coptology was held in Cairo under the auspices of the Egyptian Antiquities Organisation and UNESCO. The first two days were devoted to Nag Hammadi, and thereafter the range of interest was widened to cover other aspects of Coptic studies.

The papers submitted for inclusion in the congress volume presented something of a problem for the editor, since the resultant book promised to be both large and expensive. Moreover these papers were directed to two rather different audiences, on the one hand the specialists in Nag Hammadi and gnostic studies, on the other Coptologists interested rather in Coptic language and literature, art and architecture. Eventually the decision was taken to divide the book into two. The present volume contains all the material relating to Nag Hammadi and kindred subjects; the second, under the title "The Future of Coptology", will appear as the first of a new monograph series and will contain most of the papers from the later stages of the Congress. It is hoped that this new series will provide a medium for the publication of scholarly work in the field of Coptology, which is expected to derive fresh stimulus from the formation of an International Association for the promotion of such studies.

The material available for the second volume was still considerable in amount, and to keep the book to a reasonable size the editor gratefully accepted the offer of Professor E. Lüddeckens, editor of *Enchoria*, to publish some of the contributions in that journal. A list of these will be found in the Introduction to the congress volume, but it should perhaps be emphasised here that inclusion in the journal rather than in the congress volume does not imply relegation to a second division. The names of some of the authors concerned are in themselves sufficient guarantee of the quality of their papers.

R. McL. WILSON

THE DEMIURGE IN THE APOCRYPHON OF JOHN

by

GILLES QUISPEL

In 1896 the distinguished Coptic scholar Carl Schmidt announced in the Proceedings of the Berlin Academy of Sciences (p. 839 f.) the acquisition of a Coptic Gnostic Codex, Papyrus Berolinensis 8502, which contained among other writings the Apocryphon of John.

In the introduction to the first volume of the so-called Coptic Gnostic writings, a translation of the Pistis Sophia, the Books Jeu etc., of 1905, 9 years later, Schmidt promised that in a second volume the three still unpublished writings of the Codex Berolinensis, to wit the Gospel according to Mary, the Apocryphon of John and the Sophia Jesu Christi, were to follow.

As a provisional expedient Schmidt published in 1907 a comparison of the content of the Apocryphon of John with a chapter in the antiheretical writing of bishop Irenaeus of Lyons, *adversus haereses* I, 29, of which it was supposed to be the source.[1] The edition of the Coptic text, which was to precede the translation in the well known series of Greek Christian authors (GCS), was almost ready in 1912; but as so often happens in cases of irresponsible delay in publication, a pipe broke in the cellar of the printing house in Leipzig, and destroyed the whole impression. All this, of course, was sheer coincidence.

Only shortly before his death on 17 April 1938 Schmidt started preparing an anastatic reprint after the proofs which he had preserved. After his death it turned out to be difficult to obtain his papers from his inheritance, which was in the hands of his family, Schmidt being a bachelor. In 1939 the Coptic text of the whole edition was printed in offset.

In the meantime Johannes Munck, of Aarhus, Denmark, had taken upon himself to complete the edition, but soon abdicated. In 1941 Walter Till was charged with the same task and he indeed sent the

---

[1] C. Schmidt, in: *Philotesia*, Paul Kleinert zum 70. Geburtstag dargebracht, Berlin, 1907, 315-336.

manuscript ready for the press to the Berlin Academy. Unfortunately at that moment a war was going on, which prevented publication. Soon after the war Till understood that "a gnostic library in Coptic" had been discovered and that one of these codices, acquired by the Coptic Museum in 1946, contained two texts parallel to the Berlin manuscript. This again caused delay. In 1950 Dr. Pahor Labib most generously permitted Till to collate the Cairene manuscript and to publish the variants in the critical apparatus of his edition, which at last appeared in 1955.[2]

Nobody will ever say that Schmidt or Till suffered from the disease of unproductivity. And yet we must say that this long delay was extremely unfortunate, because Gnostic Studies might have taken a different turn if this text had been available at an early date. The debate on Gnostic origins would have been less fantastic and more firmly based upon the facts because, as we now see, the Apocryphon of John is a seminal and pivotal text in many respects. But very few people then saw its importance.

An exception should be made for two outstanding scholars, who in retrospect prove to be the great geniuses in our field, and who somehow saw that this text was basic and transmitted the then almost esoteric information that it existed to a younger generation. I speak of Erik Peterson and Henri-Charles Puech.

Erik Peterson used to hide his keen insights behind an obscure and laborious style. Towards the end of his life he came to think, like Franz Overbeck before him, that Christianity is essentially and from the very beginning an ascetic, life-denying religion. As witnesses for this thesis he adduced the Apocryphal Acts of the Apostles, which according to him were not so much Gnostic as Encratite, with a Jewish Christian background. He held that these Acts, especially the Acts of Thomas, but also Syriac Christianity in general and Manicheism, were heavily influenced by the Encratite Assyrian and Syrian from Adiabene, Tatian. With this in mind he studied the Hamburg fragments of the Acts of Paul, which Carl Schmidt had published in 1936 but which had received very little attention from patristic scholars in the troubled years before, during and after the war.[3]

---

[2] W.C. Till, *Die gnostischen Schriften der koptischen Papyrus Berolinensis 8502*, Berlin, 1955.

[3] E. Peterson, Einige Bemerkungen zum Hamburger Papyrus-Fragment der Acta Pauli, *Vig.Chr.*, 1949, 142-162, and in *Frühkirche, Judentum und Gnosis*, Rome, Freiburg and Vienna, 1959, 183-208.

There he found a remarkable depreciation of womanhood : « Woman, ruler of this world, mistress of much gold, citizen of great luxury, splendid in thy raiment, sit down on the floor and forget thy riches and thy beauty and thy finery".[4] This passage has many parallels in the other Acts and clearly shows how Encratite they all are. Somewhat further on in the same fragment we read how Paul prayed that his fetters might be broken from his hands. Thereupon there came a youth very comely in grace and loosed Paul's bonds, smiling as he did so. Peterson relates this to the "beautiful, smiling youth" of the Acts of John and similar concepts in other Acts. According to Peterson it is said in the same fragment that Paul left the prison to baptise a noble woman in the sea, a young man preceding him with a torch. This has a parallel in several passages of the Acts of Thomas (118, 119, 154, 157) and elsewhere.

All these passages seem to be allusions to the underlying idea that Christ is polymorphous and manifests himself either as a child, as a youth or as an old man. This is the way he is described in the Acts of Peter, 21 :

"Then Peter said to them : 'Tell us what you saw'. And they said : 'We saw an old man, who had such a presence as we cannot describe to you'; but others said : 'We saw a growing lad'; and others said : 'We saw a boy who gently touched our eyes, and so our eyes were opened'".

This remarkable Christology, so completely different from the *atreptōs* of Chalcedon, is said by Peterson to be explained by the theology of Tatian. As a matter of fact this Encratite teacher, in his *Address to the Greeks*, 26, asks his opponents why they divide time, saying that one part is past, and another present, and another future. As those who are sailing imagine in their ignorance, as the ship is borne along, that the hills are in motion, so the Greeks do not know that it is they who are passing along whereas in reality there is only immovable eternity, Aiōn Hestōs, as long as the Creator wills it to exist.

Christ then in the Apocryphal Acts is the *Aion*, who manifests himself as child, youth and old man, as symbols of the future, the present and the past. In 1949, when he wrote this article, Peterson knew the preview of Schmidt about the Apocryphon of John and to at least one of

---

[4] E. Hennecke and W. Schneemelcher, *New Testament Apocrypha* (transl. by R. McL. Wilson), vol. 2, London 1965, 370.

his friends he mentioned the relation of the concept of Aion to the description of Christ in the Apocryphon. Obviously he did not dare to publish his great discovery, because Schmidt's translation is hesitating and deficient here.[5] Still in the reprint in his book of 1959 (p. 192, n. 36), published after Till's edition had appeared, he only says that the passage in the Apocryphon of John: "And lo, there was manifested to me a child. I however saw the appearance as an old man» is remarkable, but unfortunately difficult to interpret. If he had known the right translation, there is no doubt that he would have said what he thought already in 1949, that in the introduction of the Apocryphon of John also, as in the Apocryphal Acts of the Apostles, Christ reveals himself as Aion in its threefold symbols of child, youth and old man. For we now know that this passage in the Berlin Codex contains a gap, in which the youth was mentioned, as transpires from the following translation of the same passage in the Nag Hammadi version of Codex II :

> "Immediately, as I thought this, the heavens opened and the whole creation gleamed in a light which came down from heaven and the whole world trembled. I was afraid and threw myself down, when I saw in the light a *youth*, who manifested himself to me. But when I saw the form of an *old man* who was great and when he changed his appearance so as to be become *a child* at the same time and thus was one in many forms in the light and the forms revealed themselves one after the other, I wondered how he could be one in three forms" (my translation).

This is very different from the text of the Berlin Codex and without any doubt the original version. The Berlin text, which does not mention the child, contains a gap and is inferior here. Therefore Peterson could not know the text which confirmed his wonderful intuition.

Henri-Charles Puech, who was also familiar with Schmidt's preview at a time when nobody knew it, was in a much more favorable position than Peterson, when he wrote about Aion in the Apocryphon of John, because he had the editions of Giversen and Krause at his disposal. He wrote with great learning and lucidity.[6] As a parallel to the threefold manifestation of Christ in the preface he adduces a passage from

---

[5] *Philotesia*, 317.
[6] H.-Ch. Puech, in : *Annuaire de l'École Pratique des Hautes Études*, 1966/67, 128-136.

Photius, according to which Jesus appears to his disciples as νέος, πρεσβύτης, παῖς.[7]

It may be that Photius alludes to lost parts of the Apocryphal Acts, but this concept is preserved in the Acts of John 88 and 89, where John reports that to James Christ manifested himself as a child, whereas to John he appeared as a comely and a fair man of a cheerful countenance or again as an old man having a head rather bald, but the beard thick and flowing.

Moreover Puech discusses the above mentioned Acts of Peter, paralleled by the *Vita Abercii*, p. 22, in which three groups of old women, or three old women, see Christ respectively as an old man, a young man and a boy. More interesting is the Martyrdom of Peter and Paul.[8] There it is said that it is Simon the Magician who changes himself in form, in age, in sex, going through the metamorphoses of child, youth, old man. The same concept of eternity lies behind the expression Ἑστώς, στάς, στησόμενος applied to Simon. This seems to reveal an awareness of the fact that this view is not limited to Christianity. Such transformations should be considered as the expression of an extraordinary power and an adaptation to the different levels of spiritual capacity in the spectators. On the other hand it is clear that this Christology is conceived after the type of the Aion, in whom past, present and future coexist. Jesus here is a personification of Aion (the Modena relief of Phanes = Aion shows us that it was very common at that time to represent this eternal god in the shape of a beautiful young man of about thirty (Q)).

Puech quotes some Christian texts, among them Marco Polo, which tell us more or less clearly how the three kings from the East, who came to Bethlehem to adore Christ, saw the new born king according to their age, as a little child, a youth of thirty years old and an aged man. The source of this legend seems to be a Diègèsis (a report) of "things which happened" in Persia, written after the middle of the fifth century in Western Syria.

This material tends to show that the passage in the preface of the Apocryphon of John concerning the polymorphy of Christ reflects a well-known Christian view, wide-spread in the second century and perhaps even related to the theology of Tatian. This confirms the general opinion of scholars that this introduction was later added to

---

[7] Photius, *Bibliotheca* 114, ed. by R. Henry, II, Paris 1960, 85.
[8] *Martyrium Petri et Pauli* 14; Lipsius and Bonnet I, 130, 18 - 132, 8.

an already existing writing and has nothing to do with the core of the myth, which is not Christian. It is for this reason that we find in this introduction a Jewish remark, which is also attested in another Christian writing. The Pharisee Arimanios accuses Jesus of having turned away his disciples from "the traditions of their fathers" (a typically Jewish expression). In the same way the Jewish highpriest Anianos in the more or less Messalian Acts of Philip (19 (14), Lipsius II, 2, 10) asks: "You do not think to turn us from the traditions of our fathers, do you?» As Warren J. Blackstone has observed, what we have here are two products of a common tradition in which the classical Judaic opposition to Christianity was expressed by the claim that Jesus sought to turn the Jews from the traditions of their fathers.[9]

There is really nothing which prevents us assuming that this introduction was written by a Christian in order to christianise an already existing document which was completely alien to Christian views.

II

These contributions of Peterson and Puech are important, because they focus our attention on the relationship of the Apocryphon of John with the concept of Aion. What they failed to see, and could hardly see at that time given the complex state of the text, is that the representation of the demiurge in this Apocryphon, which did belong to the very core of the myth, should also be linked with the views on Aion current in Hellenistic times.

As a matter of fact, this is the thesis which I want to defend in this paper; or rather, to put it more precisely, as I see it, the image of the demiurge in the Apocryphon of John is moulded after the demiurge of Orphism, Phanes or Eros, who became Aion in Hellenistic times.

In order to discern this clearly, we must translate the somewhat different versions of the birth of the demiurge that have been transmitted to us. But because this story is so confused and so confusing, we will anticipate our results here and advise the impatient reader to continue with chapter III :

A version of the Apocryphon of John did tell that the demiurge had the face of a lion and the body of a serpent, but no longer related that this demiurge was born from matter below.

---

[9] W. J. Blackstone, A short Note on the 'Apocryphon Johannis', *Vig Chr*, 1965, 163.

It is only from the "Hypostasis of the Archons" and the "Untitled Document", also found at Nag Hammadi, that an older version can be reconstructed, according to which the demiurge originates from Chaos, and ascends to the highest region of this visible world. And this concept is known to us from older sources.

A

In the twenty ninth chapter of his first book against the heresies Irenaeus summarises the principal doctrines of what he calls the Barbelognostics.[10] It has been established that Irenaeus took this information from a version of the Apocryphon of John. This contains the story of the fall of Sophia, here also called Holy Spirit and Prunikos (the whore):

> "When she saw that all the rest had a consort, but she herself was without a partner, she sought for one, with whom she might unite; and when she did not find one she took it sorely, extended herself, and *looked down into the lower regions*, thinking to find a consort there. And when she found none she leapt forth, disgusted also because she had made the leap without the goodwill of the Father. Then, moved by simplicity and goodness, she generated a work in which was ignorance and audacity.
>
> This work of hers they call the First Archon, the creator of this world. They relate that he stole from his mother a great power and departed from her into the lower regions, and made the firmament of heaven in which also they say he dwells."

This is so similar to the original doctrine of Valentinus that the learned doctor must have been familiar with a version of this myth. Irenaeus must have used in this chapter a written source similar to the one used by the author of the Apocryphon of John. It has been supposed recently that Irenaeus found it among the works the Valentinians read as sources of their own system, though they were not strictly speaking Valentinian, and that this source indeed was non-Christian.[11] We might even say that it was known already to Valentinus himself, about 140 A.D.

---

[10] I, 29, 4; Harvey I, 225-226 (translation by R. McL. Wilson, in his translation of Werner Foerster, *Gnosis* I, Oxford 1972, 104-105).

[11] P. Perkins, Irenaeus and the Gnostics, *Vig Chr*, 1976, 193-200, 200.

And yet we may say that not even this version of the Apocryphon of John contains the oldest form of the myth. It is said here, not in the other versions, that *Sophia looks down to the lower parts of this world.*

This is an old theme. It is said that Dionysus was charmed by the Titans with a mirror. This mirror causes the fall of the soul. Dionysus is dispersed owing to this mirror. And Dionysus is sometimes identified with the worldsoul.[12] This theme had been transferred from Dionysus to Sophia at an early date. In a fragment quoted by Basilides it is said that the Light (= Sophia) just felt a desire to gaze on the Darkness and threw a glance at it as it were through a mirror (the underlying idea is that the primeval waters of Chaos reflect the image of Sophia). This was only a reflection and a lustre, which they tore into pieces (like Dionysus). Therefore we find in this world only a similitude of the good.[13]

According to the Paraphrasis of Sêem there was in the beginning Light and Darkness and the Spirit between them. Darkness did not know that there was something beyond her. She was covered with water and moved. The Spirit looked down and saw the water of Darkness. Thereupon the intellect of Darkness received an image (*eine*) of the Spirit, obviously mirrored in the waters of Chaos. This intellect of Darkness *arose* and illuminated the whole underworld (the demiurge ascends from Chaos). Then the Infinite Light manifested itself to the Spirit in the shape of Derdekeas, the child, the bearer of revelation (1, 26-4, 12). Later on, it is said the light of the Spirit, which was in the womb (*physis*), from which the kosmos originated, was an *image* manifested in the shape of a serpent (*thèrion*) with many faces, which was curved below (15, 12-16). A comparison with Hippolytus, *Refutatio* V, 19, seems to show this is the demiurge.

From this we must conclude that in the primitive myth Sophia projected her image in the waters of Chaos, which reflected only a deficient likeness of her, the demiurge.[14] But in the version of Irenaeus

---

[12] R. Eisler, *Orphisch-dionysische Mysteriengedanken in der christlichen Antike*, Vorträge der Bibliothek Warburg 1922-23/II Teil, Leipzig and Berlin, 1925 (reprint, Hildesheim, 1966), 168 and 179.

[13] Hegemonius, *Acta Archelaï*, 67, 4-12; Beeson, 96-97.

[14] In the Hypostasis of the Archons the demiurge, the work of Sophia, is an image of heaven. It takes *shape from matter* like an abortion and has the form of a lion (142, 7-23). It is not said that this image is a projection of Sophia's image in matter, but the demiurge is not generated by and from Sophia, as in the Apocryphon of John. In the Untitled Document (146, 13sqq.) an image emanates from Sophia, the curtain, which casts a shadow, chaos. Then Sophia manifests herself upon the matter

we are only told that Sophia looked down, not that her image was mirrored by Chaos and produced the demiurge. On the contrary it is said that the demiurge is generated by Sophia above and comes down to create the world. That is not consistent.

B

The idea that Sophia looks down into the abyss has completely disappeared in the Coptic version of the Apocryphon of John contained in the Codex Berolinensis 8502. It is there, however, that we find *the theriomorphic appearance of the demiurge*, though in a misleading form :

> Sophia is said to have had a thought of her own. She wanted to reveal her image out of herself without the assent of her partner (*syzygos*). She brought forth because of her wantonness, *prounikos*. Her work came forth, incomplete and hateful in appearance, it did not resemble its mother.
>
> He had the face (*ha*) of a serpent and the face (*ho*) of a lion. His eyes shone with fire. She cast him away from herself, out of those places, that none of the immortals might see him because she had borne him in ignorance. She put him on a throne in the clouds and called him Jaldabaoth. He is the first Archon, who drew a great power from his mother. He removed himself from her and turned away from the place in which he had been born and occupied another place in space, an aeon flaming with shining fire, in which he now dwells. And he united with the folly, *aponoia*, which is in him (hence his name Saklas, fool). He brought forth the twelve angels of the Zodiac after the pattern of the incorruptible aeons and the seven angels of the planets (37, 16-39, 17; Till, 113-119).

This demiurge is similar to the demiurge of Plato's Timaeus in that he creates after the prototypes of the spiritual world. There cannot be the slightest doubt that he originated from Sophia above and not from the matter of Chaos below. That he is theriomorphic cannot be a secondary element, though Irenaeus does not mention it. The version of the Berlin Codex is deficient and suggests that Jaldabaoth has two faces like the Roman deity Janus *bifrons*. This has been an obstacle for the right interpretation of this figure and has led to wrong trans-

---

of chaos. From the water an archon arises, with the likeness of a lion, androgynous, who is the demiurge. These seem variations of the original myth.

lations. The parallel version of Codex III (14, 9-16, 18) from Nag Hammadi is no better. There too we read that Jaldabaoth had the face (*ha*) of a lion and the face (*ha*) of serpent.

C

In Codex II (9, 25-10, 28) the version is rather different. There too we hear that Sophia conceived a thought from herself to manifest her image without her fellow. An imperfect thing was revealed from her, different from her in appearance. "But when she saw the being that she had wanted to bring forth, ⟨that⟩ he was of a different shape (typos), ⟨the shape⟩ of a serpent with the face of a lion ⟨and that⟩ his eyes were like burning lightning which flashes, she cast him away from her out of those places, in order that none of the immortal ones should see him, for she had created him in ignorance."

She surrounded him with a cloud of light and placed his throne in the midst of it that nobody should see it. This is Jaldabaoth, the first Archon, who went down to bring forth the twelve and seven angels that dominate the world.

The version of Codex IV (15, 1-16, 6) is so mutilated that it is of no use for our purpose.

We have given a new translation of our own of the relevant passage, because we wanted to make it clear that Jaldabaoth is a monstrous figure with the body of a serpent and the head of a lion. The same representation is found very often in the first centuries of our era on amulets, called Chnoubis stones : they usually contain a thick-bodied snake with the head of a lion.[15] Abraxas too, the snake-legged god with the cock's head, is sometimes also represented with the head of a lion.[16] And this seems to put us on the right track. For Abraxas could have been moulded upon a much older iconographic type.

III

I am referring to the well known myth of the cosmic egg which, to put it in a simplified form, tells how heaven and earth were split by a demiurge originating from Chaos.

---

[15] Campbell Bonner, *Studies in Magical Amulets*, Ann Arbor, 1950, 54.

[16] Cf. the forthcoming article "Hermann Hesse and Gnosis" in the Festschrift for Hans Jonas.

The play-wright Aristophanes in his comedy "The Birds" tells us the story as follows :

> There was Chaos at first, and Darkness, and Night, and Tartarus, vasty and dismal;
> But the Earth was not there, nor the Sky nor the Air, till at length in the bosom abysmal
> Of Darkness an egg, from the whirlwind conceived, was laid by the sable-plumed Night.
> And out of that egg, as the seasons revolved, sprang Eros, the charming, the bright,
> Brilliant and bold with his pinions of gold, like a whirlwind, refulgent and sparkling!
> He hatched us, commingling in Tartarus wide, with Chaos, the murky, the darkling,
> And brought us above, as the firstlings of love, and first to the light we ascended.
> There was never a race of immortals at all, till Eros the universe blended;
> Then all things commingling together in love, there arose the fair Earth and the Sky,
> And the limitless Sea; and the race of the gods, the blessed, who never shall die.[17]

In order to put this myth in the right perspective and to show its relevance for the study of Gnosticism, I want to make a few general remarks.

It is not certain that all concerned are aware of the enormous changes in our views, which were and are being brought about by the rediscovery of the Mycenaean language and world, owing mainly to the exertions of Michael Ventris and John Chadwick,[18] combined with the data from Ras Shamra and the Canaanite civilisation in general. This has led the leading scholars in this field to underline the oriental elements in Greek religion, already integrated in the second millennium before Christ.[19]

Aphrodite is now thought to have been brought to Cyprus by the Phoenicians and from there to Cythera in the Peloponnese as early

---

[17] 693-702; translation of B. B. Rogers, Loeb Classical Library 179, 201.

[18] John Chadwick, *The Mycenaean World*, Cambridge, 1976.

[19] *Éléments Orientaux dans la Religion Grecque ancienne*, Colloque de Strasbourg 22-24 mai 1958, Paris, 1960.

as in the time of the Achaians, before the Dorian invasion. This then means that Aphrodite is nobody else than Astarte and Ishtar, the bellicose, androgynous love goddess of the Near East. But she received her immigration visa at a very early date and was a founding mother of the Greek nation.[20] Moreover it has been established recently that the classical phoenix myth was not derived from the Egyptian concept of the bird *bennu* and yet developed out of the wide-spread oriental conception of the bird of the sun. This sunbird entered the Mycenaean culture from the Semitic world, via Phoenicia. It is in the newly deciphered Linear B tablets that we find the word *po-ni-ke*, the Phoenician bird, from which the word *phoinix* later developed.[21]

We must not reject *a limine* the possibility that the cosmogonic demiurge in the cosmic egg followed the same course. This demiurge was called Eros or Phanes, the lightning one. The cult of Eros seems to have been very old and very archaic indeed. According to Pausanias[22] he was venerated in Thespiae as a stone without any image, thus representing the phallus of men and animals and at the same time the lightning which brings rain and so fertility to the earth. Phanes is an adequate name for a cosmogonic deity : "let there be light". But how is it that Eros, a unifying force, actually divides heaven from earth? This could indicate that the myth of the cosmic egg is outlandish and has been linked up with Eros. And as a matter of fact, in Egypt a similar myth is attested in a text from the period of the 11th and 12th dynasty (2130-1780) :

> "The august *god who is in his egg* has commanded that N N (the name of the proprietor of the coffin) breathes the air in the necropolis.....N N has guarded this egg of *the Great Cackler*" (translation of J. Zandee).

The myth of the cosmic egg of the Great Cackler, J. Zandee tells me, originally was characteristic of Hermopolis. It told that a Nile goose (*smn*), one of the sacred animals of Amon, laid her egg in the moor. The sungod Re was born from this egg and the two halves of the shell were preserved in Hermopolis. He functions as a demiurge who creates and arranges the world.

Our late lamented friend Siegfried Morenz supposed as early as in

---

[20] H. Herter, Die Ursprünge des Aphroditekultus, *Éléments Orientaux*, 61-76, 63.

[21] R. van den Broek, *The Myth of the Phoenix according to Classical and Early Christian Tradition*, Leiden, 1972, 397.

[22] 9, 27, 1, ed. by F. Spiro, III, 58.

1950, at a time when the Mycenaean world had not yet been rediscovered, that the Orphic concept of a cosmic egg had been borrowed from Egypt. He shows that of all the peoples of the Eastern Mediterranean only the Egyptians, the Phoenicians and the Orphics, not the Sumerians, Babylonians and Assyrians, knew this mythologeme and that the Phoenicians borrowed it from the Egyptians.[23] In the light of the present evidence this seems even more plausible nowadays. Perhaps the idea in general is rather wide-spread. But that a demiurge springs from this egg, that, as far as I know, is not so common. Moreover Amon in this myth is the life-giving, divine, fertilising wind.

There is a possibility that this cosmogonic myth was also known to the Phoenicians. According to Damascius, *de primis principiis* 125, ter (Ruelle, 323) a certain Mochus described their cosmogony in the following way : first there was Aether and Aer, from which Oulomos originates. He is Olam, Eternity or Aion. Obviously he is androgynous, because it is through selfbegetting that first Choesōros and then an egg came into being. Choesōros opens this egg and so brings about heaven and earth, which originate from the two halves of the egg. Choesōros is the old Phoenician Koscher wa Chasis, the so-called Ugaritic Hephaistos, and is considered to be an *interpretatio ugaritica* of the Egyptian demiurge Ptah.[24]

Otto Eissfeldt has taught us to take these cosmogonic theories very seriously and has given us many reasons to suppose, after Ras Shamra, that they contain sometimes authentic and very old elements.[25] We should not dismiss such information out of hand, arrogantly supposing that without the blind forces of nature nothing moves in this world that is not Greek in its origin. It has become increasingly clear that many religious and philosophical views of the Greeks are rooted in Oriental soil. This is especially true of cosmogonic theories.

It has been firmly established that the myth of the castration by Kronos of his father Ouranos is in its origin a cosmogonic representation of the splitting of heaven and earth, which lie upon each other. The prototype of this has been found in both Hittite and Canaanite religion.[26]

---

[23] S. Morenz, Ägypten und die altorphische Kosmogonie, *Aus Antike und Orient*, Festschrift Wilhelm Schubart zum 75. Geburtstag, Leipzig, 1950, 64-111, 72.

[24] Morenz, in *Aus Antike und Orient*, 81.

[25] O. Eissfeldt, Ugaritisches 1, *ZDMG*, 1944, 84-94, 84 (*Kleine Schriften* II), Tübingen, 1963, 514-528.

[26] O. Eissfeldt, Phönikische und Griechische Kosmogonie, *Éléments Orientaux*, 1-15.

If we keep this in mind, we cannot fail to see the affinity of the Orphic myth with the Genesis story, especially if we read the latter with the eyes of Otto Eissfeldt :[27]

"When God fashioned heaven and earth in the beginning — but the earth was waste and empty and darkness was upon the abyss and a mighty wind swept over the water — then God spoke : let there be light, and there was light."

So Phanes, the shining light, divides heaven and earth and so creates the universe. I do not see why this myth could not have been borrowed by the Mycenaeans from the Egyptians through the intermediary of the Phoenicians. And even if it should turn out to be more likely that it was brought forth by spontaneous generation among the Greeks there cannot be the slightest doubt that this concept is very similar to its Egyptian and Phoenician counterpart.

Its importance is still enhanced if ὑπηνέμιον ᾦόν in Aristophanes has the specific meaning of "egg submitted to the winds" rather than "wind-egg". Then the parallel with Egypt and Palestine would be more striking. The wind in myth is usually life-giving and fertilising and divine, especially in Egypt but perhaps also in the Genesis story of creation. Basilius of Caesarea has heard from a Syriac speaking exegete that in Syriac, and in Hebrew the Spirit was brooding (συνέθαλπε), and not hovering over the waters, like a bird that is sitting upon her eggs (Hexaemeron II, 6). According to Basil this shows that the Spirit is demiurgic. This, by the way, shows that Basil, the founding father of the dogma of the Trinity, like his brother Gregory of Nyssa, learned from the Syrians that the Spirit is a mother. And if we keep in mind that in the religions of the world, and also in Israel, the wind is divine and generates life, his interpretation may be correct.[28]

This then is the deeply mythological symbol from which the philosophical Eros of the Greeks originated. And its lasting mythical character, even in the lofty exaltations of Plato and Aristotle, will be obvious if we remember that love is a concomitant of the instinct of reproduction, caused or conditioned by physiological realities. It is a myth to say that the world loves God (Aristotle) or that Eros is an inclination towards Being (Plato). Discursive, analytical reasoning as

---

[27] O. Eissfeldt, Das Chaos in der Biblischen und in der Phönizischen Kosmogonie, Kleine Schriften II, 258-262.

[28] Morenz, in Aus Antike und Orient, 86.

often as not is based upon a powerful and thoroughly irrational symbol. In the latter there seems to be involved an unconscious wisdom, which fascinates reason and stimulates it to ponder upon the implications of the images. So philosophy turns out to be an evolved form of mythology, as mythology is an involved philosophy. A rationalisation makes explicit the implications of unreason and suggests a semblance of rationality.

In our times this is characteristic of dialectical reason, which is nothing but the irrational emotions of the shoemaker Jacob Boehme about the ire and the love of the *Ungrund*. In antiquity the lucubrations of unmarried philosophers about Eros have the same quality, especially when one knows what they are really speaking about.

If we ask how the myth developed within Greek religion, as opposed to Greek philosophy, no certain answer can be given. There do exist certain Orphic cosmogonies under the names of Hieronymus and Hellanicus, transmitted by the Neoplatonic philosopher Damascius.[29] Nothing is known of these two men and their date. But even if they lived in Hellenistic times certain elements of the myth they transmit could be much older. This question is not really relevant for our purpose. Nevertheless I must confess that I am astonished to see the late dates that are sometimes proposed. Is this not hypercriticism that cannot be maintained after Ras Shamra and Linear B? How can one say that the representation of Time as a monstrous figure is necessarily late? On a shield of the 8th century from Crete a lion, a bull and a horned snake are represented : this is supposed to be Dionysus, the Bull, who tries to escape the Titans in this changing form.[30] And if it is true that as a rule theriomorphic Greek divinities are to be derived from the Near East, where this sort of religion is at home, is not such an influence more probable in the still rather barbarian Mycenaean Age than later? I do think that the Orphic myth of the demiurge in the cosmic egg is very archaic, even in Greece. It runs as follows :

In the beginning there was water and mud that finally was to harden into earth. Out of water and earth was born a *serpent* with the heads of a bull and a *lion* and in the middle the face of a god and wings on its shoulders. This is called endless Time, Chronos. Out of Time are

---

[29] *De Principiis* 123 bis; O. Kern, *Orphicorum Fragmenta*, [2]Berlin, 1963, 130-131 (fragment 54).
[30] Dionysus is also found in Linear B; see Chadwick, *o.c.*, 99-100. He was the bull of the labyrinth; cf. Ch. Picard, La Formation du Polythéisme hellénique et les récents problèmes relatifs au linéaire B, *Éléments Orientaux*, 163-177.

born Aether and Chaos and Darkness. In them Chronos brought forth an egg. In this egg there was an androgynous god, with golden wings on his shoulders. Growing out of his sides he had heads of bulls. On his head he has an enormous serpent appearing with all sorts of animals. He is called in some documents Phanes, the shining one, and Eros.

The coming into being of the universe is described in different ways. Sometimes it is said that at the birth of Phanes the misty gulf below and the aether were rent.[31] Sometimes it is said that the egg was broken, so that one half became heaven and the other half became earth.[32] But in any case Phanes is, according to Hieronymus and Hellanicus also, the "diataktor", the arranger and demiurge of all things and the whole world.

Sometimes it is said that Phanes, like Chronos, has many heads, and roars like a bull and a fierce *lion*.[33] Obviously Phanes too has the head of a lion.

I cannot see why the main elements of this myth could not be Mycenaean. Orpheus himself is now held by at least one scholar to be a historical figure, who lived in the fifteenth century before Christ, an Aeolian from the Greek mainland, a bard and sorcerer, a sort of shaman.[34] And even if we are rightly critical of this extreme position, we should admit that the cosmology of the cosmic egg can be very primitive indeed. Nor should we doubt that at an early date people knew that time consists of present, past and future, obviously symbolised by the three heads of Chronos. I think I can adduce an argument to make it more probable that this view is old.

Some time ago F. St. Kapsomenos announced the discovery of an Orphic papyrus at Derveni near Saloniki. This is the oldest existing Greek papyrus ($\pm$ 350 B.C.) and contains an allegorical interpretation of an Orphic poem of the sixth century. The interpretation is inspired by the presocratic philosophy, especially of Diogenes of Apollonia, and not by the great classical philosophers Plato and Aristotle or by the Stoics. This then proves that an Orphic theology, an analytical and rational exegesis of mythological images, did exist long before

---

[31] Proclus, *In Plat. Rempubl.* II, 138, 18; Kern, 151 (fragment 72).

[32] Athenagoras, *Pro Christianis* 18; Kern, 137 (fragment 57).

[33] Proclus, *In Plat. Tim.* 30 c d; Kern, 153 (fragment 79).

[34] R. Boehme, *Orpheus der Sanger und seine Zeit*, Bern and Munich, 1970, 334 sqq.

Hellenistic times. The poem is supposed to be of the 6th century. It contains the following line :

Ζεὺς κεφαλή, Ζεὺς μέσσα, Διὸς δ' ἐκ πάντα τελεῖται.

This is of some importance. As we now see clearly, Plato alludes to this verse in Laws, IV, 715 E-716 C, where he says that according to an old story God has the beginning and the end and the middle of all things. There is now no longer any doubt that this old story is the Orphic tradition. Nor can it be denied that the author of the Pseudo-Aristotelean writing De Mundo quotes the same Orphic verse. And we should admire the acumen of Ernst Diels, who with a reference to a scholiast replaced τέτυκται by the correct τελεῖται.[35]

That this text was known to Hellenistic Jews is proved by Josephus, Ant. Jud. VIII, 280 and Contra Apionem II, 190, who alludes to the same formula.[36] When the author of the Apocalypse of John quotes God (21, 6) and Christ (22, 13) as having said : "I am ... the beginning and the end", this is an echo of the old Orphic saying, for which there is no parallel in rabbinic literature. As a matter of fact this is in my view the only passage in the New Testament where we can prove with some certainty that the author was influenced, directly or indirectly, by Orphic lore.

However, the question arises whether this verse is not a rationalisation of a still older Orphic concept according to which the all-god Chronos had three symbolic faces, representing past or beginning, present or middle, and future or end. It seems plausible that first there was the image, then the rationalisation of the poem, then the philosophical interpretation of the myth in such writings as the commentary of the Derveni papyrus. All this, I guess, took place within the Orphic school of tradition in the course of the centuries.

It is not relevant for our present research to establish whether or not Plato, as so often, was influenced by the Orphics when he described in his Timaeus the work of the demiurge, the creator of the visible world. In order to establish this, it would be necessary to establish

---

[35] H. Diels, Die Fragmente der Vorsokratiker II, ⁴Berlin, 1922, 169 : Die Konjektur bestätigen die von Helmreich edierten Galenscholien (Handschr. Studien z. Gal. I Ansbacher Progr. 1910 S. 30 n. 37).

[36] W.C. van Unnik, Het godspredikaat 'het begin en het einde' bij Flavius Josephus en in de Openbaring van Johannes, Mededelingen der Koninklijke Nederlandse Akademie van Wetenschappen, Afd. Letterkunde, Nieuwe Reeks 39, 1, Amsterdam, Oxford and New York, 1976, 7-13.

whether Plato identifies the demiurge with the highest Good or rather considers him to be the active principle of reality. As far as I can see, no preliminary studies on this subject are available. Let it suffice to say here that the Neoplatonists identified Phanes with the Platonic demiurge, Zeus, who swallowed him. Proclus says this in so many words;[37] Proclus supposes in his commentary on Plato's Timaeus[38] that Plato has followed Orpheus here (I will come back to this theme at the end of this paper).

There is, however, a philosophical exegesis of the Phanes myth, which shows no Platonic influences whatsoever, but is rather tinged with Stoic colours, which should be located in the Alexandria of the first century A.D., and is the missing link between the old Orphic views and the speculations of the Gnostics.

It is the cosmology contained in the Pseudo-Clementine writings (*Homiliae* VI, 3-26; *Recognitiones* X, 30). In all text-books and studies of Orphism this text is mentioned and considered to be an important source for the study of this mysterious religion, but mostly it is attributed to Rufinus, who was only the translator of the Greek text of the Recognitions, a revision of the so-called "fundamental writing", on which both the Homilies and the Recognitions are based. The results of critical research into the sources of the Pseudo-Clementine writings are not mentioned at all. And yet it is worth while to know that according to a plausible conjecture of W. Heintze this whole passage has been taken from a Jewish apology in the form of a dialogue between a Roman convert to Judaism and his former friend, the Alexandrian opponent of the Jews Apion, the self-same against whom Josephus wrote his well known Apology.[39] In Hom. V, 29, 1 this Apion is called a hater of the Jews and in Hom. IV, 6, 2 an Alexandrian, so that there can be no reasonable doubt that pseudo-Clement and Josephus are speaking about the same person.

Moreover there are other passages on Eros than the one mentioned, which obviously also have been taken from the same source and are

---

[37] Proclus, *In Plat. Tim.* 39 E (Diehl III, 101) and *In Plat. Tim.* 28 C (Diehl I, 314).

[38] Proclus, *In Plat. Tim.* 28 C (Diehl I, 313); cf. E. Abel, *Orphica*, Leipzig and Prague, 1885, 200 : cet Orphée que d'ailleurs Platon lui-même a *suivi* en d'autres écrits (translation of A. J. Festugière, t. II, Paris, 1967, 170).

[39] W. Heintze, *Der Klemensroman und seine griechischen Quellen*, T U 40, 2, Leipzig, 1914.

relevant for our subject. I add that it is here that we find important passages on *the spirit in matter* which could be helpful to explain the newly discovered Paraphrasis of Seem and other Gnostic writings.

This certainly is an Alexandrian allegorical interpretation of the Orphic myth, very much like the Derveni papyrus and put into the mouth of the first century philosopher Apion.

It tells us that, according to Orpheus, in the beginning there was Chaos, neither darkness nor light, neither moist nor dry, neither hot nor cold but all things mixed together, one unformed mass. It brought forth a huge egg, in which the first elements were mixed up (σύγχυσις). Through a whirlpool which drew to itself the surrounding spirit the heaviest elements went down and formed a sort of a bubble. As a *peacock's egg* seems to have only one colour, while potentially it has in it all the colours of the bird that is to be, so this living egg produces many forms. By the skill of the indwelling divine spirit (πνεῦμα) an androgynous living creature was brought forth; this Orpheus calls Phanes, because, when he appeared, the universe shone forth through him. The cosmic egg was broken by Phanes, then he, who had been formed within it, came forth, as Orpheus says :

"When the shell was broken of the capacious egg".

So by the mighty power of Phanes who appeared and came forth, the globe attained coherence and maintained order. Phanes himself took over the presidency, as it were, over the summit of heaven (ὥσπερ ἐπ᾽ἀκρωρείας οὐρανοῦ προκαθέζεται), there in ineffable mysteries illuminating the infinite Aion.

So Phanes or Eros is, according to this same source, "the eldest of all the gods". For without Eros there can be no mingling or generation either of elements, or gods, or men, or irrational animals, or aught else. For we are all instruments of Eros. He, by means of us, is the fabricator of all that is begotten, the mind inhabiting our souls" (V, 10).

This document shows us that the cosmogonic Eros, abandoned by Plato and ignored by the Stoics, continued to be celebrated in the Orphic school of Alexandria, even in the first century of our era. And if it is correct that the source of the Pseudo-Clementine writings in this case was a Jewish apology written in Alexandria, then it would appear that these Orphic speculations were known to the Jews of Alexandria at that time and were so dangerous and influential that a refutation was needed.

It needs only to be said once, but I do not think it has been said
before, that these views were known to Basilides the Gnostic. In the
report which Hippolytus transmits, *Refutatio* VII, 20-27, 13, we likewise find the view that the demiurge originates from Chaos :

When the firmament, which is above the heaven, was there, there
bubbled up and was born out of the cosmic seed and the heap of the
worldseed the Great Archon, the head of the world. When he had
been born, he lifted himself up and soared and was wholly carried
right up to the firmament (variously called Ogdoas and Akroreia)
(23, 3, 4). This Great Archon is called Abrasax, a meaningless name
which has the numerical value 365, like Mithras, thus indicating that
he is a symbol of cyclic time, and therefore Aion (25, 4). The latter is
not to be found in the Orphic source, but for the rest the concept,
and also the imagery as well as the terminology are the same :

> "Or, to make plainer what they say, just as the *egg* of a variegated
> and many-coloured bird, such as a *peacock* or some other even
> more variegated and many-coloured species, although it is only
> single, yet has within it many shapes of multiform, multi-coloured,
> and heterogeneous things, so, says he, the non-existent seed deposited
> by the non-existent God has within it the multiform seed-mixture
> of the world" (21, 5).

26, 1 : σύγχυσις for Chaos, from which the demiurge is born.

26, 9 and 27, 10 : ἀκρωρεία, the summit of this world, where the
demiurge dwells.

Basilides was not the only gnostic who had in mind the myth of
the cosmic egg when speaking about the creation of the world. According to the *Codex Brucianus* LII, 13 ff. the Mother sets up the first
begotten son who is the demiurge separating matter :

> "and he it is who separated all the matter, and in the way in
> which he spread himself over it — as it were a bird stretching
> forth its wings over its eggs — thus did the protogenitor to matter,
> and he raised up myriads upon myriads of species or races. When
> the matter was grown warm, the multitude of powers that belong
> to him were set free, and they grew in the manner of the grass, and
> they were divided according to races and according to species".

Basilides was a brilliant and profound Christian Gnostic in Alexandria of about 140 A.D. But it can be proven that this Orphic concept
had been integrated already much earlier in a Jewish shade of Gnosis.

Owing to the discoveries of Nag Hammadi we now possess the "Hypostasis of the Archons" and the "Untitled Document". The first seems to be very near to Judaism, with no evidence of Christian influence, save for an occasional gloss and an editorial expansion. And yet this text is definitely Gnostic. The "Untitled Document" or "On the Origins of the World", if not based on the former writing, is yet in one way very similar to the "Hypostasis of the Archons", with some Hellenistic additions, for instance on Eros. Christian elements are not prominent. Certain puns seem to show that the author was familiar with Hebrew and Western Aramaic and could have been a Jew living in Palestine, Syria, or Egypt.

In the "Hypostasis" it is said that the abyss is the mother of Samael, the blind ruler of this world, owing to Pistis Sophia : "he pursued it down to Chaos and the Abyss, his mother, at the instigation of Faith-Wisdom".[40] Later on in the same work we are told that Sophia who is called Pistis wished to accomplish a work alone without her mate. She projected her shadow into a certain region of space, which became matter. From this originated an androgynous being, an arrogant beast in the form of a lion, the demiurge : "Wisdom, who is called Faith, wanted to create something, alone without her consort; and her product was a celestial thing. A veil exists between the World Above and the realms that are below; and Shadow came into being beneath the veil; and that Shadow became Matter; and that Shadow was projected apart. And what she had created became a product in the Matter, like an aborted foetus. And it assumed a plastic form molded out of Shadow, and became an arrogant beast resembling a lion. It was androgynous, as I have already said, because it was from Matter that it derived." [41]

The "Untitled Document" tells very much the same story, but with interesting details.

Sophia projects her image upon (*hidzjn*) the matter of Chaos. Thereupon an Archon arises from the water with the outward appearance of a lion, an androgynous creature who is destined to rule over matter. Therefore Sophia appeals to him to ascend to the higher places of the universe, where she dwells. Therefore his esoteric name is Jaldabaoth, whereas the perfect call him Ariel, because he has the appearance of

---

[40] 135, 6-9; translation of B. Layton, in : *Harvard Theological Review*, 1974, 351-425, 396; cf. R. A. Bullard, *The Hypostasis of the Archons*, Berlin, 1970, 21.
[41] 142, 5-19; Layton, 414-416; Bullard, 35.

a lion.[42] He is the demiurge, called Samael, or Jaldabaoth, or Sakla the Fool. He reigns over the visible world. But Pistis Sophia predicts from the very beginning that he will return in the end to the abyss, which is his mother.[43]

Gershom Scholem, the third genius in this field, more specifically the genius of precision, has taught us that some of us were wrong when they believed that Jaldabaoth means "son of chaos", because the Aramaic word *bahutha* in the sense of chaos only existed in the imagination of the author of a well-known dictionary.[44] This is a pity because this name would suit the demiurge risen from chaos to a nicety. And perhaps the author of the "Untitled Document" did not know Aramaic and also supposed as we did once, that *baoth* had something to do with *tohuwabohu*, one of the few Hebrew words that everybody knows.

In the Apocryphon of John the view that the demiurge originates from chaos is not clearly defined. It would seem there that it is rather Sophia who produces the demiurge from herself. The concept of the "Hypostasis of the Archons" and of the "Untitled Document" seems to be more primitive. It would seem then that the Orphic view of the demiurge was integrated into Jewish Gnosticism even before the redaction of the myth contained in the present Apocryphon of John. Perhaps iconography can help us to determine where this happened.

Phanes is represented with the mask of a *lion*'s head on his breast, while from his sides the heads of a ram and a buck are budding forth : his body is encircled by a snake. This type was accepted by the Mithras mysteries, to indicate Aion, the new year, and Mithras, whose numerical value is 365. Sometimes he is also identified with Jao Adonai, the creator of the Hebrews. His hieratic attitude indicates Egyptian origin. The same is true of the monstrous figure with the head of a lion, which symbolises Time, Chronos, in Mithraism; Alexandrian origin of this type is probable.

There are good reasons for supposing that the figurative representation of Abraxas, with the head of a cock (or a lion) and serpentine legs, is to be located in the same town. It was among the Egyptians that according to Macrobius, *Saturnalia* 1, 20, Aion had an image of an

---

[42] 147, 23 - 148, 26; A. Böhlig and Pahor Labib, *Die Koptisch-Gnostische Schrift ohne Titel aus Codex II von Nag Hammadi*, Berlin, 1962, 40-42.

[43] 151, 24-28; Böhlig, 48.

[44] G. Scholem, Jaldabaoth Reconsidered, *Mélanges d'histoire des religions*, offerts à Henri-Charles Puech, Paris, 1974, 405-421, 408.

animal with three heads, a lion (present), wolf (past), dog (future), linked by an encircling *serpent*.[45]

It seems plausible that both Mithraic Time and Abraxas were Alexandrian variations of and inspired by the old figure of Orphic Chronos, the serpent with the head of a lion, a bull and a god. But then the theriomorphic representation of Jaldabaoth, serpent with lion's head, could easily be Egyptian and Alexandrian. And it is virtually certain that the Orphic interpretation of Phanes-Eros the demiurge was known to the Jews of Alexandria. But then both the concept as such and its symbolic representation would prompt the suggestion that it was in Alexandria that these astonishing views were formulated for the first time.

IV

In the "Untitled Document" the demiurge has the name of the archangel Ariel, which means "the lion of God". Probably this angel was chosen because traditionally the demiurge has the face of a lion. But for our purposes it is sufficient to observe that the demiurge is an angel.

In the Sophia Jesu Christi, in additions to its source, the Letter of Eugnostos, Jaldabaoth the almighty ruler of Chaos is called "the great angel" (121, 12). In Mandeism the real name of the demiurge is Gabriel the Messenger, who goes under the cover of the outlandish designation Ptahil.[46] This seems to indicate that the Orphic concept we discussed has been integrated into a Judaic system of reference in which creation was no longer attributed to God himself but rather to one of his angels or more particularly to "the Angel", namely "the Angel of the Lord".

The view, however, that the Gnostic concept of the demiurge is due to heterodox Jewish sources provokes such violent and uninhibited reactions that it seems wise to prepare the way by drawing attention to some facts which everybody knows or should know. Not infrequently in early Christian sources, and even to-day in fundamentalist circles, Christ is identified with the Angel of the Lord mentioned in the Old Testament. The reason for this is that God is held to have revealed

---

[45] See the forthcoming article mentioned in note 16.

[46] Jewish Gnosis and Mandaean Gnosticism, in J.-E. Ménard, *Les Textes de Nag Hammadi*, Colloque du Centre d'Histoire des Religions, Strasbourg, 23-25 octobre 1974, Leiden, 1975, 119.

himself even before the incarnation in the shape of a man, as the anthropomorphisms of the Old Testament show. So Tertullian could answer Marcion's criticisms of the Old Testament God in the following way :

"igitur quaecumque exigitis deo digna, habebuntur in patre invisibili incongressibilique et placido et, ut ita dixerim, philosophorum deo, quaecumque autem ut indigna reprehenditis, deputabuntur in filio et viso et audito et congresso" (*adv. Marc.* II, 27).

(Therefore all the attributes and activities you make requisition of as worthy of God are to be found in the Father, inaccessible to sight and contact, peaceable also and, so to speak, a god philosophers can approve of; but all the things you repudiate as unworthy, are to be accounted to the Son, who was both seen and heard, and held converse; translation of E. Evans, Oxford 1972, 163).

Martin Werner and Jean Cardinal Daniélou have demonstrated that this socalled Angel-Christology is characteristic of Jewish Christianity.[47] But such notions had already been prepared in pre-christian Judaism. Already in the Old Testament we see on different occasions, for instance in the story of the burning bush, Exodus 2, that the redactor has toned down the crude anthropomorphism of his source (J), according to which the Lord himself had come down to hide himself in a bush, and replaced the tetragrammaton by the veiled expression "the Angel of the Lord". In the Septuagint translation of Isaiah 9, 5 this very special Malak is conceived as the Messenger of God's privy council, identified with the Messiah and called Angel of the Great Council, *Megalès Boulès Angelos*. And Philo commonly identifies this angel with the Logos. It has been shown recently by Charles H. Talbert that it was these and similar images that lie behind the New Testament concept of a descending and ascending redeemer.[48]

Now it had already been known for a long time that the rabbis had fought against the heresy of the "two powers in heaven". But it was not quite clear what this meant. Some thought that the "heretics" who taught these views were Christians, who held that Christ was also God, or Jewish Gnostics, who derived their blasphemous ideas

---

[47] M. Werner, *Die Entstehung des Christlichen Dogmas*, Bern and Leipzig, 1941, 302-321; J. Daniélou, *Théologie du Judéo-Christianisme*, Tournai, 1958, 167-198.

[48] Charles H. Talbert, The Myth of a descending-ascending Redeemer in Mediterranean Antiquity, *NTS* 1976, 418-439.

from non-Jewish Gnostics and from them had learned that an absolute dualism opposed the highest God to the abominable demiurge who is guilty of this evil creation.

It was the discovery of the Gospel of Truth which led to a different orientation. For in that writing it is said that Christ is the Name, even the Proper Name of God. There could be little doubt that this was derived from Jewish speculations about the Name, the ineffable Šem, and about the bearer of the Name, the Angel of the Lord, called Jaoel (later Metatron) or little Jahweh, Jahweh Haqaton, because according to Exodus 23, 21, the Name of the Lord was in him. It then became clear that the doctrine of the two powers in heaven in its origin had nothing to do either with Christianity or with Gnostic dualism, but started in Judaism as an expedient to explain anthropomorphic passages in Holy Writ. Recently this whole complex of ideas has been brilliantly treated by Alan Segal in a dissertation at Yale University which has now been published by Brill's in Leyden.[49]

This book discusses all the extant rabbinic passages about Jewish heretics and possibly others who proclaim that there are two principles. The best known of these is rabbi Elisha ben Abuya, called Aher ($\pm$ 100 A.D.), who is said to have seen Metatron, sitting and writing down the merits of Israel, from which this rabbi allegedly concluded that perhaps there are two deities.

According to Segal there is no indication whatsoever that these views have anything to do with Iranian dualism. Nor are the opponents aimed at always the same. Sometimes they may have been Gnostics, at other times Christians and as often as not heterodox Jews. Before the end of the second century A.D. there is no evidence that heretics who proclaimed two powers did believe that these were opposed to each other. They were rather Jews who were worried about anthropomorphism. Biblical theophanies which picture God as a man or a fierce warrior or confuse the Lord with an angel are the basis of this tradition, which distinguishes between a completely transcendent God and His revelation in anthropomorphic shape. The rabbinic texts about the two powers in heaven can be ascribed in general to the third century. However, the earliest reports can be safely dated to the Bar Kochba revolt of the first half of the second century. And an extensive oral period must have preceded our first witnesses.

---

[49] Alan F. Segal, *Two Powers in Heaven*, Early Rabbinic Reports about Christianity and Gnosticism, Leiden, 1978.

Segal then discusses the evidence contained in Philo. He shows that
this Jewish philosopher of the first century A.D. bases his speculations upon the same ambiguous passages in the Old Testament as
the heretics opposed by the rabbis. He worries about the same anthropomorphisms and discusses the concept of a second deity, variously
called Angel of the Lord, Lord, Name, Logos. Philo calls his Logos
(and so the Angel of the Lord) a *deuteros theos*, a second God. He
also reacts to certain traditions according to which one God was
mild and the other severe, stating that these are two "measures" of
the same God. So Philo turns out to have been profoundly influenced
by, and also in part to have reacted against, these traditions, which
were then already in existence. The earliest form of this heresy involved
the assumption that any anthropomorphic description in the Bible
refers to a divinity separate from and subordinate to God. Closely
connected with this heresy were mystical and apocalyptic traditions
about the divine Name of God as a separate hypostasis, about the
Angel of the Lord (Jaoel or Metatron) and about Adam (later Adam
Kadmon, the Archetypal Man of Ezekiel 1, 28). All this is Palestinian
lore, to which Philo is indebted.

Thus Philo's Logos has not only a logical but also a religious
function. He uses this concept both for philosophical argumentation
and for explaining the anthropomorphisms in the Holy Bible. From
this we must conclude that the theories about two divine powers in
heaven, though originating in Palestine, were known in Alexandria
at the time when Philo lived there. They could have been known
to the author of the Apocryphon of John in its original version, or
to the tradition which he elaborated, if indeed this author was a Jew
and lived in *Alexandria apud Aegyptum*. There is, however, this essential
difference that in Philo and the "two principles" heretics this vicegerent
and agent of revelation is held to be a positive power, whereas in the
Apocryphon of John the demiurge is an antagonistic power.

Segal points to several sources which seem to take an intermediate
position. In the Gnosis of Baruch Elohim, the creator of the world,
is subordinate to the Good, but not yet the arrogant creature of later
Gnosticism. I add that in the well-known Leyden Magical Papyrus
the Lord and ruler of this world is brought forth by the call of God,
who pronounces Iao, but this demiurge is not evil. Segal supposes
that these distorted claims of the Gnostics about the ignorance of
Israel's God are a polemical answer to the rabbinic polemic against
"two powers" which relied heavily on Deuteronomy 32, 39: "I kill

and revive, I destroy and I heal", implying that God himself causes both good and evil.

In tracing back the origin of the concept of a lower demiurge we should not take our stand exclusively upon the witness of the rabbis and the documents of esoteric and apocalyptic Judaism. There are also the Samaritan sources, now available in excellent editions with translation, which are relevant for our purpose.

Jarl Fossum, who under my guidance is preparing a thesis on the origin of the concept of a demiurge in Gnostic texts, has found a remarkable passage in a Samaritan writing called the Malef. There it is said that the Angel of the Lord created the body of Adam, whereas God himself infused his Spirit into that frame. The text is a late composition, but there is no reason to doubt that it contains earlier traditions. For our purposes, however, the chronology is not so important. The essential point is that here for the first time we see an indubitable relationship between this angelic creator and the Timaeus.

In this dialogue Plato speaks rather mysteriously about a *demiourgos*, who fashions the visible world (and not the already preexistent world of ideas). He is called the father and maker of this universe, whom it is difficult to find and when found to relate to others. This, however, can be confidently said, that he looked up to the eternal model, especially to the idea of the Good when making the world :

"And that which has come into existence must necessarily, as we say, have come into existence by reason of some Cause. Now to discover the Maker and Father of this Universe were a task indeed; and having discovered Him, to declare Him unto all men were a thing impossible. However, let us return and inquire further concerning the Cosmos, — after which of the Models did its Architect construct it? Was it after that which is self-identical and uniform, or after that which has come into existence? Now if so be that this Cosmos is beautiful and its Constructor good, it is plain that he fixed his gaze on the Eternal; but if otherwise (which is an impious supposition), his gaze was on that which has come into existence. But it is clear to everyone that his gaze was on the Eternal; for the Cosmos is the fairest of all that has come into existence, and He the best of all the Causes" (28 C - 29 A; translation of R. G. Bury, Loeb Classical Library 234, 51-53).

The demiurge leaves the preparation of the bodies of men to his own offspring, some lower gods. They receive the immortal soul from him and envelop it in a mortal body :

"And He Himself acts as the Constructor of things divine, but the structure of the mortal things He commanded His own engendered sons to execute. And they, imitating Him, on receiving the immortal principle of soul, framed around it a mortal body, and gave it all the body to be its vehicle, and housed therein besides another form of soul, even the mortal form, which has within it passions both fearful and unavoidable — firstly, pleasure, a most mighty lure to evil; next, pains, which put good to rout; and besides these, rashness and fear, foolish counsellors both; and anger, hard to dissuade; and hope, ready to seduce. And blending these with irrational sensation and with all-daring lust, they thus compounded in necessary fashion the mortal kind of soul" (69 C-D; Bury, 179-181).

Christians are so accustomed to identify the creator with God and God with the Good that most of us involuntarily have always assumed that Plato's demiurge is the idea of the Good and that this idea is identical with the God of the Bible. But one of the greatest living experts on Greek philosophy, who is at the same time a fervent Roman Catholic, my colleague C. J. de Vogel, has protested against this view. In her book on Plato she says it is undesirable to designate this demiurge as God and Father, because that is misleading to the Christian reader, who will readily suppose that this demiurge is obviously identical with "the Good" in Plato's "State" and "Being itself" in his "Sophistes". The demiurge of the Timaeus, who produces the souls, must be located above the level of the soul, but is not identical with intelligible Being in its totality and certainly not with the Good which is beyond being and the Ground of being. "If one wants to say that the Good on the level of intelligible being manifests itself in the shape of the demiurge, then I believe one does not say something contrary to Plato's thought". Plato's terminology, de Vogel continues, is bewildering for us. He uses the word "god" for the demiurge, and for the "created gods", which are the perfect souls of the heavenly bodies, and also for the wise and good world-soul. But he never calls the highest principle and idea, viz. "the Good", God.[50] We must therefore

---

[50] C. J. de Vogel, *Plato, de filosoof van het transcendente*, Baarn, 1968, 150-152.

constantly keep in mind that according to Plato the idea of the Good is unconscious and impersonal, whereas the demiurge is personal, a craftsman, an anthropomorphic God.

Perhaps Plato here, as so often, has been inspired by Orphic lore. Since the Derveni papyrus we know that many concepts of this religion, formerly held to be late and Hellenistic, are in reality much older. It seems plausible that already in Plato's time the myth of the demiurge Phanes was circulating in Orphic circles and known to Plato. Phanes is a worldly, immanent demiurge, not the highest principle, which is Zeus according to the Orphics. In any case Plato's problem was similar to that of the Jewish rabbis : how is handicraft, a crude anthropomorphism, to be brought into accord with our notion of the dignity of the Highest? And it may be that his solution was seminal for the later developments in Palestine. For we can explain from immanent causes the stress in Judaism on God's transcendence and, corresponding to that tendency, the ever greater prominence of the Angel of the Lord : the faithful of that time became increasingly aware that God is beyond the visible world and at the same time remained firmly convinced that God sovereignly bridged the gap by revealing Himself. But it is not so easy to see why this Angel received a cosmological function and became a demiurge.

In the Samaritan text mentioned above this happened under the influence of Plato's Timaeus. And there are Jewish parallels for it. That is an adaptation of the traditional faith and the traditional exegesis of Scripture to the scientific worldview of that time. For the Timaeus of Plato was the bedside book of every civilised and not so civilised man in the centuries before and after the beginning of our era.

From now on we must ask ourselves whether the demiurge of Plato's Timaeus is not involved wherever a mediator of creation enters the scene. This is the case with the Jewish Magharians who taught that an anthropomorphous angel created the world. We wonder what relations certain apocalyptic and esoteric Jews had with them : according to the former the world had been created through the Name, the latter taught that the Creator in the Beginning was the Kabod, the glory of God, and not God himself. They all show that a subordinate being had already assumed creative functions before he was identified with the Logos, as in Philo and St John : and this explains why this creator, at least in John, always remained so personal, whereas the Greek logos of the Stoics is strictly impersonal. Christian Fathers of the Church and Gnostics wrestled with the dilemma, how God could be transcendent and yet created the world like a workman : both used the same traditional material, though in a different way.

This is also the perspective of the Apocryphon of John : it teaches that the demiurge is a lower being like the heretics who believed in "two principles", but also that this world is an image of the eons and that the bodily frame of man was fashioned by the demiurge and his fellows. These latter elements are taken from the Timaeus. And therefore it was probably under the influence of Plato's Timaeus that Jewish heretics, and the Gnostics in their wake, said that the world and the body of man had been created by a lower demiurge.

V

Does all this mean then that in the Apocryphon of John we find a distant echo of the doctrine of the two deities?

That would be too sweeping a statement. It has been shown that this view was known to the rabbis and also to Philo, and therefore must have circulated in Alexandria at the beginning of our era. But in the Apocryphon of John it is not said that the angel who creates the world is God : it is only said that this angel calls himself God, though he was ungodly in his ignorance.

This can only be understood in the perspective of Jewish mysticism. One of its main writings, 3 Enoch, or The Hebrew Book of Enoch, edited by Hugo Odeberg in 1928, has much to say about the enormous importance and privileged position of Metatron, the Angel of the Lord. He is called "Youth", like Jaldabaoth in the Untitled Document; he is clothed in a garment of glory, is crowned with a golden crown and called "Lesser YHWH"; on his crown are written the cosmic letters of the divine name by which heaven and earth were created; to him are committed the 70 angels corresponding to the nations of the world; to him wisdom and intelligence are committed more than to all the angels. And he in his turn gives wisdom unto the wise and knowledge to them that know understanding. He reveals secrets and teaches judgment and justice.

But if we should suppose that Metatron is divine, this document tells a story to make it perfectly clear that we are wrong. It is clearly directed against heretics who hold the view that there are two divine powers in heaven. According to chapter 16 of 3 Enoch Metatron was at first sitting upon a great throne at the door of the seventh hall of the heavenly palace, presiding over the celestial court. But when the arch-heretic Aher came to see him sitting there and concluded that he was a divine power, forthwith a divine voice went forth from heaven, proclaiming that this was unforgivable. Thereupon Metatron received sixty strokes with lashes of fire and was made to stand on his feet. Because this text is so unknown, it should be quoted in full:

"R. Ishmael said: Metatron, the Angel, the Prince of the Presence, the Glory of all heaven, said to me: At first I was sitting upon a great Throne at the door of the Seventh Hall; and I was judging the children of heaven, the household on high by authority of the Holy One, blessed be He. And I divided Greatness, Kingship, Dignity, Rulership, Honour and Praise, and Diadem and Crown of Glory unto all the princes of kingdoms, while I was presiding in the Celestial Court, and the princes of kingdoms were standing before me, on my right and on my left — by authority of the Holy One, blessed be He.

But when Acher came to behold the vision of the Merkaba and fixed his eyes on me, he feared and trembled before me and his soul was affrighted even unto departing from him, because of fear, horror and dread of me, when he beheld me sitting upon a throne like a king with all the ministering angels standing by me as my servants and all the princes of kingdoms adorned with crowns surrounding me: in that moment he opened his mouth and said: 'Indeed there are two Divine Powers in heaven!' Forthwith *Bath Qol* (the Divine Voice) went forth from heaven from before the Shekina and said: 'Return, ye backsliding children, except Acher!'

Then came '*Aniyel*, the Prince, the honoured, glorified, beloved, wonderful, revered and fearful one, in commission from the Holy One, blessed be He and gave me sixty strokes with lashes of fire and made me stand on my feet".[51]

With this should be compared a passage in Irenaeus, *adv. haereses* I, 30:

"Hence Jaldabaoth in exaltation boasted about all the things beneath him and said: 'I am Father and God, and above me there is none'. When his mother heard this, she called out against him: 'Do not lie, Jaldabaoth, for there is above you the Father of All, the First Man and the Man the Son of Man'."

---

[51] H. Odeberg, *3 Enoch or the Hebrew Book of Enoch*, Cambridge, 1928, 43-45.

A similar concept is found in the "Untitled Document", 151, 15-21 :

"When Pistis saw the godlessness of the great Archon, she became angry. Without being seen, she said : 'You are wrong, Sammael, that is the blind god, an immortal lightgiving man exists before you, who will reveal himself to your creatures'."[52]

The "Hypostasis of the Archons" reflects very much the same view (143, 4-8) :

"And he said to his offspring : 'It is I who am the god of the Entirety'. And Life, the daughter of Faith-Wisdom, cried out and said to him : 'You are mistaken, Sakla!' (for which the alternate name is Yalta-baoth)."[53]

In the Apocryphon of John, II, 61, 7 - 62, 15 parr. the demiurge proclaims that he is the only existing God. Thereupon a voice comes to his mother, Sophia, from the aeons above, and is heard also by the demiurge : "Man (= God) exists, and the Son of Man". It is Barbelo, the Father-Mother, who reveals that there is a God to an ignorant fool, Sakla, who thinks in his heart there is no God. Then the world of the demiurge trembles, the foundations of the abyss are shaken and owing to the waters which are upon matter the lower world was illuminated by the light of this image that she revealed. And when all the angels and the Protarchon stared, they saw the whole lower world illuminated and by the light they saw in the water the reflection (*typos*) of the image (*eikon*) (62, 24-34). Then they decided to fashion man after this image.

The underlying idea is that Barbelo, who is the Image of God, projects her reflection in the mirroring waters of the abyss and so offers the angels the opportunity to make outward Adam after the image of God. This concept is still Jewish both in imagery and in tendency. It speaks about a *bath qol*, a voice coming to the angel Meta-tron, telling him that there is only one God, not two powers in heaven.

Strangely enough, even those passages in the Apocryphon of John which at first sight seem to be inspired by an anti-Jewish animus, can only be understood when put against a Jewish background and when compared with the works of Jewish mysticism.

---

[52] Böhlig, 49.
[53] Layton, 416-418; Bullard, 36.

VI

Conclusion

In this paper we have travelled all the way from the cosmogonic world-egg in Egyptian Hermopolis to Mycenaean Greece and heterodox Palestine to trace the origins of the concept of the demiurge in the Gnostic Apocryphon of John. There can be no reasonable doubt that the Orphic Phanes, theriomorph and arising from Chaos, was the prototype of this Ialdabaoth. An immanent development within Judaism — awareness of God's transcendence, embarrassment about the crude anthropomorphisms of the Old Testament — created a situation in which it became feasible to identify the Angel of the Lord with this demiurge. But even before that it had been said that this Angel of the Lord, and not God himself, created man and the world. Perhaps this first happened among the Samaritans and it was from Samaria that this view migrated to Egypt.

So a religious theme after many wanderings returned to the place where it belonged.

The demiurge has come home to roost.

"ANAPAUSIS IN THE EPISTULA JACOBI APOCRYPHA"

by

JAN HELDERMAN

MS [a]

p. 1

```
[ιακωβος              ]ẹṬ[c2]ẹει м̄
[πιχωμε          . . .]θoc .ρнnε
[oyειρнnн αβαλ 2n̄] oyειρнnн
[oyαγαπн αβαλ 2n̄] oyαγαπн
5 oyx̣[αριc   αβαλ 2]nn oyxαριc
  oyπ[ιcтιc   αβ]αλ 2n̄ oyπιcтιc
  oyωn2 αβαλ 2n̄ oyωn2
  εϥoyααϥ επιαн ᾱκ̄ρ̄α
```

* [James wri]tes
   [this letter to Kerin]thos [the Child]
   [Peace from] peace (εἰρήνη)
   [love fro]m love (ἀγάπη)
   [grace fro]m grace (χάρις),
   f[aith fro]m faith (πίστις)
   life from holy life.

p. 3

```
   λααγε n̄тooтϥ̄ πωтn̄ πε
25 πωn2 м̄мε 6ε xε αϥρ̄πα
   2ρε αρωтn̄ ερετn̄ϣωnε
   [x]εκαc ερετnαр̄ р̄ρo oyα
   εϊ· n̄nεnтα2м̄тαn αβαλ·
   2м̄ πεyϣωnε· xε cεnαт
```

---

* Edition : M. Malinine a.o., Epistula Jacobi Apocrypha, Zürich/Stuttgart 1968.

30 ⲥⲧⲁⲩ ⲁⲛ ⲁⲡϣⲱⲛⲉ · ⲛⲉⲉⲓⲉ
ⲧⲟⲩ ⲛⲉⲧⲉ ⲙⲡⲟⲩϣⲱⲛⲉ ⲁⲩⲱ
ⲁϩⲟⲩⲥⲟⲩⲱⲛ ⲡⲙⲧⲁⲛ ⲉⲙⲡⲁ
ⲧⲟⲩϣⲱⲛⲉ ⲧⲱⲧⲛ ⲧⲉ ⲧⲙⲛⲧ
ⲧⲣⲣⲟ ⲙⲡⲛⲟⲩⲧⲉ · ⲉⲧⲃⲉ ⲡⲉⲉⲓ †

Yours is
Life. Know then that he healed
you when you were ill
in order that you might become kings.
Woe to them who have rest from
their illness for they will
return to the illness. Blessed
are those who have not been ill and
have known the rest before
they became ill. Yours is the Kingdom of God.

The first tractate in the first codex from Nag Hammadi, together
with for example the Gospel of Truth and the Gospel of Thomas,
is one of the documents which up to now have been most widely
discussed. Moreover, the enigmatic character of several expressions
presents a serious impediment to a proper evaluation and understanding
of the Epistle. In the context of a study on the gnostic concept of
ⲁⲛⲁⲡⲁⲩⲥⲓⲥ, to be published in due course, I should like to draw
attention to a possible occurrence of this concept in the Epistula
Jacobi (EJ), in order to evaluate both the gnostic rest-concept and
also the character of the letter as a whole.

The term ⲁⲛⲁⲡⲁⲩⲥⲓⲥ with its synonyms and Coptic equivalent
ⲙⲧⲁⲛ — in the sense of the gnostic concept of Rest as the ultimate
salvation — is found only at p. 3:28 and p. 3:32 of the manuscript
(at 10:2 ⲥⲙⲁⲧⲛ means "it is easy"). From a first glance at the three
translations in the *editio princeps*, however, one can clearly deduce
that it still remains to be seen whether ⲙⲧⲁⲛ here should be understood in terms of the gnostic concept of the Rest. The translators
opt for : 'genesen' and 'Gesundheit'; 'guéri' and 'santé', and 'relieved'
and 'health'. Rodolphe Kasser in a supplementary note translates by
'le bien-être' at both places. Moreover the editorial commentary on the
two passages is remarkable indeed, in that one reads at 3:32 "la santé
ou le repos : ⲙⲧⲟⲛ (SB), ⲙⲧⲁⲛ (A) traduit ὑγίεια et ἴασις aussi bien
que ἀνάπαυσις" (with a reference to Crum). This is the more remarkable

in that H. M. Schenke gives the following translation : "die Ruhe fanden von ihren Krankheit" and : "Wohl denen, die zur Erkenntnis der Ruhe kamen".

To ensure a well-founded choice in translating $\overline{\text{MTAN}}$ here, it is necessary to deal with the question of the gnostic, gnosticising or non-gnostic character of this tractate. As will be known, Dr. W. C. van Unnik (Utrecht) has on several occasions favoured a non-gnostic character : "this newly discovered apocryphon originates from a small village-church not yet affected by gnosticism between 125-150".[1] Now the editors took up an opposing stand : the Letter of James is a gnostic document. In this respect Dr. Zandee (Utrecht) tried to define that gnostic character as Valentinian. Before we decide, however, with regard to the so-called gnostic character of the letter, or seek to define its gnostic character more precisely, we should at the very outset bring into the question the readily proven Egyptian background, especially since not only van Unnik but the editors also locate the letter in Egypt. In this connection the former adduces 2 Clement and the Ascensio Isaiae, the latter the Epistula Apostolorum (EA). Now Manfred Hornschuh in his dissertation Die Anfänge des Christentums in Ägypten (Bonn 1958), as well as in his Studien zur EA (Berlin 1965 with some reservation), has demonstrated on good grounds that the EA was not written in Asia Minor as Carl Schmidt maintained (in his work Gespräche Jesu mit seinen Jüngern, Leipzig 1919), but in Egypt in about 130.

Though we cannot deal now with the concept of Rest in the EA, it is of great moment to examine that letter, first regarding the identity of the person addressed in the EJ; secondly as to the positive evaluation of martyrdom; and third in regard to the characterisation of salvation as "healing" (the two loci we are dealing with in this paper). The observations made could after all be of importance for a clearer determination of the Gnosticism which we meet with in the EJ.

I

As to the first point, the addressee, several names have been suggested for the person addressed in the poorly-preserved opening lines of the Epistle. Among those mentioned is that of Cerinthus (Schenke especial-

---

[1] W. C. van Unnik, The Origin of the recently discovered 'Apocryphon Jacobi', VC 10 (1956) p. 149-156; ad hoc see p. 156.

ly launched this idea). We encounter him also — together with Simon —
in the EA (chapters 1 and 7). In opposing Schmidt — who located EA
in Asia Minor, Cerinthus being connected with Ephesus in the tradition — Hornschuh refuted him with his own arguments (Simon and
Cerinthus being only types of early gnostic heresy as a "Gesamter-
scheinung"). It is hard indeed to deny some inconsistency in Schmidt's
argumentation, in that he connects Cerinthus with the EA as a historical
personality on *another* occasion!

On the other hand, Schmidt was right in stating that Cerinthus' name
was deeply rooted in the memory of later generations. This holds
particularly with regard to the EA, since the false teaching contested
there has in some respects the features of a Cerinthian-type Gnosticism
(separation between Creator and Redeemer God; earthly Jesus, heavenly Christ).

Something similar could be applied to the "Christology" included
in our Apocryphon of James. Finally, we should not overlook Hippolytus' information about Cerinthus being educated in Egypt and instructed in Egyptian wisdom. It is true that Schmidt — unravelling the
confused tradition concerning a gnostic Cerinthus and a judaistic-
chiliastic Cerinthus/Merinthus and separating the two — rather depre-
ciated Hippolytus' communication. In my opinion however this lacks
real proof. An Egyptian sojourn by Cerinthus would provide a sound
basis for the supposition that the beginning of the Epistle *did* have
his name. Though Kasser in an impressive way proposed ϲⲩⲙⲡⲁ̅-ⲑⲟ ϲ
or ⲙⲁⲉⲓⲡⲁ-ⲑⲟ ϲ as a reconstruction (to which one might add ⲛⲁⲅⲁ-
ⲑⲟ ϲ, see p. 5:29), I should like to follow Schenke in reading ⲕⲉⲣⲓⲛ-
ⲑⲟ ϲ, but take the word following not as ϯⲣⲏⲛⲉ (peace) but ⲡⲣⲏⲛⲉ
(the youth): *Cerinthus, the son* or something like that. In favour of
this we may note the fact that one finds in the epistle the clear
idea of the gnostics addressed being "children of the Father", of
salvation really beginning with them and they themselves surpassing
even Jesus and the apostles Peter and James (see p. 16:13; 17-19;
15:38, where we should indeed read ϣⲏⲣⲉ; and above all 16:30).
I shall return later to the subject of the gnostics being "children".

II

The *second* point we should consider concerns the evaluation of
martyrdom in a remarkable positive sense: this rather prohibits any
derivation of the EJ from the Valentinian tradition. The information

provided by Irenaeus, Clement of Alexandria and Tertullian in regard
to the Valentinian view of submission to violent death for the sake
of one's convictions and beliefs indeed speaks for itself. The famous
passage in Clement concerning Basilides — who, in what might be a
commentary on 1 Peter 4:15, compared the death of the sufferer to
that of an infant who had committed no actual sin, but nevertheless
possessed the power to commit sin — does *not* mean that for Basilides
the fact of martyrdom would be a victory over the Devil, leading to
material triumph for the saints, *but* rather that it was an act which
benefited an individual soul struggling upwards on its way to perfection. The same applies to the well-known Fragment 4 of Valentinus:
there the children of the life everlasting are, it is true, looking forward
to death, but this means only that the pneumatics will overcome death
and matter in virtue of their nature. The common gnostic spiritualisa-
tion of martyrdom is clearly found also in Valentinian exegesis of,
for example, Colossians 1:24, the Valentinians finding here not a
reference to Paul's own physical afflictions, but to his participation
in the constraining elements (pathemata) of cosmic existence, Paul
filling the 'hysteremata' of the deficient members of Christ's Body,
the ecclesia! Now in our EJ, in my opinion, we meet on the contrary a
non-gnostic evaluation of violent death, or at any rate of the trials
of martyrdom. The apostles (p. 4:29/30) ask: "Give us the means not
to be tempted by the evil devil". Christ's answer is clear: sufferings
have to be encountered. We have the same question and answer in
the EA (chapter 15 Schmidt): "O Lord, is it necessary that we take
the cup and drink it? He said: Yes, it is". The apostles — sons and
children of wisdom — will have to suffer to test their faithfulness.
By admonishing, preaching, doing good to people who mock them
and persecute them, they *are* martyrs indeed, rejected by all men and
taking their violent exit from the world. Now it was the great merit
of Wichmann, following in the steps of Volz, to have hall-marked
the notion of the "Leidenstheologie": the reflection on the undeserved
suffering and the unjustified accusation, in short on martyrdom. Odil
Hannes Steck in particular worked out the idea in his *Israel und das
gewaltsame Geschick der Propheten*, proving that early Christian reflections on martyrdom were deeply rooted in late Jewish conceptions
and traditions on the subject.[2] In my opinion the pages 4^{23}-6^{21} in our

---

[2] See Paul Volz, *Die Eschatologie der jüdischen Gemeinde im neutestamentlichen Zeit-alter*, Tübingen 1934; Wolfgang Wichmann, *Die Leidenstheologie*. Eine Form der Leidens-

EJ, which deal with temptation, persecution, accusation, suffering, being offended, despising death, being concerned about life and so on, are to be interpreted from this point of view.

One might then however make the suggestion that on closer examination this passage includes only the topic on persecution from the stereotyped *Leidenstheologie*, applied only in a *literary* manner and above all painted over in a *gnostic* sense, as often happened with Jewish, Jewish-Christian and Christian traditions. Thus p. 5:19 ⲚⲦⲀϨⲈ ϨⲰⲰⲦ — "as I myself" — could mean Christ setting an example to the gnostics, to withdraw themselves inwardly from the world of evil matter. In this case the suffering of Christ would have been evaluated unhistorically, as is done in Ev. Ver. p. 18:21-25, 20:11, 25-30. Now I for one *do* understand 5:19 in terms of the mystical union with Christ's sufferings. The passage with which we are concerned in EJ points, I should think, to *real* intimidation. It goes without saying that in the process topics and stereotyped expressions belonging to the *Leidenstheologie* were actualised, because actual suffering *was* at hand. Not in the sense of the later severe persecutions systematically organised by pagan governments: there is no real persecution yet in that sense, but a growing tendency towards it. What Carl Schmidt once said in relation to the EA — "Vexationen durch den Pöbel" — is in my opinion the point for our EJ too: vexations on account of the mob. Frend in his *Martyrdom and Persecution in the early Church*[3] convincingly informs us about the Egyptian situation from the middle of the second century. I should therefore prefer to say that the *positive evaluation* of martyrdom, as we meet it in the EA and EJ — in connection with real vexations — was deeply rooted in a Jewish-Christian *Leidenstheologie* which is attested for the *early Christian world of Egypt too*.

III

The *third* main point: the question of gnostic salvation as described in terms of *healing*. We have to deal with this topic because a *relevant*

---

deutung im Spätjudentum, Stuttgart 1930 and Odil Hannes Steck, *Israël und das gewaltsame Geschick der Propheten*. Untersuchungen zur Überlieferung des deuteronomistischen Geschichtsbildes im Alten Testament, Spätjudentum und Urchristentum, Neukirchen 1967.

[3] W. H. C. Frend, *Martyrdom and Persecution in the early Church*, A study of a conflict from the Maccabees to Donatus, Oxford 1965.

translation and a well-founded *interpretation* of 3:28 and 3:32 are involved. For a relevant translation, one should not stick to a general overall meaning, but consider the *context* and relevant *parallels*. Now the verbs most commonly used for "to heal" are ⲕⲁ⳨ⲕ, ⲣ̄ⲡⲁ⳨ⲣⲉ, and especially ⲧⲁⲗϭⲟ. As already stated, ⲙ̄ⲧⲁⲛ *can* bear the connotation of healing and health. In those days "illness" and "health" were to a large extent used metaphorically. In this connection it should be noted that God especially figures as the great physician (ever since Plato's Symposium, 189d, 193d); the figure was used by preference in early Christian literature and in gnostic writings (Jesus as physician in the Acts of Peter and the Twelve (codex VI); Acts of Thomas, Manichean Psalms, Acts of Paul). Remarkably, the idea of rest is also mentioned in some of these documents, although not in direct connection with the topic of healing. Attention may be drawn to the fact that deficiency (ϭⲱⲝⲃ̄) is hall-marked as the essence of illness, and indeed both *before* (p. 2:33, 35 by implication) and *after* our passage (p. 3:36/37; 4:1-21).

"Deficiency" certainly has the function of a key-word in the EJ. Furthermore, we should not fail to observe that this idea was given a prominent place in Valentinian Gnosticism. Together with *passion*, the *female* nature and *irresolution* it characterises "illness". One might even speak of a "*doctrine of illness*" in Valentinian Gnosticism, healing being an essential pre-requisite before one can arrive at Rest as salvation in the final sense (see Sagnard[4] pp. 260-262). The contrasting notions of fullness and deficiency, though very fundamental in Valentinianism, are not exclusively Valentinian. Thus we find ϣⲧⲁ and ⲭⲱⲕ frequently in the *Apocryphon of John*, as well as in the *Letter of Eugnostos* and the *Sophia Jesu Christi*; also in the *Gospel of the Egyptians* and *On the Origin of the World* (with the interesting passages p. 166:1 ⲁⲛⲁⲡⲁ√ⲥⲓⲥ ⲙ̄ⲛ̄ⲧ⳨ⲏⲕⲉ = rest from deficiency, because choic man was awakened by Eve on the eighth day, and p. 175 which connects perfection or fullness with the theme of kingship); and finally the *Paraphrase of Shem*, which demonstrates the relation between deficiency and perfection on the one hand and rest on the other. We should take note of the fact that the topics of *Deficiency and Perfection and Rest and Kingship* are often interrelated, as in our EJ p. 12:30 (fullness/kingship). Deficiency — the essence of illness in the gnostic sense — is also connected with

---

[4] F. M. M. Sagnard, *La Gnose valentinienne et le Témoignage de Saint Irénée*, Paris 1947.

sleep or intoxication, and not surprisingly (see our epistle, p. 3:8ff. Lines 11/12 in my opinion should be translated : "you (apostles) ought to be ashamed : though you are awake, you are asleep".). The most striking feature is, later on, the relationship (contrasting indeed!) between sleep (James and Peter) and kingship or the kingdom (p. 9:33, 10:5-6). Now the pejorative meaning of sleep in a metaphorical sense, together with drunkenness and deficiency, can be traced back not only to the philosophical tradition but in particular to the wisdom speculation of hellenistic-alexandrinian Judaism. Sleep's counterpart — a wakeful erection to knowledge, the famous "Status Rectus" — and the synonyms of these terms are in my opinion connected with each other by *kingship as a kind of Leitmotiv*. Now these categories (fullness/perfection, stability, rest and kingship) are already found in Philo's theory of virtues : the wise man is the real king. For the translation and interpretation of p. 3:28 and 32 it is of fundamental importance to realise that in Log. 2/3 of the Gospel of Thomas Kingship and Rest are interrelated in a very significant way, pointing once again — so far as the origin of the combination is concerned — to the Jewish-hellenistic sapiential literature.[5] Though this is not the place to deal with the theme of rest as the final goal in the Gospel of Thomas, it must be pointed out that in the complicated but essential interdependence (between the Oxyrhynchus logion, the remodelled Logion 2, Clement's quotation from the Gospel of the Hebrews, the Acts of Thomas, and especially the Second Apocalypse of James in Codex V) *"ruling" and "resting" point to the final goal of gnostic salvation.* Therefore, both on *contextual* grounds (deficiency, perfection, kingship) in our EJ and on *conceptual* grounds (the notions forming part of *one* complex of thought), I would give as my conclusion that the Coptic translator deliberately *chose* M̄TAN in 3:28, 32 instead of one of the common verbs for healing, precisely in order to achieve a clear contrast between the notions of illness (deficiency, sleep) and salvation (kingly rest). And this not only for the sake of the contrast, but also in view of the possibility to emphasise the *kingly worthiness* essential to the real gnostics concerned. The expression *"rest from illness"* need not be considered difficult (we may recall *Origin of the World* 166:1 : *rest from deficiency*). Moreover a possible acquain-

---

[5] Cf. E. Bammel, Rest and Rule, *VC* 23 (1969) p. 88-91 and especially M. Marcovich, Textual Criticism on the Gospel of Thomas, *J.T.S.* 20 (1969) p. 53-74; as for the point in question p. 56-58.

tance, on the part of the Coptic translator of our EJ, with the Gospel
of Thomas — used by Egyptian Manicheans, who still flourished as a
community in the middle of the fourth century and later — could
have been of some influence in his choice of ᴍᴛⲁɴ. Finally, the
proposed translation could be clarified (as I see it) by the following
interpretation. On p. 3 it is primarily the apostles Peter and James
who occupy the foreground. Jesus is rebuking them because they are
still wavering between fullness and deficiency, but then they are told
that eternal life is theirs, thanks to Jesus who himself has healed them
(ⲣ̄ⲡⲁϩⲣⲉ as a precondition before Rest is achieved).

In the preceding lines, two groups of people are characterised,
although in reality they are said to have made their appearance *after*
the apostles. First there are those who have indeed seen and heard the
Son of Man (3:17; 12:39f.), but will not attain to true belief. The woe
of 3:28 applies to them: in their self-complacency they think that
they will lose the illness of their soul merely by the purely external
hearing of the proclamation of salvation. Self-contented as they are,
they rest from their illness, that is, they imagine they have already
obtained the rest or repose of salvation. In reality, however, they
remain in their state of illness, and will return to their illness as the
situation appropriate to them. In an ironic way, *their* kind of Rest is
typified as a premature one. They do not really understand the *essence*
of deficiency, rest and martyrdom. They are would-be gnostics, church
members who live in a fatal superficiality or, to put it in the Valentinian
idiom, psychics tending to a hylic situation of life. Totally opposed
to them are the *real* gnostics, announced to appear after the apostles:
Cerinthus, the Children. The benediction of 3:32 applies to them:
they knew the Rest as final salvation beforehand, so that they could
not really become ill or deficient. One might call them Pneumatics,
the Children who surpass both the apostles. As to the qualification
"children", we may recall the Apocryphon of John, where Christ is
described as a child (ⲁⲗⲟⲩ: BG 21:4; 34:11f.), the wellknown
Valentinian predilection for this title (Heracleon; also Ev. Ver. p. 43:
2 and 22), and on the other side EA, which is anti-gnostic but sometimes gnosticising. There ᴍᴛⲁɴ is an eschatological good. Most inter-
estingly, the Christians to come are called *Children* of the Kingdom,
and also ⲧⲉⲗⲉⲓⲟⲓ (ch. 29). As to the true gnostics of the EJ with their
"ontological privilege", it is precisely their *coming* into this world
which remains problematic. The situation of James and Peter falls
remarkably between the two: one might say that they represent pneu-

matics as still latent, imprisoned in the world, often tending to a psychic way of life (cf. 12:39; 9:25-28; and especially 11:11-14), but essentially the apostles share true gnostic salvation as God's beloved, according to his providence (5:5). On the other hand the stressing of their *liberum arbitrium* ("free choice", 5:6) does not fit their rather pneumatic essence. Here it becomes clear enough that the later Valentinian distinction of three classes of men does not operate at this point.

In conclusion : the EJ in my opinion too is certainly to be located in Egyptian gnostic circles, about the middle of the second century. However, it bears witness to a gnosticism in which Cerinthian views, speculations on ⲁⲛⲁⲡⲁⲩⲥⲓⲥ as salvation in a final sense, and even a Leidenstheologie bearing on actual circumstances, could all be linked together. It is a gnosticism that defies clear-cut systematisations and classifications, for in those days boundaries were fluid; a gnosticism which may perhaps reflect some acquaintance with the beginnings of the gnostic pattern of Valentinus, but for the most part shows a remarkable closeness, both temporal and often conceptual, to the Egyptian anti-gnostic EA. With many crucial passages still unresolved, the EJ remains a most intriguing document, and one which as yet does not allow us much ⲁⲛⲁⲡⲁⲩⲥⲓⲥ!

THE COLOPHON OF THE *GOSPEL OF THE EGYPTIANS*: CONCESSUS AND MACARIUS OF NAG HAMMADI

by

P. BELLET, O.S.B.

I have published elsewhere a review[1] of the critical edition of the *Gospel of the Egyptians* by A. Böhlig and F. Wisse.[2] My present paper was originally meant as a review-study of the edition, in which were discussed the colophon in Codex III and related questions in the Nag Hammadi corpus. The historical character of my review, however, dealing as it did with authorship, onomastics, epistolography, dialect characteristics, and the general question of the possible origin of the Gnostic Corpus, seemed less fitting for publication in a biblical periodical. So I intend now to present the results of my research, trying to prove the conclusions I announced in my review. I intend to keep the inductive method of my research, even if the very title of my paper seems to tell the most important information about the content of the colophon, the identification of the scribe and his colleague, and their importance in the history and culture of the gnostic cenacle.

Some of the hypotheses on textual criticism and grammar were formulated before the publication of the facsimile edition of Codex III and, in my view, proved to be essentially correct. So I left them unchanged, because this working process leads the reader to a better understanding of some important details in grammar and dialect.

The Colophon

From my point of view the most important part of the text in III is the colophon, which is lacking in IV, at least by mutilation. According to the editors, it was probably absent, unless it was written

---

[1] *Catholic Biblical Quarterly* 39 (1977) 275-7.

[2] A. Böhlig and F. Wisse, in coöperation with P. Labib, *Nag Hammadi Codices III.2 and IV.2, The Gospel of the Egyptians* (*The Holy Book of the Great Invisible Spirit* [*Nag Hammadi Studies* IV]). Leiden: E. J. Brill, 1975. I would like to thank my colleague Msgr. P. W. Skehan for reading my paper and assisting me in discussing problems of onomastics, textual criticism, dialects, and patristics.

on the (lost) lower part of page 82 which was left blank, an entirely improbable thing (pp. 8, 22, 31 note 7, 37 note 4, 167, 206).

To facilitate control of the discussion it seems necessary to give the text of the colophon. Naturally I follow my criteria for the editing of Coptic texts. The present translation differs in several points from that given by B.-W.

Colophon III.69.6-17

```
6    πεγαγγελιον ⟨ν⟩νρμνκημε
     τβιβλος νςραϊ ννουτε τριε
8    ρα ετρηπ τεχαρις τςυνρεςις
     τεςθηςις τεφρονηςις μνπε
10   ρςρητς · εγγνωςτος παγαπη
     τικος ρμπεπνα ρντςαρξ ·
12   παρενπε γογγεςˋςˊος μννα
     ωβρογοειν ρνογαφθαρςια
14   ις πεχς πωηρε μπνουτε
     πςωτηρ · ιχθυς θεογραφος
16   τβιβλος τριερα μπνοб ναρο
     ρατον μπνα ραμην > > > ——
     > > > > ——
```

The Gospel of the Egyptians. The God-written, holy, secret book. Grace, understanding, perception, prudence (be) with him who has written it, Eugnostos the loving in the Spirit — in the flesh my name is Goggessos — and with my partners in the lights in incorruptibility. Jesus Christ, Son of God, Saviour. IXΘΥΣ. God-written (is) the holy book of the great, invisible Spirit. Amen.

The editors dedicate a few lines of commentary to the colophon (pp. 31 and 206), but have not tried to identify the name of the scribe and the problem which it presents, probably because they were not convinced by the explanations of other scholars. Thus they have left matters in the colophon as they are and have simply given the scribe the *spiritual* name EYΓNΩCTΩC and the *fleshly* name ΓOΓΓECCOC. To begin with the latter name, Doresse seems to be the only one to have discussed it, and he gave to the name Goggessos the sense 'murmurer', because according to the religion of Zoroaster the faithful did not recite their prayers but *murmured* them. Or, following the opinion of Scholem, they talked confidentially, as though *murmuring* or *whispering* the secret mysteries.[3] There is a categorical reason which makes this overly complicated explanation unacceptable. It would give the name an esoteric or initiate sense, which is exactly the opposite of what the colophon says. And phonetically it is difficult to place it in relation to the Greek γόγγυσος, especially with the correction of the name in the colophon by a contemporary hand. The solution to the problem of the name is automatically given in itself: ΓΟΓΓΕϹϹΟϹ = ΚΟΝΚΕϹϹΟϹ = Concessus.

The colophon, then, brings us into contact with a Latin, who had become Egyptian to such an extent that his speech no longer distinguished palatals. Given this identification, our imagination can freely picture a Latin, a disciple and follower of the school and teachings, perhaps, of Valentinus, the master of gnosticism at Rome in the second half of the second century, who followed him to Egypt; or a Latin, a second- or third-generation Copt, one perhaps of the many veterans, administrative functionaries or the like who became established in Egypt. After examining scores and scores of works relative to documents and onomastics in Greek, Coptic, and Latin, we have been able to add only one example to the work of Preisigke (1922, repr. 1967) and the *Onomasticon* of the *TLL* II (1913). The *Onomasticon* bears witness that the masculine form of the name was known at Ostia, Germania Superior, Dacia, Numidia (8 examples), Byzacena (1 example), and Provincia Proconsularis (5 examples). The feminine 'Concessa' was known at Ostia, Nimes, Narbonensis, Rhaetia, Dalmatia, Baetica, Numidia, Mauretania Sitifensis, and Provincia Byzacena. It seems, then, to be a Latin name belonging mainly to Africa in the region around Carthage. We know of its existence in Egypt first from the documents adduced by Preisigke: *P.Teb.* II.338.13 of the years A.D. 194-196, in the reign of Septimius Severus. This is a revenue-return to Philoxenus, *strategus* of the divisions of Themistes and Polemon in the Fayum, by order of the *epistrategus* Calpurnius Concessus. This *epistrategus* is also known from *BGU* 1022.21 of the fourth year of Severus and from *P.Kar.* 425.1 (Youtie), August A.D. 198. The variants of the name in inscriptions and documents, 'Comcesus', ΚΟΝΚΕϹΤΟϹ etc., do not detract from the identity of the name, and no scholars have seen any difficulty here. The Latin form of our scribe would be the normal 'Concessus'.

---

[3] *JA* 256 (1968) 325 and 360 nn. 199-200.

With reference to the name ΕΥΓΝΩϹΤΟϹ, it does not appear in Preisigke *NB*, while the *Onomasticon* of the *TLL* has reached only the letter *D*. Nor does it appear in Forcellini or in *CIL* VI, Pars VII (1975). My researches in other documents have yielded nothing. One must search much further. But research up to now seems to me to justify the conclusion that if the name existed it must have been quite rare, and, in view of what I shall have to say, perhaps related only to gnostic circles. In the present case, I believe that one must consider the name as a hypocoristicon of γνωστικός, and not as a passive form. Rather it is a synonym of εὐγνώστης, in so far as the word would signify, not 'well-known', but 'good at knowing', 'knowing well'' (the secret), 'divining', and, with the εὐ- -prefix, 'good at divining', 'the skilful diviner', 'sage'. If γνωστός in Gen 2:9 is doubtful (Lampe), Philo understood it as active in his commentary : γνωριστικός (var. γνωστικός) (*De opif. mundi* I.54.3 [= ed. Cohn]), and so did Origen : τὸ γνωστὸν καλοῦ καὶ πονηροῦ ξύλον (*C. Celsum* IV.39 = I.311.11 [= ed. Koetschau]). Concessus, in taking this other name, or his 'fellow-lights' or 'partners in the lights' in giving him this name, would have used the same terminology as the Christian gnostic Clement of Alexandria : ὁ ἄρα γνωστικός, τοῦ ἑνὸς ὄντως θεοῦ...ἀγαπητικὸς ὑπάρχων (*Strom.* III.49.13 [= ed. Stählin]). The resemblance to the colophon is striking. This brings us to the sense of the word ἀγαπητικός not as 'beloved' (p. 166), but as 'loving, charitable' toward the brothers, of course, 'in the Spirit'. The 'Spirit' is not the Spirit of Christian theology, but the 'great and invisible Spirit' of which the colophon speaks at the end and which gives the real title of the book described by the author in the first lines of the tractate.

The editors (pp. 31 and 206), and scholars in general, speak of the *spiritual* name Eugnostos and the *fleshly* name Goggessos. This is not a false description. But it is not properly so expressed in the colophon, because 'in the Spirit' does not refer to Eugnostos, except in so far as it is a moral quality of his love. The translation 'beloved' seems to me to imply that Eugnostos was already dead and a venerated figure in the gnostic circle. This does not agree with the following statement in the colophon about the fleshly name. The word 'loving' gives a quality to the person of Eugnostos and to the mission he exercised in the cenacle. Eugnostos is the 'good divine' and the 'loving' divine of the gnostic group. Concessus, then, is the leader, the master, the divine. Eugnostos is the *charismatic*, official name, in the way that *Apa* defines Pachomius, or *archimandrites* Shenoute.

Another important word for the understanding of the colophon is
ϣⲃⲣⲟⲅⲟⲉⲓⲛ. The word appears also in the *Pistis Sophia* 135.4-5.[4]
The editors translate it 'fellow lights', which are rightly understood as
'fellow gnostics' (p. 206), rightly if the word is understood as an
allegorical application, on the human level, of gnostic mythology. The
word is inspired by the section about 'consorts' (σύζυγοι) 'of the lights'
(III.52.3-16; IV.63.24-64.10). But while the 'consorts' which make up
the ogdoad of Autogenes (grace, understanding, perception, prudence,
the four concepts which appear in the colophon in Greek form) have
this Greek form as well in the body of Codex III, the text of IV translates
them into Coptic with the exception of αἴσθησις,[5] and keeps in Greek
the word φωστήρ, a technical word in gnostic theology for the divine
element of the ogdoad. This the text of III translates by ⲟⲩⲟⲉⲓⲛ
except for the case where it presents the theme (III.52.6). Here
logically it too uses the technical word φωστήρ. The text of IV would
then have said ϣⲃⲣⲫⲱⲥⲧⲏⲣ, and would not have had a colophon
exactly identical with that of III. In this case also III seems to me
to manifest a more primitive character, while the Coptic terminology
of IV.63.24-64.10 is the consequence of a later exegesis to explain
text III and to make clear the symmetry between the four lights, the
pleroma, on the divine level, and the four consorts on the human
level, — in plain terms, the four virtues of gnostic morality. Thus,
the Greek word corresponding to ϣⲃⲣⲟⲅⲟⲉⲓⲛ would have been
formed not with συν-, which would make the gnostics 'fellow-lights'
with the divine element, a false idea, but rather with φιλο-, ὁμο- or
'partners of the lights', the four σύζυγοι or moral virtues Concessus
demands.

The editors (p. 23) believe that the colophon was translated from
the Greek. The theory is possible, but not necessary. If true, the literary
activity of Concessus would have to be placed at the end of the
second century, if this be the date of the composition of the tractate.
But the colophon could have been written in Coptic exactly as it is
and precisely according to the Coptic of III, and not for any Greek
Vorlage. We do not see that "the benediction 'grace ... (be) with ...'

---

[4] C. Schmidt, ed., *Pistis Sophia* [*Coptica* II] (Copenhagen 1925).

[5] The order in the colophon is different from that in the body of *GE*. It is
worth noting that Coptic theology has always been uneasy in translating αἴσθησις,
'perception through the senses or the mind'. Prov 2:3-6 shows that αἴσθησις as a
Coptic word translated the Greek αἴσθησις (vs. 3 add. against B*S), ἐπίγνωσις (5),
γνῶσις (6).

reflects the Greek since Coptic would *normally* require a verb" (p. 206; italics mine). Let it suffice to cite the Sahidic of 1 Thes 5:28; Tit 3:15; Phlm 25; Heb 13:25 among many other examples to show that the colophon in this case could have been conceived in Coptic. That it has a strongly Greek character means nothing in a colophon or in a Coptic work of the period.

This also is the explanation which must be given to the acrostic IXΘYC and to the reading which the author of the colophon makes of it. The editors (p. 206) find a reason for their theory of Greek influence, in so far as "the added monogram IXΘYC refers to the Greek text." Another explanation seems better. The acrostic — to call it 'monogram' is incorrect — is, in the mind of the author of the colophon, an authentic *ideogram*, such that Concessus gives it a reading that was natural to him : Coptic, and uniquely Coptic. The use of the complete title is not Greek, as the authors would have it, nor is it anything remarkable. Concessus expressed himself as he had to, in Coptic. It does not seem to me out of place to give another example which brings us not very far from the period and the geography of the Corpus of Nag Hammadi : *P. Bodmer* VI, Prov.[6] The scribe of the fourth-fifth century appears uncertain of himself, and his orthography resists all attempts at classification. But it seems evident that the *nomina sacra* in *Greek* in 3:9 and 5:21, ̄м̄ογ, and in 16.11, ναϩρμκγ, suppose the *Coptic* reading πνογτε and πχοειс, which explains the assimilation of the preceding consonant. The Greek reading makes no sense. It is contrary to the textual tradition of other Coptic texts, Akhmimic and Sahidic, of Prov (on which P depends), is erroneous as to the genitive which it supposes, and, as we said, does not explain the assimilation. The scribe of P, then, very deficient in Coptic culture, saw and read the *nomen sacrum* as an ideogram which he himself had created (both times at the end of a line to save space). That is exactly what Concessus has done in his colophon.

The editors note repeatedly that the tractate is only marginally Christian, and Christ appears only six times and in a syncretistic context. But the existence of the acrostic and of its expansion would seem to indicate a complete Christianity. All in all, this Christianity is only apparent and in the words, the context of which is transformed from a Christian sense to a Sethian gnostic sense. Σωτήρ in the

---

[6] R. Kasser, ed., *Papyrus Bodmer VI : Livre des Proverbes* (*CSCO* 194; Scr. Copt. 27). Louvain 1960. Quoted as P.

colophon is Seth. The word appears only once in the tractate and is
clearly applied to Seth 'the great saviour' (III.68.22), whose mission, in
passing through the three parousias, is to *save* (ⲚⲞⲨϨⲘ) the race "who
went astray" (III.63.8). The editors in their commentary (pp. 191-197)
on sections III.63.4-64.9 'On the Work of Seth' and III.64.9-65.26 'On
the Bringers of Salvation', clearly demonstrate the equation of Seth =
Jesus and their common "dwelling-place in heaven". The sense, then,
of σωτήρ in the colophon is a normal application of the term, borrowed
for the second conclusion of the tractate (III.68.22). The affirmation
of the tractate seems explicit: "The great Seth wrote this book ...
in order that ... it may come forth and reveal this ... holy race of
the great Σωτήρ" (III.68.10-22). And the whole expansion of the
acrostic refers not to the Christ of the Christians, but to Seth of the
sect. I cannot tell from where Concessus took the knowledge and the
application of the acrostic. But it does not seem to me that "the symbol
of the fish was known at that time [at what time?] in Egyptian
Christianity" (p. 106; cf. 35f.) only by the authority of Clement of
Alexandria (*Paid.* III.11.59.2 [= ed. Stählin p. 270.8]) whom the editors
cite. The symbol in Clement has not the well-known christological
meaning. It is one of five symbols which Clement admits as modest
on the rings worn by women at Alexandria: a dove, a fish, a ship,
a lyre, an anchor. And with reference to the fish, the reason is clear:
"if it is a fisherman, it will recall the apostle and the young men who
were pulled out of the water." The christological symbol was known
from literary documents such as the Sibylline Oracles and Tertullian,
and from archaeological documentation such as the inscriptions of
Abercius (Phrygia) and Pectorius (Gaul), and different monuments at
Rome, perhaps later, but always within the period possible for the
literary activity of Concessus. The symbol, then, does not point to
Egypt as a possible "place of origin of the tractate" (p. 36). In point
of fact, we do believe that the tractate is Egyptian, but not for that
reason. And if it were to be demonstrated that the colophon belonged
originally to the Greek redaction in its primitive second-century form
or in the actual compilation of the second-third centuries, the witness
of the colophon could be the oldest literary witness to the acrostic.
The expansion did not create the symbol. It is the symbol that created
the expansion. However, the symbol could have been understood
originally in gnostic terms, without relation to the orthodox Christian
sense. The symbol, then, must be read according to the thought of
the person using it. It is to be found as well in another Sethian tractate,

The Three Steles of Seth (Codex VII.5.118.8), but in this case I do not know how the symbol is to be interpreted.

Dialects and Palaeography

The editors dedicate some pages to the dialect and palaeographic peculiarities of the two codices. Publication of the whole collection will permit the study of the influence of one dialect on another, and it seems that it must serve for localization of dialects and for establishment of the provenance of MSS. With reference to Codex III, the editors indicate that "there are almost no unusual or non-Sahidic grammatical features in the tractate" (p. 7). A careful reading of the Coptic index seems to me to show a deeper influence of A, A², ME. For the present I shall limit myself to two details which seem important for the morphology of the Coptic verb and which put us in touch with the culture of Concessus. Of the Perfect Relative the editors cite *once* the form єp- (III.60.26). To this must be added also 69.9-10, precisely in the colophon. The form has been treated with sufficient documentation by Crum (*Dict.* 57b) for the Sahidic of the *Pistis Sophia* from Akhmim and the Subakhmimic of John, and also by Kasser[7] for the dialect called 'Middle Egyptian proper' (ME), according to the terminology of Kahle, for which the name 'Oxyrhynchic' has been, perhaps in premature fashion, proposed. Kasser's documentation for ME is based above all on the codex G67 of Acts, which seems to me to indicate a localization towards the south of the area of the dialect, much in accord with the influence on Codex III of Nag Hammadi. The form belongs to A² and ME, but we do not see it quoted by Quecke[8] for the Milan MS of the epistles of Paul in ME dialects. The other dialect peculiarity seems to reinforce yet again the extension of ME towards the south. The editors (p. 7) indicate "a unique expression for the passive by means of an impersonal third person feminine singular instead of the usual third person plural" in III.2.66.6 and also in III.1.33.17, "in a relative clause both times." To this add III.1.36.8

---

[7] *Compléments morphologiques au dictionnaire de Crum* (*BIFAO* 64 [1966]) 64.

[8] In T. Orlandi, *Papiri della Università degli Studi di Milano* V (Milan 1974); cf. M. Krause/P. Labib, *Gnostische u. hermetische Schriften aus Codex II u. Codex VI* (Glückstadt 1971). This old prefix is also found four times in P. Bodmer III of John in Old Bohairic of the fourth century (?), cf. Kasser in *CSCO* 177 (Louvain 1958) p. xi. This fact and the relation to *Pistis Sophia* is irrelevant to the question of supposed gnosticism in this old version, *pace* Kasser (*ibid.*, p. xii) and E. Massaux (*NTS* 5 [1958-1959] 210-212).

and 11. This form seems to me all by itself to define a dialect and a locality. The parallel texts of the *Apocryphon Johannis* of Codices II and IV published by Krause[9] and of *BG* 8502 published by Till[10] have the form ⲉⲧⲟⲩ-, common to all dialects. Only Codex III, connected with the scribe Concessus, presents this peculiarity, which is a normal form of the Present I *Relative* in ME as opposed to *all* other dialects. But the concept of *impersonal* does not seem to explain anything. It is simply a matter of a third person plural ⲉⲧⲥⲉ- which the scribe, through a hearing error, wrote as third person feminine singular ⲉⲧⲥ. Or it could establish the existence — not hitherto attested in Coptic — of a popular form common to singular and plural as in Demotic,[11] in such a way that the difference between third person feminine singular and third person plural was in older ME only morphographic, not phonetic or morphologic. The error, then, if error there was, was an easy one to make. Once again, this detail leads us to an influence of ME, and of it alone, on the codex of Concessus and, moreover, to a localization of ME towards the south. The correction of the text by Krause, albeit in a note, is uncalled for. Another important point for palaeography is the reading ⲡⲛⲟⲩⲧⲉ in III.63.2 which the editors rightly correct to ⲡϯ (gift), and which the copyist of III would have taken erroneously for a compendium of the *nomen sacrum*. On p. 191 the editors amply illustrate other examples of misunderstanding of this false compendium in *BG*. But the affirmation of the editors, following Till, that the form of the compendium ⲛ̄ϯ or ⲡ̄ϯ is owed to Fayumic influence (difficult to explain in Sahidic MSS) does not seem convincing. The abbreviation ⲡ̄ϯ/ⲛ̄ϯ, or better ⲡⲛϯ, is the only case where ME proper has the final iota in agreement with Fayumic and Bohairic as Kahle indicated (*Bal* I.222). However, in the present case the confusion comes from an influence neither Fayumic nor Bohairic, but rather ME proper, upon the scribe of III, a simple and easy case of distraction not evidenced in the other tractates of his codex. It was an error which could have been committed by the scribe of the first exemplar who was working on the original of the translation. Therefore palaeographically the copy of *GE* in III could have been the first library copy. To say that "this passage proves

---

[9] M. Krause/P. Labib, *Die drei Versionen des Apokryphon des Johannis im Koptischen Museum zu Alt-Kairo* [*ADAIK*, Kopt. Reihe I] (Wiesbaden 1962).

[10] *Die gnostischen Schriften des koptischen Papyrus Berolinensis 8502* [TU 62] (Berlin 1955). We could not see the second edition by H.-M. Schenke (1972).

[11] Cf. G. Steindorff, *Lehrbuch der koptischen Grammatik* (Chicago 1951) § 312.

that we are not dealing with *the first Coptic copy* [italics mine] of this version of GEgypt" (p. 191) seems to me to be saying nothing at all. Hitherto there has been presented, so far as I know, no proof that *GE* of Codex III is *not* a first copy of the original of the translation. But we cannot any the more say that it is. The *first* copy in a literary hand depends always on the private original copy. These are the details which oblige us not to hold an opinion until the complete publication of the whole Nag Hammadi collection.

The Work of Concessus

To give some coherence to the previous discussion about the content of the colophon and to give some precision to our results, we must grant that the scribe bore the name Concessus and the cognomen Eugnostos. The reason for the second name was not only that it is a hypocoristic form of 'gnostic', but also a proper appellation for his role, 'divine' of the cenacle. If the two Eugnostoi, the one of the colophon of Codex III and the one of the Letter of Eugnostos the Blessed, are to be identified as the same person, it must be said that the colophon comes originally from Concessus but the copy is not by him. If the two persons are different, the MS *could* have a known scribe, Concessus, who copied *GE*, perhaps his own version, and gathered together other tractates of a previous Eugnostos, a venerated figure in the gnostic circle and perhaps his predecessor as 'divine' of the group. Naturally so, if μακάριος means 'blessed'. With reference to the relationship between the two Eugnostoi and between the Greek original and the Coptic translation and to the period of the literary activity of the author, translator and copyist, perhaps four hypotheses could be made, which scholarship must work out, and all of which suppose that Concessus was the colophon's author.

A. One could place the redaction of the work in Greek by Concessus in the second-third centuries, in such a way that we are dealing only with a Coptic translation of a Greek text and colophon.

B. The MS may be giving us a copy made by Concessus at the end of the third century from a pre-existent Coptic version of which he was only the copyist. The verb in III.69.19, then, ⲡⲉⲣ̄ⲥϩⲏⲧ̄ⲥ, would mean 'the one who copied'. Or, perhaps Concessus worked on the text and the translation, in such a way as to merit the name of the author, and then the verb could be understood as meaning 'the one who wrote'.

C. Concessus may be writing his own Coptic version in calligraphic form, in such a way that he was both translator and scribe. The MS would then be the original library copy. This would call for two Eugnostoi. Concessus could not include in his volume a work by himself where he called himself 'blessed', if this be the sense of μακάριος in the Letter of Eugnostos.

D. The scribe may be giving us the Coptic version of Concessus, according to (C), or the original of Concessus translated, according to (A), and at the end preserving the colophon of the Coptic archetype or of the Greek original, in such a way that Concessus was the author or translator of the tractate and author of the colophon, but not the copyist of the codex.

There are many questions to be resolved before making a scientific decision. But we would incline toward this last hypothesis, for a very simple reason, namely the error of the first hand in the name of the scribe, as I indicate in my transcription. It does not seem possible that the scribe made a mistake in his own name. Whether the correction is by the first or a second hand, the hand of the codex itself cannot be that of Concessus.

The fact that in the copying of earlier works the colophon of the archetype is preserved has nothing strange about it. I shall cite the case of the colophon of Evagrius Ponticus in the Coislinianus (H) of the Bibliothèque Nationale, Paris, of the sixth century, and then in the Neapolitanus, Lib. n°. II.A.7, of the twelfth century. Both reproduce the colophon of Evagrius of the second half of the fourth century, both the colophon and naturally the biblical text which was joined with it.[12] The codex of Concessus, then, would give us his work, *GE*, of which he was the author or translator, but not his own hand. The scribe, unknown, would have added other Sethian works, which might or might not be by Concessus.

Letter of Eugnostos the Blessed?

Finally we enter *in medias res* with a few words about the so-called *Letter of Eugnostos*. The name seems to have been sufficient to identify him with the person of the colophon, without our having seen a

---

[12] Colophon published by J. A. Robinson, *Euthaliana* [*Texts and Studies* III.3] (Cambridge 1895) 3. Diplomatic edition and plate of Coislinianus in H. Omont, Notice sur un très ancien manuscrit grec en onciales des Épîtres de Saint Paul, *Notices et extraits...* 33.1 (1890) 189 and Plate II. Cf. J. Finegan, *Encountering New Testament Manuscripts* (Grand Rapids 1974) §§ 41-42.

serious effort at research. So, as far as the relation between the two Eugnostoi is concerned, the editors (p. 206) have only this sentence : "the name Eugnostos is interesting in that there is a tractate by that name in Codex III and V, 'The Letter of Eugnostos'". I acknowledge that the name and above all the appellation 'blessed' bothered me continually in my research. But at the end I think I have found the solution. The *Letter* bears no resemblance to the superficial Christianity of *GE*. They are alike perhaps only in a stylistic frequency of self-citation.[13] The completely or almost completely pagan character of the *Letter* does not seem to be in agreement with the appellation 'blessed', which supposes rather a Christian ideology, which one could attribute to Concessus. The appellation is necessarily late, and quite inapplicable to the Eugnostos of the *Letter*. It is inapplicable, unless we are dealing not with an appellation, 'blessed', but with a proper name, 'Macarius', exactly as in the case of Concessus. Both have a name 'according to the flesh', viz. Concessus, Macarius. Both have a 'spiritual' name, to put it thus, a name proper to the head of the gnostic cenacle, viz., Eugnostos, which in both cases is given first. There was, then, an order of succession in the direction of the group. Who preceded or followed whom, we cannot say — nor whether each belonged to a different group. It does not seem to me that the article before the name, which makes it an appellation, presents any difficulty in Coptic. It would indicate only the lateness of the title and a certain degree of christianization posterior to the date of the letter and of the author : second-third century for the Greek, end of the third century for the Coptic translation. In an opposite case to Gal 1:1, and elsewhere in Paul : Παῦλος ἀπόστολος, the translator of the *Letter* of Εὔγνωστος Μακάριος has given a translation equivalent to the biblical text : ⲉⲅⲅⲛⲱⲥⲧⲟⲥ ⲡⲙⲁⲕⲁⲣⲓⲟⲥ = ⲡⲁⲩⲗⲟⲥ ⲡⲁⲡⲟⲥⲧⲟⲗⲟⲥ. The article is erroneous in both cases. The duality of the two Eugnostoi is apparent in and of itself.

Letter of the eugnostos *Macarius*

The translator, then, from a title and a name has made a name and a title. I doubt whether one could present another example in all of

---

[13] The expression 'as I have already mentioned' or the like is to be found many times in both works. E.g. : *GE* IV (III is missing) 58.5; 59.3-15; III.50.9.16 (and parallel); 55.11 (and parallel); 62.11 (and parallel); 63.5 (and parallel); *Letter* : translation p. 28.3, 8; 29.11; 30.10 *infra*; 32.10, 15,29; 34.2, 5.

the Coptic, Greek, or Latin epistolography of antiquity where the
rules for heading letters are not kept, even in the latest versions and
including men like Pachomius, Horsiesi, Shenoute, Athanasius and a
thousand others. To put it bluntly, it is difficult to imagine Pachomius
writing to his monks at Chenoboskion, the supposed neighbors of the
gnostic group : "Apa the blessed to his own." In the case of the *Letter*,
we do not find ourselves facing a liturgical reading. Not even in the
liturgy would it have been expressed that way and no more so for a
citation by a disciple who revered the master. It is simply an *inscriptio*,
classical in style, written by the author. And no one could have written
the form in which it has been presented by scholars, least of all the
author of the *Letter/Tractate*. Evidently even this impossible *inscriptio*
would have ended with χαίρειν, in both cases, in the imaginary one of
Pachomius and the real one of Macarius.

So we come to examine the beginning of the letter of this *eugnostos*.
The text is preserved in Codex III of Concessus and in Codex V by an
unknown scribe. The latter very mutilated text is published in facsmile
edition. It entered the tractate *Sophia Jesu Christi* (*SJC*), if one admits
the priority of the *Letter* to that work, or else came from it, if one
admits a backwards movement from Christian thought evident in *SJC*
towards the almost total paganism which can be seen in the *Letter*.[14]
It would be necessary to consult the two Coptic texts of III and V
of the *Letter* and that of the *SJC* in III for a complete study of their
textual relationship. My knowledge of the *Letter* is limited to the
German and English translations by M. Krause and R.McL. Wilson,
the critical apparatus of Till's edition of the *SJC* in *BG*,[15] and the
reproduction of the mutilated Codex V.

All scholars seem to have stopped before χαίρειν in the *inscriptio*,
making it the beginning of the *Letter*. By my reading, it seems one must
say that Krause-Wilson, in their translation and note, sum up the actual
state of research on and understanding of the opening : "The blessed
Eugnostos to his own : Rejoice in this, that you know ...", with
the following note : "Instead of 'Rejoice in this', the parallel text in

---

[14] Discussion of the opinions on this question in the *Letter* and in gnostic literature
in general, often badly focussed as literary and textual criticism and more often
affected by school prejudices (and not always creditable ones), would be endless. One
can find information in E. M. Yamauchi, *Pre-Christian Gnosticism: a survey of the
proposed evidences* (Grand Rapids 1973) 104-107 (the *Letter*); R. McL. Wilson, *Gnosis
and the New Testament* (Philadelphia 1968) 111-117 (on the *Letter*).

[15] In W. Foerster, ed., *Gnosis: a selection of gnostic texts, II: Coptic and Mandaean
sources* (New York 1974) 24-39. For Till, see n. 10 above.

V.1.3 offers the better reading : Greetings! I wish ..." If this translation and note have any value, it is that they permit us to read the complete Coptic text of the *inscriptio* and beginning of the *Letter*, a Coptic text which has not been given complete by any scholar, even those who described the codices technically. Putting the English-German translation over against the Coptic, the reading and sense of the Coptic which result are so clear that, even supposing a difference of reading, the reading we propose in the note would appear a necessary critical correction. Epistolography and grammar demonstrate the error committed in the translation of the text. The art of letter-writing demands the reading of χαίρειν as belonging to the *inscriptio*. The wrong separation was made by the first scholars to deal with the *Letter*. It stems from a misunderstanding of ϩⲛⲛⲁⲓ, translated 'in this', or better by the German 'in diesen', and which other scholars have, evading responsibility, omitted in translation. But the sense is clear : 'I wish' from ϩⲛⲉ, exactly as the other witnesses : ϯⲟⲩⲱϣ. The variant, material but not real, shows that Codex III by Concessus has the original reading in the Coptic translation with perfect smoothness : "Eugnostos Macarius to those who are his, greetings. It is pleasing to me that you know ..." The verb can be translated by 'I wish', but perhaps we are right in attributing to Macarius a certain style, which renders the Coptic even better. The spelling ⲛⲛ = ⲛ is very common at Nag Hammadi, and has given rise to the double error. The reading ϯⲟⲩⲱϣ is explained only as an introduction to the teaching of Jesus in *SJC*. In the *Letter* it is simply an affirmation of the doctrine accepted in the gnostic cenacle. *SJC* is shown to be secondary, and its reading could have influenced the textual tradition of Codex V. In the codex of Concessus, the causative infinitive depends on ϩⲛⲛⲁⲓ to express finality, not on χαίρειν as in the translations, an error in Coptic grammar. The copyist of III knew the difference between a subordinate clause of finality with causative infinitive dependent on an impersonal verb or verb of wishing, and a co-ordinate clause which would have been expressed with ϫⲉ- and the I Present, or rather simply with the circumstantial present.[16] The grammar supposed by the translators is impossible.

---

[16] In order to discuss this question, I posit the following *inscriptio* and beginning of the *Letter* : ⲉⲩⲅⲛⲱⲥⲧⲟⲥ {ⲡ}ⲙⲁⲕⲁⲣⲓⲟⲥ ⲛ̅ⲛⲉⲧⲉⲛⲟⲩϥⲛⲉ ⲭⲁⲓⲣⲉ · ϩⲛ̅ⲛⲁⲓ ⲉⲧⲣⲉ-ⲧⲛ̅ⲉⲓⲙⲉ ... For the reconstruction we can make use of the partial Coptic title in Krause, *Die drei Versionen...*, p. 19 n. 9; a partial translation by Robinson, *NTS* 14 (1968) 393; the erroneous observation of Till *BG 8502* 80.5; the translation of Krause-

There is, then, a certain fineness of style to the beginning of the *Letter*, which perhaps permits us to attribute to Macarius — in Greek or in Coptic — a certain intellectual eminence, which is illustrated

---

Wilson (*Gnosis* II.27 and n. 3); the incomplete, mutilated and interpolated translation of Doresse (*VC* 2 [1948] 143; *The Secret Books* ... [1960] 192); and a reproduction of the mutilated Codex V. 1. The epistolary formula 'A to B χαίρειν' is the most common in familiar letters, both from a superior to an inferior and vice versa. The omission of χαίρειν is found only a dozen times from the third century B.C. to the third century A.D., and only once in familiar letters (*P. Lond.* I.42, 172 B.C.). In business letters the first example of the omission seems to be *PSI* IV.344, 256 B.C. : letters of fiscal officials copied into registers. It is also lacking — and with reason — in *P. Tebt.* II.424, IIIc. A.D. : Sarapamon is angry with Piperas who owes seven years' rents and dues. Χαίρειν is missing there, of course. Cf. F. J. Exler, *The Form of the Ancient Greek Letter* (Washington 1923). For the addressees, τοῖς ἰδίοις, no explanation is necessary. The formula of introduction, γιγνώσκειν ὑμᾶς θέλω, very common in familiar letters, is often found in the resumption of epistolary style in the body of the letters of St Paul. But the most important word in the beginning of the *Letter* of Macarius is the verb ϩⲛⲉ, which occasions my note. The meaning can be expressed by θέλω, βούλομαι, but the verb has as well a sense of 'pleasure, gladness, contentment, acquiescence', and, still more important, its use seems to lead in a very precise way to the ME dialect area. The verb naturally belongs to the general linguistic wealth of Coptic, but ME has a predilection for it. The vocabulary of the Milan fragments of Paul (cf. n. 8 above) is instructive. According to the Index, of the thirteen times *P.Mil.* uses ϩⲛⲉ, five times Sahidic ϩⲛⲉ is preserved, eight times it represents Sahidic ⲟⲩⲱϣ, very often, if not always, as a question of style and nuance of the concept of will. Our case is illustrated in the Coptic of Col 2:1 : Sah: ϯⲟⲩⲱϣ ⲅⲁⲣ ⲉⲧⲣⲉⲧⲛⲉⲓⲙⲉ; ME : ϩⲛⲉⲓ [ⲅⲁⲣ ⲉⲧⲣⲉⲧⲛⲉⲓⲙ]ⲉ (fol. 48v. 12). The very mutilated formula of the *inscriptio* of the *Letter* in Codex V is different, much longer, and we do not see how Codices III and V could be in agreement. At the end of the *Letter*, the *SJC* of *BG 8502* and Codex III, with variants in the two witnesses, are in agreement in having a plural for the addressees : ⲛⲏⲧⲛ, ⲉⲣⲱⲧⲛ; as opposed to *Letter* : ⲛⲁⲕ. The reading of the *Letter* seems preferable, and the change of number is part of the epistolary style proper to a Letter/tractate, better than the plural of *SJC* in a preaching context. The *Letter* is addressed to the reader; the *SJC* to the listeners.

Addendum : The study in the text and the discussion in the note above were based on my reading of translations and partial editions. Before sending my notes to the printer, I received the transcription of the first three lines of the letter in Codex III from Fr G. W. MacRae, S.J., through the kindness of my former student, Fr D. W. Johnson, S.J. I thank them for their help.

Afterwards I have subsequently been able to see the facsimile edition of Codex III and can be more precise in my note. My discussion deals with the patterns of epistolography, grammar and dialect characteristics. I am happy to see my theories confirmed by the reading :

ⲉⲩⲅⲛⲱⲥⲧⲟⲥ {ⲡ}ⲙⲁⲕⲁⲣⲓⲟⲥ ⲛ̄ⲛⲉ-
ⲧⲉⲛⲟⲩ ϥ ⲛⲉ ϫⲉⲣⲁϣⲉ ϩⲛ̄ⲛⲉ-
ⲉⲓ ⲉⲧⲣⲉⲧⲛ̄ⲉⲓⲙⲉ ϫⲉⲣⲱⲙⲉ ⲛⲓⲙ

On the authority of Codex V, I supposed the letter had the normal Greek χαίρειν. The Coptic ⲣⲁϣⲉ means nothing else. The spelling ϩⲛ̄ⲛⲁⲓ attributed to III according to the Sahidic is really ϩⲛ̄ⲛⲉⲉⲓ. So we have two examples in one word of the very common Nag Hammadi spellings : ⲛⲛ = ⲛ; ⲉⲉⲓ = ⲉⲓ. And the Sahidic pronominal ϩⲛⲁ⸗ presents the proper ME form ϩⲛⲉ⸗ as in the quotation of Col 2:1 given in another place at the beginning of the tractate. The *Letter* also shows an exceptional capacity for the creation of philosophical language in Coptic, to which we are accustomed in no other Coptic writer and which helps to place Macarius in the history of philosophical thought in the second and third centuries. The study of gnostic thought on cosmogony is not my field. I shall limit myself to an observation on the Coptic language of the *Letter*, which seems to me to demonstrate that Macarius had a vocabulary worthy of Epicurus, the best Stoics, and Plotinus. That does not dispense him from being wrong in his gnostic theories, but it seems that editors, lexicographers, translators and commentators have not succeeded in seeing the etymon and the internal and semantic unity of certain key words. From the beginning Macarius presents and refutes three theories upheld by philosophers about the ordering of the world. The translation of the designations of these theories : (a) 'self-controlled', (b) 'providence', and (c) 'something that is destined to happen', and especially that of the designation of the objections : (a) 'that which derives from itself', (b) 'providence is foolishness', and (c) 'what is approaching is something that is not known', does not seem to be consistent — with the exception, naturally, of (b), 'providence' — and does not recognize the sense of the Coptic qualitative, among other errors. The philosophical language of the beginning of the *Letter* merits a serious investigation, as the work must perhaps be considered an exposition on cosmogony by the master of the school. It will be sufficient to cite the same *status quaestionis*

---

above. There is, then, a new proof that Codex III is older than Codex V in its text and in the character of the dialect.

The use of ⲣⲁϣⲉ for ⲭⲁⲓⲣⲉ points to an older epistolography. According to the Coptic concordances the verb ⲣⲁϣⲉ translates χαίρειν sixty-four times. Only in Lk 19:48 does it correspond to ἐκκρεμαννύναι, which the concordances indicate with 'A' (*aliud*). But ⲣⲁϣⲉ in this case is clearly due to dittography : ⲛⲉⲣⲉⲡⲗⲁⲟⲥ ⲅⲁⲣ {ⲣ}ⲁ-ϣⲉ. So the MSS and editions are wrong, and ⲁϣⲉ is to be read : 'the people were *in suspense* listening to him'. That is also the verb in Bohairic. Crum (*Dict.* 88b II s.v. ⲉⲓϣⲉ) indicates the essential correction. Dittography existed before the addition, by a corrector, of ⲧⲏⲣϥ after ⲅⲁⲣ in cod. 53 (tenth century). MS Morgan 569 has the addition. As a substantive it translates χαρά fifty-nine times. Only in Acts 21:17 does it translate ἀσμένως : 'with joy'. Besa (*CSCO* 157 p. 78.16-18) has one example which seems to resolve the difficulty found by scholars in the beginning of the *Letter* by Macarius : ⲃⲏⲥⲁ ⲡⲉⲓⲉⲗⲁⲭⲓⲥⲧⲟⲥ ⲡⲉⲧⲥϩⲁⲓ ⲛ̄ⲛⲉϥⲙⲉⲣⲁⲧⲉ ⲛ̄ⲥⲛⲏⲩ ϩⲙ̄ⲡϫⲟⲉⲓⲥ · ⲉⲓϣⲁⲛϫⲟⲟⲥ ϫⲉⲭⲁⲓⲣⲉ · ⲧⲉⲛⲟⲩ ⲣⲱ ⲉϥⲧⲱⲛ ⲡⲣⲁϣⲉ ·

Besa writes in grief about the lack of unity in his community, and expresses his sorrow with a double break in the normal formula of salutation : 'Besa, this most humble one, writes to his beloved brethren in the Lord ... If I say "greetings" ... but now where is the joy?' The normal salutation in writing letters is to be found, for example, *ibid.* p. 129.21-23; cf. also Jas 1:1.

that Epicurus expounded : Ἐπίκουρος...φησὶ...ὅλως πρόνοιαν μὴ εἶναι μηδὲ εἱμαρμένην, ἀλλὰ πάντα αὐτοματισμῷ γίνεσθαι.[17]

The four witnesses of the *Letter* are not always in agreement, but it seems that αὐτοματισμός (ἀνάγκη of the Stoics) is perfectly expressed by the Coptic ⲛⲧⲁⲩⲁⲅⲉ ⲙ̄ⲙⲟϥ, which supposes a quite comprehensible and even acceptable etymology for ἀνάγκη, and which gave rise to the nonsensical reading of *BG* 8502.81.7 ⲡ̄ⲛⲁ ⲉϥⲟⲩⲁⲁⲃ (ἄγειν-ἄγιον), as Till has noted (p. 304 n. 1). But the most important word is ⲧⲉⲑⲟⲛⲧ — i.e. ⲧⲉⲧⲥⲟⲛⲧ — which perfectly mirrors the structure, the meaning, and even the gender of the Greek ἡ εἱμαρμένη or, if you will, ἡ Μοῖρα. We do not know if the word is indicated in any other place in the Coptic intellectual tradition. It appears only in the *Letter* and *SJC* and the two texts are not always materially in agreement. The *Letter*, *SJC* in Codex III and *SJC BG* 8502.82.7 have ⲧⲉⲑⲟⲛⲧ, but ⲧⲉⲑⲟⲛⲧ of *BG* p. 81.11 is rendered in the *Letter* and *SJC* of Codex III by ⲡⲉⲧⲏⲡ ⲉϣⲱⲡⲉⲡⲉ which is an exact explanation, corresponding to the cogent sense of the Greek δεῖ, ἔξεστι, ὀφείλει and which in *BG* p. 118.12 — out of the context of the *Letter* — translates the technical term ἀκόλουθον, *consequens*. Crum (*Dict.* 691b) considered the word a qualitative of unknown sense in both places in *BG*. Till left the word untranslated, and provided a note attempting to explain it as a relative proposition of a second — or secondary? — form of ϩⲱⲛ 'order, command'. He believed his explanation open to question. And it is, both by the sense, which cannot be allowed to pass, and by the form, since the qualitative of ϩⲱⲛ is attested in Coptic neither in first nor in second form. The root is ϩⲱⲛⲧ, 'approach, be near', which in Sahidic must regularly yield the form ϩⲟⲛⲧ in the qualitative, even if the only form attested is ϩⲏⲛⲧ which seems to me simply a form influenced by the synonym ϩⲱⲛ 'approach, be near', with the normal qualitative ϩⲏⲛ. Moreover it is normal, i.e. common, in many dialects to use the one verb for the other since both mean the same thing. The Sahidic NT uses ϩⲱⲛ only at Acts 22:6. ϩⲱⲛⲧ is to be found only in codex *a* (paper, and late). What is more, ϩⲟⲛⲧ, not ϩⲏⲛⲧ, explains the Subakhmimic form ϩⲁⲛⲧ (which would also be the Middle Egyptian form), these being the other two dialects which could influence the language of the thinker of the *Letter*. The rendering of ἡ εἱμαρμένη is perfect : 'the thing allotted,

---

[17] According to Hippolytus, *Philos.* 22.3, in H. Usener, *Epicurea* (Leipzig 1887) § 359; cf. also Doresse, *JA* 256 (1968) 361 n. 207.

determined; destiny'. Other gnostic treatises use the word ἡ εἱμαρ-μένη, e.g. *Pistis Sophia, passim*. As far as I know, apart from gnostic texts only the *Manichaica* have a technical use of ϩⲱⲛⲧ, e.g. *Ps.* 39.28.

It does not seem out of place here to illustrate this use of ϩⲟⲛⲧ, since it is important for the understanding of the theological language of Macarius and the Coptic *Manichaica*. G. Quispel[18] has said that the quotation of the logion about good and evil in the Pseudo-Clementine *Hom.* 12.29 (to be found also in a Manichaean source[19]) does not mean that Mani agreed with it. The Jewish Christians of the Pseudo-Clementine homilies were related to, if not identical with, the Elkesaites, and stressed that good and evil were willed by God. But Mani's dualism was meant to relieve God of any responsibility for evil. The Coptic version of this logion in the Manichaean Psalms shows, by its language alone, the exactness of Quispel's observation. Comparison of the Greek and Coptic texts shows the latter to be theologically more exact, and helps to interpret Manichaean thought.[20]

1a   τὰ ἀγαθὰ ἐλθεῖν δεῖ,
 b   μακάριος δὲ δι' οὗ ἔρχεται.
2a   Ὁμοίως καὶ τὰ κακὰ ἀνάγκη ἐλθεῖν,
 b   οὐαὶ δὲ δι' οὗ ἔρχεται.
27a ⲡⲁⲅⲁⲑⲟⲛ ⲥϩⲛⲏⲩⲧ ⲁⲉⲓ
 b   ⲛⲉⲓⲉⲧϥ̄ ⲙ̄ⲡⲉⲧϥⲛⲏⲩ ⲁϣⲱⲡⲉ.
28a ⲡⲉⲧϩⲁⲩ ⲁⲛ ϩⲁⲛⲧ ⲁϣⲱⲡⲉ
 b   ⲟⲩⲁⲓ ⲙ̄ⲡⲉⲧϥⲛⲏⲩ ⲛ̄ⲧⲉϥⲗⲁⲓϭⲉ.

The translation from the Greek by Quispel keeps the same Greek ambiguity, while the translation from the Coptic by Allberry does not seem to do justice to the meaning of the verbs and to the cogent and definite result expressed by the Coptic qualitative.

Quispel (p. 109)

1a The good is *destined* to come,
 b blessed is he by whose hand it comes;
2a the evil is *destined* to come,
 b cursed is he through whom it comes.

---

[18] Jewish Gnosis and Mandaean Gnosticism : some reflections on the writing *Bronté*, *NHS* 7 (1975) 82-122; cf. p. 109.

[19] *A Manichaean Psalm-Book II*, ed. C.R.C. Allberry (Stuttgart 1938) 39.27-28.

[20] The quotation from John Damascene, *Parall.* I c. 28, has the same text, except that in 2a he has δεῖ for ἀνάγκη (*PG* 2.323C).

Allberry

27a The Good is *destined* to come :
  b blessed is he by whom it comes;
28a the Evil too *is near* to be :
  b woe unto him because of whom it comes.

The Coptic translator of Manichaean thought could not be happy with the same Greek verb applied to good and evil, and expressed the Manichaean dualism perfectly. The two Coptic qualitatives express a definite result. But the different meaning of the verbs has to be kept : they cannot be used one for another. The qualitative of ca2ne expresses the rational concept of *provision, command*; *pre*destination, *pre*ordination. That of 2ωnt expresses more than *nearness*; it expresses rather the inevitable character of destiny's *arrival*, εἰμαρμένη or ἀνάγκη. The Coptic translator had a reason for choosing these verbs : c2nhyt speaks of divine *predestination* and can be said of the Good; 2ant implies the inevitability of *Destiny*. Good comes from God; evil from Destiny. Both writers, the one who used the two verbs in the *Manichaica* and the one who used 2ont in Macarius' Coptic, were not far from recognizing here the superiority of the Egyptian language to the Greek, expressed by the author of *Corpus Hermeticum* XVI in his theory about translations into Greek. His theory originated in his acceptance of the magic value of words that lose their power when translated; but also in linguistic pride. The translators of Mani and Macarius had shown that Coptic in this case is superior to Greek. The use of ca2ne and 2ωnt avoided the confusion of 2ωn with its double meaning and lack of some forms, which made it less apt for use in philosophical language. So the note about te0ont by Till is to be emended accordingly.

It seems, then, that the lemma 2ont in Crum *Dict.* 691b ought to be included as the qualitative of 2ωnt, preserved only by the *Letter* and related texts. The translation which scholars give of mececoane (*BG* 82.8) is of itself contradictory, and more so if we understand that Macarius uses the negative *consuetudinis* with the precise intention of avoiding the passive sense of ἀναίσθητος which translators give it.[21] The verb is simply the definition of te0ont.

---

[21] Gnostic theory about the negative attributes has given rise to a very abundant use of negative concepts, above all with at-, in the Nag Hammadi texts, which deserves an attentive semantic study. The use of the negative of habitude in our case is one of the ways, and a very stylistically effective one, to express the same idea with more essential

Conclusion

In coming to the end of these notes, it seems opportune to give the results we consider we have obtained. The name of the scribe in the colophon of Codex III must be identified with Concessus. His work, and the date of his activity as writer and copyist, must be investigated with greater precision, but it seems that we can affirm that the character of the Sahidic of his MS represents the Coptic of the area from Chenoboskion to the north of Akhmim at the end of the third century. The existence of the position of *eugnostos* in the school or schools of the sect seems to me to be certain. This institution, and the conventions of epistolography, surely demand that the author of the *Letter* bore the name of the *eugnostos* Macarius, not of 'Eugnostos the Blessed'. The *Letter* is an exposition of gnostic doctrine, with very technical philosophical terms. When we speak of Nag Hammadi, we are speaking *only* of the collection of gnostic MSS, which need not be considered as a unity in origin and in content, in so far as it seems clear that all the works belong to a gnostic culture that represented as a whole the institutions supposed to be established between Akhmim — or rather south of Assyut — and Qena.

Scholars have established, or tried to establish, some relationship between the gnostics and the Pachomians, institutions whose centres are supposed to be very near to one another. But while the Pachomians belonged, and are seen to have belonged, to the mountain, the river, the arid plain and the fertile flat land, the agriculture and the literary culture, the art and the worship, that is to say to the concrete history of the fourth and fifth centuries in Egypt, the gnostics had no contact with their land and their time. Along these lines we have tried to give precision and concreteness to two names, to scribes, institutions, dialect characteristics of MSS which, at least in my view, place the gnostic group within Coptic culture of the third to fifth centuries in a tangible way, and in the same geographical surrounding as the Pachomians.

---

content, almost like the qualitative. Cf. also *SJC, BG* 117.2 : ⲁⲧⲱⲓⲃⲉ; *Letter* : ⲙⲉϥϣⲓⲃⲉ; and in a negative relative sentence the use of the positive tense of habitude in the plural ϣⲁⲩ- for a passive meaning. In this way one must understand, and correct, the edition of M. Krause of VII.2.57.24 (*The Second Treatise of the Great Seth*) in F. Altheim/R. Stiehl, *Christentum am Roten Meer* II (Berlin/New York 1973). Read ⲙ̄ⲡⲉϣⲁⲩϣⲁⲭⲉ (= ⲙ̄ⲡⲉⲧⲉϣⲁⲩϣⲁⲭⲉ) which supposes the Greek ὁ ἄρρητος (cf. *ibid.* 61.36; 69.26) or the like. The editor's division does not make sense, least of all in a nominal sentence. And in point of fact, in spite of the translation, ⲡⲉϣ is not in the index, and with reason.

To conclude, we cannot omit indicating one fact which we think
has not been considered and which perhaps may explain, or help
explain, the formation of the general unity and the very concrete
diversity of the gnostic corpus, and its presence — perhaps historically
meaningful, perhaps only accidental and late — at Chenoboskion
as well, and may also determine the time of composition of the corpus
and explain the disappearance of the MSS under the sand. I refer
to the action of Shenoute, at the beginning of the fifth century, against
the temple of Pneueit near Akhmim. His actions have been explained,
long before the discovery of the gnostic corpus, as actions against
the *pagan* temple of that locality. But a simple reading of Shenoute's
own account of his deeds demonstrates that the archimandrite was
acting against a *gnostic* group, and specifically a *Sethian* group. The
description Shenoute gives seems to express the opinion of a stranger
to the group; and he speaks (88.11-16) using almost the same terms
as the ecclesiastical canons.[22] He was acting against a group that
called itself 'without a king', ⲍⲉⲛⲁⲧⲣ̄ⲣⲟ : ἀβασίλευτοι (88.20). The
word is typical of the Sethians and is often found in Nag Hammadi
literature.[23] Before the Coptic gnostic corpus, the word appeared only
here in Shenoute, and it would be a *hapax* in Coptic literature outside
of the gnostic tradition. By an oversight on the part of Crum, the
word was not entered in his *Dictionary*! It seems, then, that Shenoute
knew it from the Sethians, and no one knew it but Shenoute. He
probably gave it a political value, or used it sarcastically in order to
compel the group to accept the imperial Christian regime and to join
the Church. His final insistence on accepting Cyril as *illuminator*
(ⲣⲉϥⲣ̄ⲟⲩⲟⲉⲓⲛ, 88.28) of the Church seems a very clear reference
to Sethian theories of the φωστήρ of the sect. These two words alone
suffice to point to definite Sethian gnostics, whom he described before
as *pagan-heretics* (85.16), unbelievers in their *demiurge* (85.22), who

---

[22] J. Leipoldt, *Sinuthii archimandritae vita et opera omnia* III (*CSCO* 42; Scr. Copt.
II.4) (Louvain 1908). For the *canones ecclesiastici* cf. P. de Lagarde, *Aegyptiaca* (Göttingen
1883) can. 10, p. 242.

[23] Outside of authors who use the word in a general sense ('not ruled by a king',
cf. *LSJ*), the word appears, so far as I know, only among the Naassenes and Sethians,
similar sects. On the Naassenes Hippolytus gives us two citations: *Haer.* 5.8.2.30
(p. 89.12; 94.27 [Wendland] = *PG* 16.3139B; 3147C). Cf. Lampe *PGL s.v.* In the
Coptic corpus the idea and the word appear many times in Sethian writings. Cf.
Gnosis II.22, the text referring to n. 22 (Apocalypse of Adam); 29 n. 11 (Letter of
Macarius); 52 n. 36 (Hypostasis of the Archons). Also in A. Böhlig/P. Labib, *Die
koptisch-gnostische Schrift ohne Titel aus Codex II von Nag Hammadi* (Berlin 1962)
173.2, 6; 175.14. Cf. E. M. Yamauchi, *Pre-Christian Gnosticism*, 108.

was of course God for Shenoute. That is the only instance of the use of the word *demiurge* in Shenoute, a clear echo of gnostic terminology.

One who knows Shenoute cannot doubt for a moment that he meant what he said. After a categorical address to the people of the country : 'Do not be afraid; I am not hiding' (88.11) — the words ⲉⲓⲕⲏⲡ ⲁⲛ define the life of Shenoute — he addresses his adversaries, offering them the answer : to accept the Empire, the Church, and Cyril, or else exile : 'I shall make you acknowledge the kings who will make you subject to the Church and to its illuminator, our most holy father and martyr, the archbishop Cyril. Or else the sword will wipe out most of you, and moreover those of you who are spared will go into exile' (88.27-89.3). That the group left Pneueit would be only natural, and if they went away it would not be to the north, towards the area under the influence of Alexandria. And they took away with them the books of the sect, if any remained in their possession, since Shenoute had seized 'books full of abomination' (87.25) which he kept among other cultic 'spoils'. He speaks also of a 'book full of every kind of magic' (89.15). If he had opened to Codex III p. 44 or 66, or Codex IV p. 54, he could be describing the *Gospel of the Egyptians* in the Nag Hammadi corpus. (To say nothing, of course, if he had seen the *Book of Jeu*.) All these things he had kept (89.12), perhaps in case he lost his case before the magistrates of Antinoe. These events can be dated to the beginning of the episcopate of Cyril, A.D. 412. Did this exile bring into being or reinforce the Chenoboskion group? Have the Sahidic codices — and even more the Subakhmimic ones — of Nag Hammadi no deep influences of the A, A², and ME dialects? Does Akhmim not in large part explain the character of the Nag Hammadi corpus, and of *all* the gnostic texts in Coptic even before those of Nag Hammadi? If Chenoboskion was important for the Pachomians, what about Tsē and Tsmine "in the land of Akhmim"?[24] The hiding of the corpus under the sand is usually put around A.D. 400. But there is no evidence to justify such precision.*

---

[24] Cf. L. Th. Lefort, *Les vies coptes de Saint Pachôme* (Louvain 1943) 120 nn. 1-2; idem, Les premiers monastères pachômiens, *Muséon* 52 (1939) 403-404.

* Addendum to note 16 : Codex PPalau Rib. Inv.-Nr 181 edited by H. Quecke (Das Lukasevangelium Saïdisch, [PC 6; Barcelona, 1977]) has the true reading ⲁⲱⲉ (Lk 19:48) which the editor (p. 37) wrongly emends < ⲣ > ⲁⲱⲉ.

REPORT ON THE *DIALOGUE OF THE SAVIOR*
(CG III, 5)

by

ELAINE PAGELS

Reporting on research prepared collaboratively with

HELMUT KOESTER

Form critical analysis of the *Dialogue of the Savior* indicates that the present text is composed of several sources and traditions (as noted on the outline that follows). The first section (120, 2-124, 22), consisting of gnostic discourse about the passage of the soul through the heavenly spheres and the hostile powers, apparently derives from the final author. Although this section incorporates a prayer (121, 5-122, 1) that may come from liturgical tradition, both the discourse and the prayer are closely related to the author's own language. Both refer frequently to the New Testament, especially to the Pauline and deutero-Pauline epistles, to Hebrews, and to the Catholic epistles. Among such New Testament expressions are not only phrases that could be considered generally gnostic terms, such as "stand in the rest," (120, 5-7), and "power of darkness" (122, 4, 16; although these too may be related to Heb 4:1-11 and Col 1:13); one also finds such expressions as "to believe the truth" (121, 2; 2 Thess 2:12); to "redeem one's soul" (121, 22-23); cf. James 1:21; I Pet 1:9), the phrase "through (Christ's) sacrifice" (121, 20; Eph 5:2; Heb 10, 10-19) and the metaphor of the armor of God (121, 10; I Thess 5:8ff.; Eph 6:11-17). The first section of the text also reveals other peculiarities of the author's diction. The term "Savior" occurs only in the *incipit* and the *explicit*, and in passages which are seams connecting the author's composition with one of his sources. Elsewhere, Jesus is called "the Lord."

A second section (127, 23-131, 15) offers a creation myth based on Gen 1-2. The myth speaks of "darkness and water and a spirit" (127, 23-128, 1), recalling Gen 1:2; "the signs that are over the earth," (129, 18; Gen 1:14), and the lack of water on the earth (129, 20ff.; Gen 2:5). Although this section of the text is rather badly damaged, we note that the myth intends to explain the earth's fruitfulness, and its dependence upon God. Here, however, the author does not attempt, in typical gnostic fashion, to restate the creation myth, but reflects only on the term "spirit." In this, his exegetical method seems closely related to Philo's.

A third section (133, 16-134, 24) presents a traditional wisdom interpretation of a cosmological list, *darkness, light, fire, water, wind*. Yet the traditional list is interrupted in three places with Christian (and specifically *gnostic* Christian) interpolations, apparently inserted by the final author (see below, p. 69).

A fourth originally independent section (134, 24-137, 3) is a fragment of an apocalyptic vision. Here the seams of the source and redactor are clear. The original source relates that only one person receives the vision, and the third person singular occurs in several places (135, 13-15; 136, 17). In the present *Dialogue*, however, the text relates that *three* persons received the vision : Judas, Matthew, and Miriam.

The fifth section noted on the outline is the primary source used by the author — a dialogue between Jesus, called "the Lord," and the three disciples, Judas, Matthew, and Miriam. This original dialogue, which constitutes about sixty percent of the present text, is woven throughout the whole of the present *Dialogue of the Savior*. After the opening discourse and prayer, the author picks up the original dialogue (124, 23-127, 22), then interrupts it again with the creation myth (127, 23-131, 15). Following this, the original dialogue, into which the apocalyptic vision (134, 24-137, 3) is placed, forms the final third of the present text. This original dialogue source contains no discourses. Instead, questions and answers follow one another in rapid succession. Rather than following a literary pattern of dialogic composition, this dialogue is based on traditional sayings of Jesus which are explained and interpreted. The original dialogue is based on a traditional collection of sayings, analogous to the synoptic sayings source Q, or the Gospel of Thomas, or the collection used by 2 Clement and Justin Martyr. Here it is the three disciples, Judas, Miriam, and Matthew, who introduce the sayings of Jesus, inquiring about their meaning, and "the Lord" replies, giving interpretation of the traditional saying.

The sayings quoted and interpreted have parallels in Matthew (ten times, alternatively in Mark, but only if they occur in Matthew); Luke (at least twice Luke only among the synoptic gospels); John (once or twice) and the Gospel of Thomas (sixteen times). The predominance of sayings with parallels in the Gospel of Thomas is striking, and suggests that this primary source of the present *Dialogue of the Savior* may directly continue the tradition of sayings represented in the *Gospel of Thomas*.

We could go farther, and suggest that the original dialogue source intends to carry out the instruction of the first saying of the *Gospel of Thomas*, that is, to "find the interpretation of these sayings" in order not to "taste death." Correspondingly, discussion of the sayings proceeds in an order indicated by the second saying of the *Gospel of Thomas*, which speaks of an *ordo salutis* of *seeking, finding, marvelling, ruling, resting*. Sayings about seeking and finding predominate in the first section; following this, when the disciples receive the visions, they *marvel*; then they ask the Lord about *ruling*, and finally, about *resting*. The intention, clearly, is to indicate to the disciples their place within the eschatological timetable. Although they are those who have *sought* and *found*, they are still in the situation before *ruling* and *resting*; they still are carrying the burden of earthly labor; and Miriam, who recognizes this, receives the highest praise.

Following our form-critical analysis, we can begin to look at the present *Dialogue* as a whole, to describe its structure and theological concerns. We discover a duality that is sustained throughout the *Dialogue* : first, an emphasis on realized eschatology; second, juxtaposed with this, clear evidence of futuristic eschatology. This duality seems to be integral to the structure of the present *Dialogue*. An examination of passages that clearly reveal the hand of the final author confirms this impression. At the opening of the dialogue, for example, the Savior announces that "already the time has come" (120, 3) for him and his disciples to "leave labor behind" and to "stand in the rest" (120, 3-7) : here the context indicates that the author interprets "rest" in terms of present realization.

Following this invitation to "dwell in heaven always" (120, 9-10) the Savior teaches the disciples a prayer (121, 5-122, 1) and instructs them that they must be prepared "when the time of dissolution will come." He explains not only that "the first power of the darkness will come upon you" (122, 4-5) but also reveals the identity of that power ("truly, fear is the power of darkness," 122, 16). Thereby he teaches that they face a terrifying passage : if they undertake it in fear, that fear (the "power of darkness") will swallow them up; but if they face this transition without fear, they will pass safely through dissolution, through death.

The author then inserts other sections of the original dialogue (124,

23-127, 18; 128, 13-129, 16), and follows these with the account of
the origin of the cosmos (127, 23ff.:129, 20-131, 18). Following this
account, a section of dialogue resumes : the Lord explains that the elect
is to "enter into [the place of life], in order that he may not be con-
fined in this impoverished cosmos" (132, 3-5). When Matthew
responds that he wants to see that "place of life, [that place] in which
there is no evil, but rather the pure light" (132, 6-9), the Lord replies
that he cannot see it, "so long as you wear the flesh" (132, 11-12).
Although in the present he cannot see the place of life, the Lord tells
Matthew that "everyone who has known himself has seen it" (132,
15-16).

Following this saying concerning self-knowledge, the author places
the cosmological list, which explains that the disciple must understand
the origin of the *fire* (134, 1-4), of the *water* (134, 5-8), of the *wind*
(134, 8-11) and of the *body* (134, 11-14). The major part of this list, as
noted above (p. 67), consists of traditional material. But when his
source mentions the water, the author chooses to insert a rhetorical
question : if one does not understand the water, "what is the use
for him to receive baptism in it?" (134, 6-8). At the conclusion of
the cosmological list, the author adds that "whoever does not understand how he came will not understand how he will go, and is not a
stranger to the cosmos" (134, 19-24), recalling the famous gnostic
statement concerning baptism from *Exc. Theod.* 78, 2 (ἔστιν δὲ οὐ τὸ
λουτρὸν μόνον τὸ ἐλευθεροῦν, ἀλλὰ καὶ ἡ γνῶσις, τίνες ἦμεν, τί
γεγόναμεν · ποῦ ἦμεν, ἢ ποῦ ἐνεβλήθημεν · ποῦ σπεύδομεν, πόθεν
λυτρούμεθα · τί γέννησις, τί ἀναγέννησις).

What pattern do we observe so far? According to the structure of
the present *Dialogue*, the Savior first invites the disciples to "enter
into rest," instructs them in prayer, prepares them to face the "time of
dissolution," explains to them that the cosmos has originated from a
place beyond, and urges them to pass beyond the cosmos into the
"place of life." He instructs them to know themselves, and to understand the elements of the cosmos, in order to receive the effect of
baptism, and concludes in phrases that recall gnostic baptismal for-
mulae.

We suggest that the whole of the present *Dialogue* offers an interpretation of baptism as a process that involves going through dissolution, that is, through death, and entering into the "place of life." This
interpretation receives confirmation when we note that while the
original dialogue contains no explicit reference to the NT writings,

the author incorporates frequent reference to them into the present *Dialogue*. Those the author cites most often are from the Pauline corpus, and specifically from those passages which NT scholars identify as referring to baptismal liturgy. The author apparently follows the pattern of Romans 6:3f., interpreting baptism as a process of going "into death" (6:3), being "buried" with Christ "through baptism into death" (6:4). But unlike the Paul of *Romans* 6, this author understands this process as it is interpreted in *Eph.* 2:1-6 and *Col.* 3:1-4: those baptized, having died, already have attained true life (121, 18-122, 24; cf. *Col.* 1:1-3); already they "dwell in heaven" (120, 9-10; cf. *Eph.* 2:6). Like other gnostic teachers, this author adapts Pauline and deutero-Pauline statements on baptism in the direction of realized eschatology. So *Exc. Theod.* 77, 1-2 declares that "therefore baptism is called death, and an end of the old life, when we take leave of the evil principalities; but it is called life according to Christ, who is its sole Lord." The author of *A Valentinian Exposition* (CG XI, 2) similarly describes how those who receive the second baptism "die" (44, 32), and are "brought out of the world (κόσμος) into the aeon" (ὁ αἰών); 41, 23-38; 42, 16-19).

Following the invitation and the instruction, with its reference to baptismal initiation, the author describes how the Lord takes the three elect disciples, Judas, Matthew, and Miriam, "in order to show them the whole of heaven and earth" (134, 24-135, 2). This author, however, frames the traditional vision narratives with the words, "and when he placed his hand upon them, they hoped that they might see" visions (135, 2-4). Could this statement allude to an element in baptismal ritual as the author understands it — that the laying on of hands which follows baptism is understood as the possible prelude for receiving visions? If so, the practice of laying on of hands during initiation into the Marcosian circle might offer a parallel (AH 1, 13, 3-6).

In our text, at any rate, the disciples do receive visions; but, surprisingly, the account of the visions does not conclude the present *Dialogue*. Instead, through the visions and the dialogue which follows, the disciples receive a new — and more complex — understanding of their own situation, as baptized and elect disciples. When they have received a second vision in addition to the first (136, 17f.) a section of dialogue resumes to interpret it (137, 3f.). Now the Lord teaches them that they must discriminate between what is merely a "temporal vision" and the "eternal vision :" of the "One Who Is Forever" (137, 10-14). The former they have received already : the latter is reserved for the eschatological future. Here, contrary to what we have been led to expect of gnostic theology, we find the author of the *Dialogue* dealing with the tension between what the disciples have received "already" through baptism, initiation, and through visions, and what they anticipate as "not yet."

According to the schema of the saying we have mentioned as programmatic for the *Dialogue*, the saying about *seeking/finding/marvelling/ruling/resting*, the disciples, having received baptism, are those who have already *sought* and *found*, and who have *marvelled* (in the vision sequence). They have attained *rest*, but now they discover that this rest is, in a sense, only provisional. As we noted before, the dialogue resumes as the disciples inquire about the next stages in the process — *ruling* and *resting*. Now Judas asks, "who will rule over us"?, assuming that "surely, the archons who dwell in heaven will rule over us" (138, 13-14). The Lord replies that "you will rule over them" (138, 14-15); that is, the elect *will rule*, but their reign lies in the future. Second, Matthew asks, "why do we not rest ourselves at once?" (141, 3-4). The Lord answers, "(you will rest) when you lay down these burdens" (141, 4-5), for they are still burdened by existence in the flesh (143, 11-15), in this cosmos.

Clearly this is a paradox, since in the opening invitation the Savior had invited them to "enter into rest" (120, 3ff.) : now they discover that although they have left their labor behind (120, 4-5) and attained some rest, they still must carry the burden of their present existence! The disciples now recognize that the baptismal initiation, which involved passage through death and entrance into "the place of life", is itself an anticipation of the future time of their actual death, when they will "come forth from the corruption of the flesh" (143, 11-15) and enter into eternal life (143, 15f.). Only then will they leave behind them the temporal visions, and enjoy the eternal vision of the "One Who Is Forever."

Finally Miriam asks the crucial question : *why?* "Tell me, Lord, why have I come to this place? To gain, or to suffer loss?" (140, 15-18). The Lord replies, "Because you reveal the greatness of the revealer" (140, 18)—a rather extraordinary answer. The elect are not here to gain anything for themselves, for what more could they gain than what they already have received—the awareness that the Living God dwells within them, and they in Him (137, 22-138, 2)? Nor are they here to suffer any purgation for themselves. The meaning of their burdensome present existence is that they are not here for their own sake, but for the sake of others. They have come into the world, as the Lord himself came into it, to "seek and to save" others (137, 16-21).

Miriam expresses her new understanding of three traditional sayings, which the author takes as interpreting the present situation of the elect : first, the saying on the "evil of each day" (139, 8-9; cf. Mt 6:34b); second, "the laborer is worthy of his food (τροφή)" (139, 9-10; Mt 10:10); third, "the disciple is like his teacher" (139, 11; Mt 10:25). That is, according to the interpretation suggested here, first, the present time is tainted with evil; second, the elect is the laborer, who, like the Lord, anticipates future reward for his work : third, the elect disciple, like his Lord, shares in the same task of revelation,. revealing "the greatness of the Revealer" in the world. Her insight gains her the greatest praise : "this word she spoke as a woman who knew the All" (139, 12-13). As the *Dialogue* closes, the disciples are instructed how to perfect their work (141, 20ff.), how to pray (144, 14-16), and to "destroy the works of femaleness" (144, 19ff.). Unfortunately, this section of the dialogue is badly damaged.

We can see, nevertheless, that the author of *Dialogue of the Savior* juxtaposes realized eschatology with futuristic eschatology for a specific purpose. The first describes what baptism effects and conveys (as in *Eph.* 2:1-6); the second, what remains, after baptism, the presently unrealized hope of the elect. The author uses traditional material—the prayer, the original dialogue, the creation account, the cosmological list, the visions, as means of interpreting the paradoxical situation of the elect in the world. Through baptism the elect already have *found* what they *sought*, the awareness of the Living God dwelling within, and they have *marvelled*. But although they have left labor behind, having "died to the cosmos" to become "alive to God" (cf. *Exc. Theod.* 80, 2), they have now taken up the Lord's own burden : they have, in effect, *become* the Revealer in the world, and bear the burden of present existence in order to reveal His greatness to others. Only when this work is completed and they leave off the body in death, will they finally come to *reign*, and to their final *rest*.

DIALOGUE OF THE SAVIOR
(CG III, 5)

Brief report on introduction prepared by

HELMUT   KOESTER

and

ELAINE   PAGELS

Part I: Form-critical analysis of CG III, 5 indicates that the present *Dialogue* is composed of several sources :

First : 120, 2-124, 22 : Gnostic discourse on the soul's passage through heavenly spheres and hostile powers. NT (especially Pauline and deutero-Pauline) allusions occur often in this section, which probably derives from the final author.

Second : 127, 23-131, 15 : *Creation myth* based on Genesis 1-2 : a traditional myth which explains the origin of the world's fruitfulness and its dependence upon God.

Third : 133, 16-134, 24 : *Wisdom interpretation* of a *cosmological list* (fire, water, wind, body).

Fourth : 134, 24-137, 3 : *Apocalyptic vision* : the original vision is told in terms of one person : the redactor introduces three persons, Judas, Miriam, and Matthew, corresponding to the *dramatis personae* of the original dialogue.

Fifth : 124, 23 ff. ; passim : *Dialogue* between "the Lord," Judas, Miriam, and Matthew. This original dialogue is the other's *primary source*. It is woven throughout the whole of the present *Dialogue of the Savior*; is based on a traditional collection of the sayings of Jesus, analogous to the synoptic *Sayings Source*. Parallels with *Matthew* occur more frequently (10 times) than those with *Mark*, *Luke*, or *John* : yet parallels to the *Gospel of Thomas* occur 16 times.

Part II : Structure of the present *Dialogue*

The first section (120, 2-124, 22), the *discourse*, introduces a duality : realized eschatology is juxtaposed with futuristic eschatology.

The second section, the *creation myth* (127, 23-131, 15) is used to demonstrate that the cosmos originates from a place "beyond," and to urge the elect to pass beyond this cosmos to that "place of life."

The third section, the *cosmological list* (133, 16-134, 24) is used to explain that whoever knows himself must understand the origin of fire, water, wind and the body, in order to receive the true effect of baptism, which is apparently γνῶσις.

The fourth section (134, 24-137, 3) describes how, following the invitation and instruction, the disciples receive the *laying on of hands* and *see visions*. Now they are taught to discriminate between the *temporal vision*, which they have already received and the *eternal* vision, reserved for the eschatological future.

The fifth section, the *original dialogue*, attempted to carry out the instruction of the first saying of the *Gospel of Thomas*, to "find the interpretation of (Jesus') words" in order not to "taste death." It describes an *ordo salutis* of *seeking*, *finding*, marvelling, ruling and resting. The present version, the *Dialogue of the Savior*, intends to interpret the present experience of the elect in terms of this *ordo salutis*. This may indeed prove to be a *topos* in other gnostic literature as well.

DIE PARAPHRASE
ALS FORM GNOSTISCHER VERKÜNDIGUNG

von

BARBARA ALAND

In dem Handschriftenfund von Nag Hammadi sind uns ganze gnostische Schriften erhalten.[1] Dieser Satz ist nicht als Binsenweisheit gemeint, sondern als Aufforderung zu einer ganz bestimmten Interpretation dieser Texte, nämlich einer Interpretation, die versucht, die Schriften als ganze nach Inhalt *und* Form zu verstehen. Daß das bei den vorliegenden Texten viel leichter gesagt ist als getan, liegt auf der Hand. Jedem, der auch nur einige dieser Schriften liest, werden sogleich die Schwierigkeiten eines solchen Unternehmens deutlich werden. Mir scheint aber, daß nur so der Vorteil genutzt werden kann, den uns dieser Handschriftenfund gegenüber den Nachrichten über die Gnosis aus den Exzerpten bei den Kirchenvätern bietet. Dort sind nur Fragmente erhalten. Selbst wenn wir einmal voraussetzen, daß sie — wenigstens zum Teil — sachlich richtige Auszüge aus gnostischen Werken sind, so lassen sie doch über Stil, Form, Aufbau und Eigenart der gnostischen Verkündigung keine sicheren Schlüsse zu. Aber auch darin spricht sich aus, was Gnosis ist. Will man sie also verstehen, wird man auch auf die Wechselbeziehung zwischen Inhalt und Form in gnostischen Schriften zu achten haben.[2]

Wie man eine solche Interpretation ganzer Schriften aus Nag Hammadi angehen könnte, möchte ich versuchsweise an der "Paraphrase des Sēem" (VII, 1) skizzieren. Diese 1973 von Martin Krause edierte

---

[1] Auf die schwierige (und immer häufiger negativ beantwortete) Frage, ob alle Schriften aus Nag Hammadi "gnostisch" sind, soll hier nicht eingegangen werden. Sie ist vielleicht nach unserem heutigen Wissensstand auch noch gar nicht befriedigend zu lösen. Zumindest scheint mir eine Schrift nicht schon deswegen nicht gnostisch sein zu müssen, weil ihr bestimmte materielle Einzelheiten gnostischer Lehre zu fehlen scheinen. Vgl. dazu unten S. 87 Anm. 29.

[2] Dafür, die Texte von Nag Hammadi "als ganze zu begreifen" und nicht etwa zu voreilig die "Schere der Literarkritik" anzusetzen, spricht sich jetzt auch O. Betz aus, Das Problem der Gnosis seit der Entdeckung der Texte von Nag Hammadi, *Verkündigung und Forschung* (Neues Testament) 2, 1976, 46-80, vgl. 69.

Schrift³ ist noch wenig behandelt worden.⁴ Das ist nicht zu ver-
wundern. Denn sie ist zwar gut überliefert, erscheint dem Leser aber
wirr, ohne verständlichen Zusammenhang und Aufbau, reich an Bildern
und dunklen Anspielungen.⁵ Karl Martin Fischer, der kürzlich in
Vorbereitung seiner Übersetzung der Schrift eine erste Gesamtanalyse
versuchte, endet im Grund mit einem non liquet: "Die Schrift will
nicht in erster Linie verstanden werden, sondern auf der Grundlage
einer gemeinsamen Geisteshaltung meditativ weitergesponnen werden"
(266). So sehr der zweite Teil dieser These zu bedenken ist,⁶ so ist
doch der erste mit dem Sinn von Sprache kaum vereinbar.

Den Schlüssel zum Verständnis der Textes bietet, wie mir scheint,
der Titel der Schrift: "die Paraphrase des Sēem", ergänzt durch die
einleitenden Worte: "Paraphrase über den ungezeugten Geist". Hier
ist jedes Wort zu beachten. Es geht um den ungezeugten Geist, d.h.
jenen, der nicht dem Zeugen als dem Charakteristikum der Finsternis-
macht unterliegt, also jenen Geist, der vom Licht stammt, der aber
in das Dunkel gefallen ist und aus ihm wieder befreit werden muß
(vgl. 1, 28-30). Dieser bekannte gnostische Zentraltopos wird im ganzen
folgenden Text in jeweils immer neuen Bildern und Wendungen wieder-
holt und umschrieben, d.h. mit andern Worten: er wird "paraphrasiert". "Paraphrase" meint also in unserer Schrift in erster Linie nicht
die umschreibende Wiedergabe eines bestimmten vorgegebenen Textes,⁷
sondern die einer grundlegenden Einsicht und Überzeugung.⁸

Im folgenden möchte ich nun den in diesem Sinne "paraphrastischen"
Charakter der Paraphrase des Sēem aufzeigen, um daran dann einige

---

³ In: F. Altheim und R. Stiehl (Hrsg.), *Christentum am Roten Meer*, 2. Bd., Berlin
1973, 2-105.
⁴ Mir sind bisher folgende Arbeiten darüber bekannt geworden: F. Wisse, The
Redeemer Figure in the Paraphrase of Shem, *Novum Testamentum* 12, 1970, 130-140.
Darauf geht jetzt kurz ein (insbesondere auf Wisses Deutung des Begriffes Paraphrase)
L. Abramowski, Notizen zur "Hypostase der Archonten" (ed. Bullard), *ZNW* 67, 1976,
280-285, bes. 285; der Beitrag des Berliner Arbeitskreises für koptisch-gnostische
Schriften, Die Bedeutung der Texte von Nag Hammadi für die moderne Gnosis-
forschung, in: K.W. Tröger (Hrsg.), *Gnosis und Neues Testament*, Berlin, 1973, 13-76,
bes. 57-60; K.M. Fischer, Die Paraphrase des Sēem, in: *Essays on the Nag Hammadi
Texts, in Honour of Pahor Labib*, Leiden 1975, 255-267; J.-M. Sevrin, A propos de la
"Paraphrase de Sēem", *Le Muséon* 88, 1975, 69-95; M. Krause, Die Paraphrase des
Sēem und der Bericht Hippolyts, in *Proceedings of the International Colloquium on
Gnosticism* (Stockholm 1973), Stockholm 1977, 101-110.
⁵ Vgl. dazu auch Wisse, a.O. 131.
⁶ Vgl. dazu unten S. 83f.
⁷ Vgl. aber unten S. 81.
⁸ Zu anderen Deutungen des Begriffes Paraphrase bei Wisse und Sevrin s. unten
S. 81 Anm. 18.

Erwägungen über Verbreitung, Sinn und Konsequenzen einer solchen Ausdrucksform anzuschließen.

Die Paraphrase gibt sich wie viele gnostische Schriften als Offenbarung, und zwar an einem gewissen Sēem, der bisher noch nicht näher identifiziert werden konnte.[9] Ihm eröffnet der Offenbarer Derdekeas zunächst eine Prinzipienlehre, wie wir sie ähnlich aus andern gnostischen Dreiprinzipien-Systemen kennen:[10] Drei Kräfte (bzw. "Wurzeln") bestanden von Anfang an: Licht, Finsternis und Pneuma. Das Licht ist "Denken", es ist "voll von Hören und Sprechen" (1, 32ff.), mit andern Worten, es hat Bewußtsein, und zwar nicht nur von sich selbst, sondern auch von der Eigenart der andern Kräfte (vgl. 2, 10-14). Demgegenüber ist die Finsternis als entgegengesetzte, aber nicht "ebenbürtige" Wurzel "ohne Wahrnehmung" (ⲁⲛⲁⲓⲥⲑⲏⲧⲟⲥ). Sie erkennt weder ihre eigene wesensmäßige "Unordnung" noch das Licht, das über ihr ist (2, 13-17). Sie besitzt aber den Nus, d.h. jenen in ihren Herrschaftsbereich gefallenen Funken des Lichts, der sie überhaupt erst zu irgendeiner Art von Handeln befähigt.[11] Es ist wichtig festzustellen, daß die Paraphrase den Fall des Lichtes von vornherein voraussetzt, ihn nicht erst darstellt.[12] Zwischen Licht und Finsternis befindet sich als dritte Wurzel das "freundliche, demütige" Pneuma, im weiteren Verlauf anscheinend auch als "Duft" (ⲱⲗⲙⲉ) bezeichnet.[13] Diese Wurzel tritt, wie in allen sog. Dreiprinzipiensystemen, offenbar in Erscheinung, um den Teil des Lichtes zu markieren, der in die Finsternis gefallen ist. Um der Unantastbarkeit des Lichtes willen kann das nicht ein Teil des Lichtes selbst sein, sondern muß eine von ihm getrennte Kraft sein, die aber ihrem Wesen nach dem Licht zugehört.

Auf diese feierliche Schilderung der Prinzipien, d.h. der Voraussetzungen für das gnostische Heilsdrama, folgt nun in langer (der rasch ermüdete Leser möchte sagen in endloser) Folge die Schilderung der Befreiungsaktionen des Lichts bzw. der dagegen gerichteten Versuche der Finsternis, den Nus als die Quelle ihrer Handlungsfähigkeit in sich festzuhalten. Diese einzelnen Aktionen und Reaktionen werden

---

[9] Vgl. dazu Fischer, a.O. 260 Anm. 1.

[10] Insbesondere aus Hippolyts Bericht, Refutatio 5, 19-22.

[11] Vgl. 3,7ff. et passim. Aus der Tatsache, daß die Finsternis den Nus in Besitz hat, ist auch schon die Aussage von 2,17f. zu erklären. Vgl. dazu unten S. 79.

[12] Das ist wichtig, weil schon damit angedeutet wird, daß der Autor der Paraphrase keinen zusammenhängenden kosmogonischen Mythos bieten wollte. Er berührt sich auch darin wieder mit dem Exzerpt bei Hippolyt, Ref. 5,19.

[13] Vgl. 25, 18 u.ö.; vgl. im Index bei Krause s.v.; eine ähnliche Charakterisierung des Pneumas wieder bei Hippolyt 5, 19, 3.

nicht als ein fortlaufendes mythisches Geschehen geschildert — selbst
der aus Wiederholungen bestehende gnostische Mythos hätte nicht die
Kraft, eine derart große Folge von im Prinzip gleichartigen Aussagen
in ein Geschehen zu integrieren. Nur ein ganz lockerer zusammen-
fassender Rahmen ist, wenn überhaupt, bemerkbar, insofern zunächst
nur von der Vermischung der Prinzipien die Rede ist und im zweiten
Teil mehr von deren Konsequenzen für den in dieser Welt lebenden
Menschen gesprochen wird.[14] Entscheidend ist vielmehr festzustellen,
daß es sich um aneinandergereihte Variationen zum Thema Gefangenschaft und Befreiung des Lichts handelt. Das Gliederungs- und Dar-
stellungsprinzip dieser "Variationen" sei im folgenden an einigen Beispielen erläutert.

Auf die Vorstellung der Urprinzipien (bis 2,17) folgt eine kurze
Schilderung ihres Verhaltens zueinander, das in sich und ohne nähere
Erklärung kaum verständlich wäre (2,17-35): Die Finsternis kommt
zum Bewußtsein der ihr mit dem Nus gegebenen Handlungsfähigkeit,[15]
sie sieht, daß sie "mit Wasser" (stets Symbol des Bösen) "bedeckt"
ist und bewegt sich. Daraufhin erschrickt und flieht das Pneuma über
ihr. Das "Denken des Geistes", d.h. das eigentlich wirkende und gute
Prinzip, sieht herab und blickt auf die unendliche Lichtfülle, die in
der Finsternis versklavt ist — das ist die Schilderung der gnostischen
Grundsituation — und wird aktiv. Auf seine Veranlassung hin spaltet
sich nämlich die Finsternis, steigt empor, und brüstet sich des Besitzes
des Nus. Sie tut das in törichter Unwissenheit, ohne Kenntnis davon,
daß sie vom Licht zu diesem Tun getrieben wird, das damit im
Endeffekt die Befreiung des Licht-Nus aus der Herrschaft der Finsternis
bezweckt (2,33f.).

Damit endet die erste Vorstellung des Themas. Der mit gnostischen
Mythen vertraute Leser — und einen solchen setzt die Paraphrase
voraus — erkennt einzelne Motive sofort wieder (Das Sich-Brüsten
der Finsternis erinnert z.B. an Jaldabaoths: "Ich bin Gott und außer

---

[14] Vgl. zum "Rahmen" der Schrift auch Fischer, a.O. 255-259, der allerdings unter
dem Stichwort Rahmen schon eine genauere Inhaltsangabe zu liefern versucht. Interes-
santerweise stellt auch er dabei mehrfach plötzliche Neuanfänge im Fluß der Er-
zählungen, miteinander konkurrierende "Entwürfe" zum selben Thema (263), Rück-
bezüge und Verweise fest, ohne diese allerdings, wie ich es versuche, als Elemente des
immer neu ansetzenden "Paraphrasierens" des Autors zu verstehen und so mit dem
Titel der Schrift in Beziehung zu setzen.
[15] "Als sie aber ihre Schlechtigkeit ertragen konnte ..." 2,17f.; s. dazu oben S. 77
Anm. 11; vgl. dazu auch Hippolyt, Ref. 5, 19, 6.

mir ist keiner"), ohne daß jedoch der Zusammenhang der einzelnen angedeuteten Motive schon deutlich würde.

Das geschieht nun teilweise im nächsten Durchgang, d.h. in der ersten "Variation" des Themas. Der Autor der Paraphrase greift plötzlich (2,35 b, vgl. 2,19 f.) zurück, erwähnt erneut, daß sich die Finsternis bewegt und das Licht sich daraufhin offenbart habe (2,35-3,1; vgl. 2,19 f. und 25) und schildert nun breiter als bei der ersten Vorstellung des Themas die Reaktion der Finsternis. Sie, die vorher nicht wußte, daß es eine Kraft gibt, die erhabener ist als sie selbst (3,3 f.), wird sich ihres Minderseins bewußt. Sie entbrennt in Schmerz und Eifersucht und "erhebt ihren Verstand in die Höhe" (2,7 f.) in dem — vergeblichen — Versuch, dem geschauten Licht-Geist ebenbürtig zu werden (2,3-18). Damit wird jetzt ausführlich motiviert und erläutert, was bei der ersten Vorstellung des Themas mit dem "Emporsteigen" und "Sich-Brüsten" der Finsternis (2,31-35) nur kurz angedeutet war. Zugleich werden die Folgen des Sich-Brüstens deutlicher als zuvor (vgl. 2,33 f.) veranschaulicht: Die Finsternis kann dem Lichte nicht ähnlich werden. Alles, was sie vermag, ist, kraft des erhobenen Nus in einem "Feuerlicht" über die Unterwelt zu leuchten. In der Tatsache des Feuerlichtes, das die Finsternis nur aufgrund des von ihr gefangen gehaltenen Lichtes (d.h. des Nus) zustande bringt, offenbart sich schon die Verwandtschaft dieser Nuskraft mit dem Licht und d.h. ihre grundsätzliche Verschiedenheit vom Wesen der Finsternis (3,18-26). Damit deutet sich die zukünftige Befreiung des Lichtes, die in einer Bewußtwerdung seiner eigenen Qualität besteht, bereits an. Der Zusammenhang wird klar: die Offenbarung des Lichtes bedeutet eine bewußte Provozierung der Finsternis, die dadurch zur "Erhebung" angeregt werden soll, damit sie im Laufe dieser Erhebung ihrer Nuskraft verlustig gehe.[16]

Dieser aus anderen gnostischen Mythen bekannte Gedanke wird nun im dritten Durchgang des Themas (3,30-5,2) deutlich ausgesprochen. Wieder wird die Offenbarung des Lichtes erwähnt und jetzt ausführlicher als zuvor geschildert und begründet (3,30-4,10; vgl. 2,36 f. und

---

[16] Der folgende Satz (3,27-29) spielt darauf noch einmal an: "Der Geist" — gemeint ist der in der Finsternis gefangene Geist — "hatte von jeder Gestalt der Finsternis Nutzen". D.h. welche Gestalt die Finsternis auch immer annimmt, sei es, wie beschrieben, die eines "Feuerlichtes", sei es, wie im folgenden, die einer Wolke, eines Mutterschoßes (4,22 ff.), eines "Furchttieres" (15,5) o.ä., der Geist in der Finsternis, der sie erst zu diesem verschiedenen Gestaltwerden befähigt (so deutlich z.B. 15,10-16), zieht daraus seinen Nutzen, "weil er" — auf diese Weise — "in seiner Größe in Erscheinung trat" (3,28 f.) und d.h. damit der erste Schritt zu seiner Befreiung getan ist.

2,25f.). Derdekeas, der "Sohn des unbefleckten, grenzenlosen Lichtes"
(4,2f.), bzw. sein "Strahl" oder "Abbild" (4,4f. bzw. 3,34) tritt in
Erscheinung, "damit der Nus der Finsternis nicht in der Unterwelt
bleibe" (4,8-10). Im folgenden wird kurz auf die — dem Leser nun
schon bekannte — Reaktion der Finsternis angespielt (8,10-12) und
dann noch deutlicher der Zweck der Offenbarung des Lichtes ange-
geben: "damit die Finsternis sich selbst verdunkle nach dem Willen
der Größe" (4,13-15),[17] zu ergänzen ist: durch ihre immer wieder-
holten Versuche, dem geschauten Licht ähnlich zu werden. Es wird
nun auch klar dieses Vorgehen des Lichtes charakterisiert: "dies war
Irreführung" (ⲡⲗⲁⲛⲏ, 4,26f.). D.h. der Leser begreift jetzt — bzw. hat
es schon bei der Andeutung im ersten Durchgang des Themas begriffen,
weil er den Mythos kennt — daß die Finsternis vom Licht planmäßig
zu ihren Aktionen provoziert wird, damit ihr dabei das gefangen-
gehaltene Licht abhanden komme. Die in diesem Durchgang geschil-
derte Aktion der Finsternis zur Erlangung der Ebenbürtigkeit mit
dem Licht besteht — parallel dem Sich-Brüsten und dem Emporsteigen der Finsternis — in der Schaffung einer Wolke. In ihr empfängt
der "Mutterschoß" Gestalt (vgl. Hipp. 5, 19, 19ff.). Die Finsternis
gerät in sexuelle Begierde zu ihrem eigenen Werk, sie "reibt" den
Mutterschoß, mit dem Erfolg, daß sich ihr Nus "in die Tiefen der
Natur hinab auflöst" und "ihr Auge (d.h. das "der Kraft der Bitterkeit
der Finsternis" 4,33f.) bricht". Damit ist die Niederlage der Finsternis
hier schon ausgesprochen, allerdings nur in einer grundsätzlichen Weise.
Der Prozeß des Kampfes zwischen Licht und Finsternis ist noch nicht
am Ende. Denn da sich der Nus "in die Tiefen der Natur hinab"
aufgelöst hat, befähigt er jetzt die Natur zum Handeln, wie vordem
die Finsternis. Er wird der "Same für die Natur" (4,37f.).

In der folgenden Variation des Themas (5,2-36) wird geschildert,
wie nun die Natur, parallel der Finsternis, aufgrund des Nus handelt
und Werke hervorbringt (5,3-6). Wieder ist von einer — leuchtenden —
Wolke die Rede, in der der Nus wie ein "schädigendes Furchtfeuer"
in Erscheinung tritt (5,14-16). Er stößt auf den ungezeugten Geist
(5,16-18). Damit ist wieder auf die Offenbarung des Geistes angespielt,
die in allen vorhergehenden Variationen eine Reaktion der Finsternis

---

[17] Vgl. ebenso auch im folgenden (4,16-18): "damit die Finsternis untätig werde
(ⲁⲣⲟⲥ) in jeder Art der Kraft, die sie hatte". D.h. es ist das Bestreben des Lichtes,
der Finsternis ihre gesamte Lichtkraft zu entziehen, damit sie zur Untätigkeit ver-
dammt werde, wohingegen die Finsternis gerade diese Lichtkraft betätigen und damit,
wie sie fälschlich meint, erhalten will (vgl. 3,18ff.).

bewirkte. So auch hier. Die Natur spaltet sich (πωρ͞x 5,23) in vier
Teile, die zu verschiedenen Wolken werden. Von einer "Spaltung"
der Finsternis auf Veranlassung des Lichtes hörten wir schon oben
(2,28-30 πωρ͞x). Ihr Sinn wird jetzt deutlich. Die Natur soll "entleert"
(5,20), d.h. der zum Licht gehörige Nus soll aus Finsternis und Wasser
herausgezogen werden, "damit das schädigende Feuer nicht an ihm
hafte" (5,30-36). Zu Beginn der nächsten "Variation" (6,1-35) wird
diese Begründung der "Spaltung" noch einmal ausdrücklich bestätigt:
"Deshalb wurde die Natur nach meinem" (d.h. des Offenbarers
Derdekeas, also des Lichtes) "Wunsche gespalten; damit der Nus sich
zu seiner Kraft hinauf zurückwende, die die Finsterniswurzel" (d.h.
das Prinzip Finsternis, aus dem auch die Natur stammt), "die mit
ihm vermischt war, von ihm genommen hatte" (6,1-6).

Wir brechen hier ab. Mir scheint, das Prinzip, nach dem der Autor
vorgeht, ist deutlich geworden. Er fügt "Variation" an "Variation"
über das immer gleiche Thema der Gefangenschaft und Befreiung des
Lichtes. Dabei verknüpft er die einzelnen Variationen, indem er Begriffe
und Vorstellungen aus vorhergehenden Durchführungen des Themas
aufgreift und sie in "paraphrasierender" Weise jetzt breiter ausführt
und verdeutlichend umschreibt. D.h. unser Text ist nicht nur seinem
gesamten Aufbau nach eine Paraphrase, insofern die einzelnen "Variationen" dasselbe Thema immer neu "umschreiben", sondern auch die
einzelnen Durchführungen sind durch eine Technik des Paraphrasierens
untereinander verbunden. Trägt die "Paraphrase des Seem" ihren Titel
auch zweifellos aus dem ersten genannten Grund,[18] so unterstreicht

---

[18] Eine ganz andere Deutung des Terminus Paraphrase geben Wisse a.O. 130
(übernommen von Abramowski a.O. 285 u.a.) und Sevrin a.O. 69f. Wisse geht dabei
nicht vom Titel der Schrift aus, sondern von dem einzigen Vorkommen des Begriffes
im Text in 32,27: "das ist die Paraphrase". Wisse versteht diesen Satz, der "after a
formal ending of the main section of the tractate" stehe (?), als Einleitung eines folgenden
Kommentars zu einer kurz zuvor (31,4-32,5) genannten Reihe von magischen Namen,
die der Gnostiker beim Aufstieg in das Brautgemach des Lichtes zitieren muß. Nur
dieser "Kommentar", in dem erklärt wird, wofür die merkwürdigen Namen stehen
(32,27-34,16), sei also die eigentliche Paraphrase. Von dort her habe der gesamte Traktat
seinen Titel bekommen. Die dieser Deutung zugrundeliegende Beobachtung ist richtig.
In der Tat werden in dem Abschnitt 32,27-34,16 jene Namen ausgedeutet und zwar
mit Bildern und Begriffen, die dem Leser aus früheren "Variationen" des Themas
schon bekannt sind (Staunen, Wolke, Gewand etc.). Allerdings werden die Namen
auch bei ihrer ersten Nennung nicht nur aufgezählt (so nur 31,5-7), sondern schon
mit ersten andeutenden Attributen versehen (31,22-32,5). Der von Wisse so genannte
"Kommentar" greift diese erklärenden Ansätze auf und erweitert und umschreibt sie.
Mit andern Worten: Wisse hat in dem "Kommentar" eine paraphrasierende Partie
entdeckt, die aber nicht einmalig ist, wie er meint, sondern dem Stilprinzip des gesamten Traktates entspricht. — Was nun den Satz "das ist die Paraphrase" (32,27)

doch diese paraphrasierende Technik im einzelnen ihr Anliegen. Es fehlt dem Autor also, wie mir scheint, durchaus nicht an einem bestimmten Willen zur Form, auch wenn die erste Lektüre der Schrift diesen Eindruck erwecken mag. Man muß sich allerdings nicht nur auf Sprache und Bilder, die der Autor benutzt, einlassen, sondern auch auf die Art seiner Darstellung. Nur dann besteht die Chance, wirklich zu verstehen, was er ausdrücken will. Offensichtlich genügt eine — häufig geübte — Art der Interpretation gnostischer Texte nicht, bei der etwa die einigermaßen verständlichen Einzelheiten und Einzelpartien aus dem Ganzen herausgegriffen werden und von dort aus dann entweder der Mythos des Autors in Umrissen rekonstruiert wird oder Aussagen zu Einzelproblemen gemacht werden.[19] Eine solche Interpretation bleibt bei dem "Material" stehen, mit dem der Autor arbeitet und fragt nicht, wozu er es benutzt. Erst wenn man das tut

---

anlangt, der Wisse erst zu seiner Deutung führte, so ist keineswegs sicher, daß er als Einleitung des Folgenden gedacht ist. Vielmehr läßt der Kontext, in dem er steht, eher darauf schließen, daß er den Abschluß des Vorherigen bildet (so auch Sevrin a.O. 69f.). Unmittelbar vor jenem Satz stehen nämlich grundsätzliche Mahnungen des Offenbarers Derdekeas an Sēem, er solle sein Denken vor der Finsternis bewahren und reinhalten (32,19-24). Sie klingen in den feierlich bekräftigenden Sätzen aus: "Das, was ich dich lehre, ist gerecht! Das ist die Paraphrase." (Fortsetzung neu ansetzend und erklärend: "Was nämlich das Firmament anlangt, so hast du nicht daran gedacht ..."). Für Sevrin ist der letzte Satz des Zitates zu verstehen als "das ist die Offenbarung". Denn "paraphrase" bedeute "révélation", wie sich aus den untertitelartigen ersten Zeilen des Gesamttraktates ergebe (1,2-3 bzw. 3-5, vgl. a.O. 70 mit Anm. 4). Mir scheint er damit zwar zu vereinfachen und die Wortbedeutung von παράφρασις ungebührlich zu vernachlässigen, in 32,27 scheint er mir aber den Sinn des Gemeinten richtig zu treffen. In einem eigenen paraphrasierenden Versuch würde ich den Abschnitt 32,19-27 etwa folgendermaßen umschreiben: halte dich an das, Sēem, was du wirklich bist, nämlich Geist (vgl. dazu Monoimos bei Hippolyt, Ref. 8, 15, 1), und laß diesen Geist nicht (wieder) dunkel werden, indem du ihn mit Körperlichem befleckst. Diese Mahnung, die ich dir sage, ist gerecht. Sie ist der Kern der Paraphrase" (d.h. sie ist der eigentliche Inhalt der ganzen Schrift).

[19] So folgt Wisse bei seiner Inhaltsangabe des Traktats (a.O. 131ff.) ausdrücklich nicht "the flow of the tractate, since the revelation does not follow a chronological pattern, but rather frequently back-tracks, repeats, expands, changes terminology and generally tends to confuse and obscure." Wenn das so ist, scheint mir, muß man gerade darauf eingehen. Bei jedem anderen Vorgehen verstellt man sich den Zugang zu der zu interpretierenden Schrift. — Bei dieser wie anderer Kritik an Wisses allererster Behandlung der Paraphrase des Sēem möchte ich aber ausdrücklich hervorheben, daß er in einer sehr viel schwierigeren Lage war als alle späteren Interpreten und daß er angesichts dessen, noch bevor eine Edition des Textes erschienen war, eine ausgezeichnete erste Vorstellung der Schrift geboten hat, auf die man immer wieder zurückgreifen muß. Nur im Sinne des gemeinsamen Bemühens um ein immer besseres Verständnis der gnostischen Texte ist es daher zu verstehen, wenn ich sage, daß man m.E. an eine neue Schrift nicht unter einem Einzelaspekt wie etwa dem der "Redeemer Figure in the Paraphrase of Shem" herangehen sollte.

und dabei möglichst Satz für Satz zu verstehen sucht, auf jeden Fall
aber den Zusammenhang des Ganzen bewahrt und nicht zerreißt,
kann die Intention des Autors deutlich werden.[20] Im Fall der Paraphrase des Sēem ordnet sich dann nicht nur der scheinbar wirre und
spröde Text, sondern man versteht auch den Sinn des Stilprinzips der
ständigen Wiederholungen. Wem dienten sie sonst als dem dringenden,
ja glühenden Anliegen des Autors zur Verkündigung : Das Licht ist
der Finsternis überlegen. Ihr aber (s. dazu im folgenden) gehört dem
Licht an!

Der weitere Verlauf der "Paraphrase" folgt dem beschriebenen
Prinzip. Zwar sind die einzelnen Variationen nicht immer eindeutig
voneinander abzugrenzen, sondern gehen zuweilen auch ineinander
über. Ihre Verknüpfung untereinander ist ebenfalls nicht immer deutlich erkennbar, wohl auch nicht immer durchgeführt. Dennoch bleibt
der Charakter und Stil der Schrift gewahrt, wie sich in einer durch-
gehenden Einzelkommentierung zeigen ließe. Ein Handlungs-oder Ge-
dankenfortschritt in der Folge der einzelnen Variationen ist nicht zu
erwarten und auch nicht zu bemerken. Es wird lediglich immer deutlicher herausgearbeitet, daß die Finsternis sich schließlich in ihren
immer erneuten Versuchen, den Nus in ihren Hervorbringungen festzuhalten, erschöpft. Die "Winde aus dem Wasser" (Metapher für die
Finsternis) bringen schließlich nur noch "jegliche Unreinheit" bzw.
"unfruchtbare Männer und Frauen" hervor (23,26-35). Die Finsternis
hat den Nus, aufgrund dessen allein sie ja handeln kann, verbraucht.
"Am letzten Tage" wird sie wieder zu dem — handlungsunfähigen
— "Finsternis-Klumpen" (ⲃⲱⲗⲟⲥ ⲛ̄ⲕⲁⲕⲉ) werden, der sie "von Anfang an" — d.h. vor In-Besitznahme des Nus — war (45,14-20). Eine
zusammenhängende Kosmogonie nach Art des gnostischen Mythos
ist nicht beabsichtigt. Das schließt gelegentliche Anklänge nicht aus.
So wird z.B. von der Schaffung von Himmel und Erde, der Tiere und
Pflanzen berichtet (20,2ff.). Aber auch das ist wieder einbezogen in
den Gesamtcharakter der Schrift. Denn Himmel und Erde sind wieder
Werke der Finsternis, zu denen sie von dem Lichtoffenbarer in sie
täuschender Absicht provoziert worden ist.[21] Sie weiß nicht, daß mit

---

[20] Zögernd verweise ich als Parallelbeispiele etwa auf die Tragödien Senecas oder
das Epos des Statius u.a., die auch an einem vorgegebenen mythologischen Stoff ihre
Intentionen zum Ausdruck bringen. Die Formkraft des gnostischen Autors kann mit
der eines Seneca sicher nicht verglichen werden. Auch sonst ist vieles in diesen ganz
verschiedenen Literaturgattungen unvergleichlich, aber nicht alles.

[21] Er nähert sich ihr in einer Tiergestalt — vgl. das gleiche Motiv bei Hippolyt,
Ref. 5, 19, 19f.

dem scheinbar glänzenden Werk von Himmel und Erde wieder schon
ein Schritt zur Scheidung von Licht und Finsternis hin, um die es
allein geht, getan worden ist (20,25 ff., vgl. 22,20 f., aber auch schon
5,19-22 u.ö.).

Als feste Markierung in der gleichförmigen Abfolge der Bilder und
Motive tritt die erste deutliche Anrede an die Menschen hervor (24,2 ff.)
— vielleicht nicht zufällig fast genau in der Mitte der langen Schrift:
"Euretwegen trat das Abbild des Geistes auf der Erde und dem Wasser
(d.h. im Finsternisbereich) in Erscheinung. Denn ihr gleicht dem Licht.
Ihr habt nämlich teil an den Winden und Dämonen (d.h. an den
Finsterniskräften) *und* am Denken vom Licht der Kraft des Staunens"
(24,2-9).[22] Diese prononcierte Anrede an die Gnostiker, die ihnen
ihre wahre Zugehörigkeit und damit das Heil offenbart, enthüllt auch
den Sinn der ganzen Schrift. Denn keinen andern Zweck haben die
nicht endenwollenden Darstellungen des Kampfes zwischen Licht und
Finsternis als den, den Menschen, die noch in der Welt, d.h. in der
Finsternis befangen sind, mitzuteilen: ihr gleicht dem Licht. Das Licht
aber *hat* schon über die Finsternis gesiegt. Deren Niederlage wurde in
jeder einzelnen Durchführung des Themas offenbar. Also seid auch
ihr im Prinzip schon von der Finsternis frei.[23]

Die Form der Anrede, sei es an Sēem, den Offenbarungsempfänger,
sei es an sein "Geschlecht", wird im folgenden gewahrt. Ihnen, den
schon erleuchteten Gnostikern, kommt es zu, die Offenbarung an andere
Menschen weiterzugeben (26,20-25). Damit sie diese Aufgabe erfüllen
können, wird wiederum in erneuten Variationen des Themas die Befreiung des Lichts geschildert (26,25 ff.; vgl. auch 24,27 ff. u.ö.). Die
Erwähnung der Missionspflicht der Gnostiker dient also als Stilmittel,
um erneute Durchführungen des Themas zu ermöglichen.[24] In 28,22

---

[22] Die Kraft des Staunens (ⲑⲁⲩⲙⲁ) wird schon in 6,14-35 als die Kraft erklärt,
aus der heraus sich der zum Bewußtsein gekommene Lichtgeist von der Last der ihn
bedrückenden Finsternis frei macht.

[23] Diese gnostische Grundüberzeugung wird im folgenden vielfältig umschrieben.
Besonders eindrücklich und deutlich in 24,16-27: Selig werden die Menschen genannt,
denen "Anteil (am Geist) gegeben wird", d.h. denen durch Offenbarung (vgl. 24,28)
zu verstehen gegeben wird, daß ihre Seele ein sie bedrückendes Werk der Finsternis ist,
das nicht zu ihnen gehört und das sie ablegen und dadurch in das Denken des Lichtes
eintreten können. Ähnlich 47,16-20 und bes. 48,8-30. Diese Partien hebt auch Fischer
(a.O. 265) als Zentralstellen der Schrift hervor, die als "Ausgangspunkt der ganzen Interpretation dienen" müßten. Er macht aber nicht deutlich, inwiefern die ganze übrige
Paraphrase eben diese Gedanken und nichts anderes verkündigt und durch ständige
Wiederholungen einschärft.

[24] In ähnlicher Weise wird immer wieder Gelegenheit zu wiederholenden Umschreibungen des Themas genommen. Zuweilen weist der Autor auch direkt auf frühere Partien

beginnt schließlich eine lange Apokalypse (bis 41,21), die — wiederum in vielfacher Wiederholung — das Fazit aus dem Bisherigen zieht: zwar werden noch viele Bedrückungen kommen, aber die Geistmenschen, die der gnostischen Offenbarung "Glauben" (ⲡⲓⲥⲧⲓⲥ, 35,6 ff. u.ö., vgl. s.v. πίστις im Index bei Krause) schenken, sind schon gerettet (vgl. 34,16 ff.; vgl. auch 42,16 f.). Sie sollen ihr Denken vom Leib, dem Werk der Finsternis, freihalten (32,21-25; 34,25 ff.; 41,5 ff.; 48,8 ff. u.ö.). In den letzten Zeiten werden sich ihre Gedanken ganz von der Finsternis trennen (vgl. 48,19-22). Denn "sie können nicht besiegt werden" (48,12 f.).

In welcher sachlichen Beziehung steht nun diese Verkündigung der Paraphrase des Sēem zu ihrer merkwürdigen Form? Besteht überhaupt eine Beziehung? Mir scheint, durchaus. Warum? Die ständig wiederholte Überzeugung des Autors von der Überlegenheit des Lichtes über die Finsternis und den sich daraus ergebenden Konsequenzen beruht auf Offenbarung. Sie ist in keiner Weise aus der Welt, sei es der sinnlich wahrnehmbaren, sei es der intelligiblen, ableitbar, sondern muß dem einzelnen als Offenbarung "gegeben" werden (37,10-12).[25] Von der Welt — und Welt ist hier im umfassenden Sinne gemeint — kann überhaupt nur geredet werden als der, die schon "zerstört" ist (42,17), die "wertlos" (48,8) ist. Der einzelne Mensch wird, anders als im Christentum, nicht als der Sünder in der Welt angesprochen, sondern als der, der die Welt schon überwunden hat. Was bleibt dann dem gnostischen Prediger noch zu tun übrig? Wenn die Welt weder Analogiecharakter hat, noch auch als Gegebenheit, in der der einzelne Anzuredende steht, Bedeutung hat, so bleibt ihm nichts anderes zu tun als die eine Offenbarung immer und immer wieder zu wiederholen. Das führt literarisch zur immer erneuten Umschreibung der Offenbarung, bzw. zu dem, was unser Autor "Paraphrase" nennt.

Eine Schrift, wie die Paraphrase des Sēem — mag sie uns auch als wirr und überladen erscheinen — ist daher vom inneren Gesetz der Gnosis her durchaus konsequent. Mehr noch, sie zeigt, wohin

---

seiner Paraphrase zurück, z.B. 38,3 ff. "Ich sagte nämlich schon ..." (Verweis auf 30, 21 ff.).

[25] Daß Offenbarung notwendig ist und daß der Mensch nicht etwa von sich aus zur Einsicht kommen kann, geht nicht nur daraus hervor, daß der ganze Traktat in die Form einer Offenbarung gekleidet ist (1,4 f.), sondern wird auch mehrfach expressis verbis gesagt. 36,2 ff. : "Ich bin es, der die Tore für immer geöffnet hat, die von Anfang an verschlossen waren"; 37,6 f. : "Es ist notwendig, daß das Denken vom Wort (ⲗⲟⲅⲟⲥ) gerufen wird ..." etc.

sich die Gnosis im Laufe der Zeit mit Notwendigkeit entwickelte.[26]
Gerade das Wirre der Schrift, das aus dem Wunsch erwächst, die
Offenbarung wieder und wieder anders zu umschreiben, ist charakteristisch. Offensichtlich trägt die Gnosis mit ihrer ausschließlichen Kon-
zentrierung auf die Offenbarung den Keim ihrer Auflösung schon in
sich. Damit widerspricht ein Werk wie die Paraphrase des Sēem
übrigens auch der bekannten These von Hans Jonas, wonach sich die
mythologische Gnosis zur "mystischen Philosophie" hin entwickelt
habe.[27] Vielmehr zeigt sich : Der allen mythologischen Systemen inne-
wohnende, von Jonas so bezeichnete "Mangel", nämlich die "Ent-
wicklungslosigkeit der *praktischen* Seite der Gnosis" (II, 126) und die
fehlende Möglichkeit zu "menschlicher *Selbstrealisierung* des gnostischen Prinzips" (II, 124, *v. Vf.*) weist nicht schon über sich hinaus
auf eine grundsätzliche Überwindung der Mythologie hin. Die mystische
Philosophie ist nicht insofern die Konsequenz der mythologischen
Gnosis als in ihr der vorher nur geschaute Seinsbegriff nun auch
gedacht "und gedacht eben getätigt" (II 165) wird. Zwar kann in
der mythologischen Gnosis der Mythos wirklich nur geglaubt und nicht
im eigentlichen Sinne erkannt werden, weil Erkenntnis die Reproduzier-
barkeit des erkannten Seinsgesetzes aus sich heraus implizieren müßte.
Aber das ist, so scheint die Paraphrase des Sēem zu lehren, ja gerade das
Zentrum gnostischer Verkündigung : sie will wirklich nur "geglaubt"
werden. Der Gnostiker bleibt entsprechend auf Offenbarung ange-
wiesen und die vornehmste, ja einzige Aufgabe des erweckten Pneu-
matikers in dieser Welt bleibt es, diese Offenbarung verkündigend
an andere weiterzugeben. Drängte die Gnosis in ihrer Konsequenz
wirklich zur Philosophie, so würde die Offenbarung entbehrlich. Ihren
Platz würde, wenn er nicht ganz verwaist bliebe, allenfalls eine Art
sokratischer Mäeutik einnehmen müssen. Denn der einzelne potentielle
Gnostiker müßte ja kraft seiner Anteilhabe an der eigentlichen Welt im
wesentlichen aus sich heraus diese Teilhabe auch realisieren können,
indem er erkennt.

Diesen Weg geht aber die gnostische Literatur gerade nicht, sondern
sie paraphrasiert den zentralen Gehalt der gnostischen Offenbarung
immer erneut. Denn dieser paraphrasierende Grundzug eignet, so
scheint mir, nicht nur der hier behandelten Schrift, sondern im Prinzip

---

[26] Mit Fischer a.O. 266 bin ich der Ansicht, daß die Paraphrase des Sēem eine
gnostische Spätschrift ist.

[27] Vgl. schon den Untertitel des zweiten Teils seines Werkes Gnosis und spät-
antiker Geist : "Von der Mythologie zur mystischen Philosophie", Göttingen 1966[2] et
passim.

aller gnostischen Literatur. Deutlich ist das bei den großen varierenden Wiedergaben des Mythos, die wir kennen;[28] deutlich aber auch bei der Fülle der im weitesten Sinne "exegetischen" Literatur der Gnosis[29] oder anderen Formen : immer wird mit Hilfe jeweils anderen Materials — auch Homer kann dazu dienen — die eine Uroffenbarung zur Sprache gebracht. Ja, der gnostische Mythos selbst ist in sich schon paraphrastisch, insofern als das immer erneute Auftreten und Handeln der verschiedenen Erlösergestalten darin auch nur die eine Grundtatsache der Überlegenheit und Befreiung des Lichtes verdeutlichen soll.

Von hier aus fällt nun auch, so scheint mir, ein anderes Licht auf die schon mehrfach behandelte Frage nach dem Verhältnis der uns vorliegenden Paraphrase des Sēem und der bei Hippolyt zitierten und offensichtlich exzerpierten Paraphrase des Seth. Martin Krause hat zweifellos recht, wenn er in einem demnächst erscheinenden Aufsatz feststellt, daß unsere Paraphrase nicht identisch mit der Quelle Hippolyts gewesen sein kann.[30] Aber damit ist die Frage noch nicht erledigt. Denn daß eine starke Verwandtschaft zwischen den Exzerpten bei Hippolyt und der Paraphrase des Sēem nicht nur in der Prinzipienlehre, sondern auch in den einzelnen verwendeten Bildern und Motiven besteht, ist ebenso sicher. Wenn man nun den paraphrastischen Charakter der gnostischen Literatur bedenkt, so muß darin durchaus kein Widerspruch liegen. Sondern die Ähnlichkeit erklärt

---

[28] Beispiele sind etwa das Apokryphon des Johannes, die Schrift vom Ursprung der Welt, die Hypostase der Archonten u.a.

[29] Dazu rechne ich Schriften wie die Naassenerpredigt, die Apophasis Megale (vgl. dazu Frickels Arbeiten), aber auch das Thomasevangelium bzw. alle jene gnostischen Schriften, in denen an beinahe jedem beliebigen vorgegebenen Stoff immer das Gleiche demonstriert wird. Ich meine also jene Schriften, die Hippolyt charakterisiert, wenn er sagt : "Sie (die Gnostiker) gehen ohne Sorgfalt vor, wenn sie das, was alle möglichen Menschen sagen und tun, nach ihrem eigenen Sinn auslegen und behaupten, alles sei pneumatisch (zu interpretieren)", Ref. 5,9,7. Weil das so ist, weil also nahezu jeder beliebige Text gnostisch verstehbar war, deshalb ist es so schwierig, ein Urteil darüber zu fällen, ob alle Texte aus Nag Hammadi gnostisch sind oder nicht. Denn natürlich muß man dann auch mit jeder Art von nur andeutender oder auch mehr verhüllender als klar aufdeckender Schriftstellerei der Gnostiker selbst rechnen, die dennoch für ihresgleichen verständlich war. Jedenfalls scheint es mir nicht zu genügen, die Mannigfaltigkeit der Bibliothek von Nag Hammadi damit zu erklären, "daß ihre Besitzer Gnostiker waren, die nichtgnostische Werke, die ihre asketischen Anschauungen teilten, in ihre Sammlung heiliger Bücher aufnahmen" (so F. Wisse, Die Sextus-Sprüche und das Problem der gnostischen Ethik, in : *Göttinger Orientforschungen* VI,2 p. 83). Die Askese ist als verbindendes Moment der vielfältigen Nag Hammadi-Texte viel zu eng. Verbindend ist das starke und alles in den Dienst nehmende Bewußtsein, erlöst zu sein. Daraus ergeben sich *auch* asketische Konsequenzen.

[30] Vgl. oben S. 76 Anm. 4.

sich daraus, daß beide Paraphrasen für ihre gnostische Verkündigung
offenbar das gleiche Bild- und Gedankenmaterial benutzen, das sie
unabhängig voneinander beide paraphrasierend weiterspinnen. Sie stam-
men offenbar aus der gleichen gnostischen Umgebung, d.h. sie sind
zwei der "unzähligen" Schriften der "Sethianer", von denen Hippolyt
weiß.[31]

Wir werfen zum Schluß noch einen Blick auf den Begriff der
Paraphrase in der antiken Literatur, um damit das spezifisch gnostische
Verständnis dieses Terminus zu vergleichen. παραφράζειν meint zunächst ganz allgemein das Umschreiben eines bestimmten Begriffs oder
Gedankens in anderen Worten.[32] Bei christlichen Schriftstellern ge-
winnt der Begriff den Beiklang des — unlauteren — Entlehnens. Clemens
von Alexandrien führt eine lange Reihe von Beispielen dafür an, daß
bestimmte Sätze und Verse aus heidnischen Schriftstellern lediglich
"Umschreibungen" gewisser Stellen aus den Propheten und Psalmen
seien.[33] In demselben Sinne wirft Hippolyt den gnostischen Häresiar-
chen vor, sie hätten nur die Lehren der Magier und Philosophen "als
ihre eigenen paraphrasiert".[34] Bemerkenswert für unseren Zusammenhang ist dabei, daß also durchaus — ähnlich dem Gebrauch des Terminus in unserem Text — von einem Paraphrasieren einzelner Gedanken und Gedankenkomplexe die Rede sein kann, nicht nur von dem
bestimmter zusammenhängender Texte. In diesem letzten Sinne hat der
Begriff seine Bedeutung im antiken Rhetorikunterricht. Quintilian
empfiehlt den Rednern das Paraphrasieren als ein außerordentlich
geeignetes Mittel, um rhetorische Kraft und Genauigkeit zu erlangen.
Er gibt Regeln dafür an. Es ging nicht nur darum, daß ein Text mit
anderen Worten wiedererzählt wurde,[35] sondern den Namen paraphrasis verdiente nur, was mit dem Original in einen Wettstreit um die
beste Formulierung der Gedanken eintrat.[36] Kürzungen oder Er-

---

[31] Ref. 5,21,1. In einem ähnlichen Verhältnis wie die Paraphrase des Sēem und des
Seth zueinander stehen die verschiedenen Fassungen des Apokryphons des Johannes
untereinander und zu den Berichten bei Irenäus, adv. haer. 1,29 bzw. 1,30.

[32] Vgl. Philo, De Vita Mos. II 38. Philo hebt die Besonderheit der einheitlichen
Übersetzung der Septuaginta hervor, die umso erstaunlicher sei, als das Griechische
doch reich an Ausdrucksmöglichkeiten sei καὶ ταὐτὸν ἐνθύμημα οἶόν τε μεταφράζοντα
καὶ παραφράζοντα σχηματίσαι πολλαχῶς.

[33] Stromata, ed. Stählin Bd. II p. 121,24; 393,4; 442,1f. weiteres vgl. s.v. im Index.
Als Synonym gebraucht Clemens ἐκεῖθεν ἔσπακε τὴν διάνοιαν II 413,21 u.ä. Vgl. auch
II 424,9ff.

[34] Refutatio, ed. Wendland p. 64,14f. (= 4, 42, 1).

[35] Institutio oratoria 1,9,2.

[36] Inst. or. 10,5,5. In diesem Sinne empfiehlt Quintilian besonders die Übertragung

weiterungen des Textes waren dabei erlaubt, aber jeweils nur dann, wenn sie den Sinn des Gemeinten nicht antasteten, sondern exakt zum Ausdruck brachten. Diese Forderungen blieben nicht rein akademisch, sondern wurden im Schulunterricht vielfältig befolgt. Noch Augustin berichtet anschaulich darüber, wie er als Schüler bestimmte Partien der Aeneis in Prosa paraphrasieren mußte.[37] Entscheidend ist nun, daß diese Übung zum Selbstzweck wurde. Es entwickelt sich eine Art Kunstgattung der Paraphrase, d.h. eine als Kunstwerk gedachte Umsetzung bestimmter Werke in einen anderen Stil.[38] Im christlichen Bereich ist vielleicht am bekanntesten Nonnos' epische Paraphrase (μεταβολή) des Johannesevangeliums in Hexametern (5. Jh.), in der sich der Verfasser seiner Vorlage Satz für Satz anschließt. Aber auch die unter dem Namen des Apollinaris von Laodicea überlieferte Psalmenparaphrase (μετάφρασις), sowie in lateinischer Sprache die Evangelienharmonie des Juvencus (um 330), die Paraphrase einzelner Psalmen des Paulinus von Nola, das Epos über die Apostelgeschichte des Arator (544) u.a. sind zu nennen.[39] Daneben gibt es im Bereich der philosophischen Schulen und ihrer Überlieferung seit dem ersten vorchristlichen Jahrhundert paraphrasierende Kommentierungen, insbesondere des Aristoteles. Sie sind von dem Bestreben geleitet, den Text des Aristoteles nicht nur zu verdeutlichen, ihn einheitlicher und leichter zugänglich zu machen, sondern auch, sich mit ihm auseinanderzusetzen, indem Nicht-Befriedigendes eliminiert und durch Besseres ersetzt wird.[40] Diese Kommentare haben eine lange Tradition; im 4. nachchristlichen Jahrhundert erlangt der berühmteste Sophist des Jahrhunderts, Themistios, mit seinen ausdrücklich so genannten Paraphrasen aristotelischer Werke hohen Ruhm.

Wir sehen also: das Genos der Paraphrase ist der Antike in vielfacher Form vertraut. Zwar entspricht keine dieser Formen dem, was wir als gnostische Paraphrase kennenlernten, genau. Das war aber auch

---

von Poesie in Prosa, hält aber auch die Paraphrasierung lateinischer Redner bzw. die Neufassung (transferre) jeweils eigener Werke für nützlich (10,5,5ff.).

[37] Conf. 1,17.

[38] Vgl. dazu E. R. Curtius, *Europäische Literatur und lateinisches Mittelalter*, Bern 1973[8], 157f. und 453ff.

[39] Darüber hinaus finden sich in der byzantinischen Literatur des späteren Mittelalters Paraphrasen in großem Umfang, und zwar als Umsetzungen älterer Literaturwerke in die Volkssprache. Sie sind gleichzeitig Umarbeitungen und -dichtungen der Originale. Vgl. dazu Krumbacher, *Geschichte der byz. Literatur* 221 und 909f.

[40] Vgl. dazu P. Moraux, *Der Aristotelismus bei den Griechen. Von Andronikos bis Alexander von Aphrodisias*. 1. Band: *Die Renaissance des Aristotelismus im 1. Jh. v. Chr.*, Berlin 1973, mit Beispielen 101f., 469ff. et passim.

nicht zu erwarten. Denn das Paraphrasieren der Gnostiker ist ja die Form ihrer Verkündigung, die sich folgerichtig aus ihrem Inhalt ergibt, und nicht Nachahmung fremder Stile ist. Dennoch war durch die in der Antike verbreitete Übung des Paraphrasierens der Boden für die spezifisch gnostische Paraphrase bereitet, und zwar insofern, als die Gnostiker das, was sie vom Inhalt ihrer Predigt her ohnehin zu tun genötigt waren, nämlich zu wiederholen und zu umschreiben, nun auch als "Paraphrase" empfinden, es so benennen und ausdrücklich üben konnten. Paraphrasen in diesem Sinne sind hier wie dort ein Zeichen von Spätform, einer Spätform aber, die Altes zu bewahren und lebendig zu machen bestrebt ist.[41]

Trifft das zu, so gilt für die hier behandelte Schrift und darüber hinaus für die gesamte Nag Hammadi-Bibliothek : Trotz des absonderlichen Wustes von Zeichen und Bildern in ihren Schriften soll doch auch damit nur das zentrale Anliegen gnostischer Verkündigung bewahrt und neu zur Geltung gebracht werden. Dieses Anliegen — und das heißt auch das Wesen der Gnosis — besser zu verstehen (m.E. muß es durch die Stichworte Offenbarung und antwortender Glaube umschrieben werden), kann Nag Hammadi deshalb mit der Fülle seiner gnostischen oder doch gnostisch interpretierbaren und so interpretierten Literatur in einzigartiger Weise dienen.[42] Es lohnt sich also, dem nachzugehen. Das kann aber nicht ohne Berücksichtigung der jeweiligen Form der Verkündigung geschehen.

---

[41] Nicht zufällig wird das Paraphrasieren zur Zeit der zweiten Sophistik beliebt, einer Zeit, die auf die Pflege und nicht selbst schöpferische Wiederholung des Alten gerichtet ist. Als Beispiel nacherlebender und nachschaffender Umsetzung von Kunstwerken in ein anderes Genos ist auch auf Philostrats Bildbeschreibungen hinzuweisen.

[42] Zur Frage, ob die Paraphrase des Seem christlich ist oder nicht, nur so viel : Mir scheint keinerlei Schwierigkeit zu bestehen, sie als aus christlichem Milieu erwachsen zu verstehen (ähnlich jetzt, wenn auch zögernd, Fischer, a.O. 266f.). Die Frage nach der Christlichkeit von Nag Hammadi-Texten entscheidet sich m.E. nicht in erster Linie daran, ob bestimmte christliche dogmatische Einzelheiten oder christliche Namen erwähnt werden. Denn wenn es stimmt, daß die Gnostiker ganz verschiedenes "Material" benutzen können, um daran ihre pneumatische Einsicht zu demonstrieren, dann konnte auf derlei auch verzichtet werden. Mir scheinen daher die gnostischen Texte aus Nag Hammadi durchaus als Nachwirkungen und Weiterbildungen der christlich gnostisierenden Mission des 2. Jahrhunderts von Alexandrien aus zu begreifen sein. Die Tatsache, daß in den Ledereinbänden der Nag Hammadi-Codices christliche Papyri aus pachomianischen Klöstern gefunden wurden (s. dazu J. Barns, Greek and Coptic Papyri from the Covers of the Nag Hammadi Codices, in : *Essays on the Nag Hammadi Texts, in Honour of Pahor Labib*, ed. Krause, Leiden 1975, 9-18), die damit eingebundenen Texte also zumindest in christlichen Klöstern der ersten Hälfte des 4. Jh. gelesen wurden, spricht ja auch eine deutliche Sprache.

UN RITUEL IDÉAL D'INTRONISATION
DANS TROIS TEXTES GNOSTIQUES DE NAG HAMMADI

par

MADDALENA SCOPELLO

Trois textes de la Bibliothèque copte de Nag Hammadi, l'*Authentikos Logos* (VI.2), l'*Exégèse de l'âme* (II.6)[1] et la *Protennoia Trimorphe* (XIII.I)[2] décrivent le processus gnostique du salut et font état d'un rituel qui paraît ne s'être déroulé que sur un plan idéal. Il nous a paru possible de retrouver sous ce rituel gnostique les fragments d'un rituel d'intronisation royale tel qu'il nous est attesté dans deux Pseudépigraphes de l'Ancien Testament, le *Testament de Lévi*[3] et le *Livre des Secrets d'Hénoch.*[4] Dans ces deux textes, en effet, ainsi que G. Widengren l'a bien montré,[5] et précisément au chapître 8 de *Lévi* et au chapître 9 de II *Hénoch*, on décrit l'intronisation céleste des Patriarches à l'aide d'un rituel d'intronisation royale, dont les origines lointaines sont à chercher en milieu mésopotamien. Rappelons ici le schéma proposé par Widengren,[6] illustrant le rituel d'intronisation tel qu'on le reconstitue à partir des deux Pseudépigraphes juifs :

   ascension
   présentation
   ablution
   onction
   repas
   investiture

---

[1] Ed. M. Krause, P. Labib, *Gnostische und Hermetische Schriften aus Codex II und Codex VI*, Glückstadt, 1971, pp. 133-149 et pp. 68-87. On utilise pour l'*Authentikos Logos* la traduction de J. E. Ménard, *L'Authentikos Logos*, Laval, 1977.

[2] Ed. Y. Janssens, La Protennoia Trimorphe, *Le Muséon*, 87 (1974), pp. 360-391.

[3] Ed. R. H. Charles, *The greek versions of the Testaments of the twelve Patriarchs*[2], Oxford, 1960, pp. 27-65.

[4] Ed. A. Vaillant, *Le Livre des Secrets d'Hénoch*, Paris, 1952.

[5] G. Widengren, *Sakrales Königtum im alten Testament und im Judentum*, Stuttgart, 1955, pp. 49-53. Cf. aussi du même auteur, Royal ideology and the Testaments of the twelve Patriarchs in *Promise and Fulfilment*, *Mélanges S. Hooke*, Edinburgh, 1963, pp. 202-212.

[6] Le schéma est proposé à la p. 53 de *Sakrales Königtum*.

dénomination
proclamation
intronisation
participation aux mystères

Des trois textes cités de Nag Hammadi, les deux premiers, l'*Authentikos Logos* et l'*Exégèse de l'âme*, décrivent la remontée de l'âme au plérôme par l'intervention de son Noûs. Dans l'*Authentikos Logos*, le Noûs, ministre du rituel, apporte à l'âme qui s'est prostituée un repas et une onction qui lui permettent de se reconnaître et de retrouver ses attributs royaux. Ainsi, revêtue de majesté, l'âme écrase ses ennemis avant de remonter au ciel : là elle accomplira le hiéros gamos avec le Noûs, atteignant ainsi la connaissance des mystères. On lit, en effet à la page 28 de l'*Authentikos Logos* : "ainsi en est-il de l'âme (ψυχή) chaque fois qu'elle reçoit un logos (λόγος) pour le poser sur ses yeux comme un baume afin qu'elle voie et que sa lumière fasse disparaître les ennemis (πόλεμος) qui la combattent (πολεμεῖν), qu'elle les aveugle par son éclat et qu'elle les encercle lors de son avènement (παρουσία), qu'elle les écrase par sa vigilance et qu'elle se manifeste ouvertement (παρρησιάζεσθαι) dans sa puissance (κράτος) et sa parure royale. Et ses ennemis la contemplent, honteux, alors qu'elle monte vers le ciel, dans son trésor".

Dans l'*Exégèse de l'âme*, le retour de l'âme au salut débute par une ablution baptismale coïncidant avec le retournement de la matrice de l'âme; suivent une onction et une investiture, qui préparent l'âme à l'union avec son Noûs. Après avoir accompli le hiéros gamos, l'âme est couronnée par le Père et remonte au plérôme où elle participe aux mystères divins.[7]

Quant à la *Protennoia*, le rituel d'intronisation concerne le Fils du Sauveur, — entendons le Gnostique —, qui, dépouillé de son vêtement de chair et de toute ignorance (*Protennoia* 49) rejoint le plérôme. On lit en *Protennoia* 48 : « Je l'ai revêtu de lumière brillante, c'est-à-dire la connaissance de la pensée de la paternité; et je l'ai transmis à ceux qui donnent la robe (στολή) : Ammon, Elassô, Aménai, et ils l'ont revêtu d'une robe (στολή) d'entre les robes (στολή) de lumière; et je l'ai transmis à ceux qui baptisent (βαπτιστής); ils l'ont baptisé (βαπτίζειν) : Micheus, Michar, Mnesinous; et ils l'ont plongé dans la source (πηγή) de l'eau de la vie; et je l'ai transmis à ceux qui donnent le trône : Barièl, Nouthan, Sabénai; ils lui ont donné un trône

---

[7] *Exégèse de l'âme* II.134.19-24; 135.29.

venant du trône de la gloire; et je l'ai transmis à ceux qui rendent gloire :
Eriôm, Elièn, Phariel; ils lui ont rendu gloire dans la gloire de la
paternité; et ils ont pris possession de lui ceux qui prennent possession :
Gamaliel, ...], Samblô, grands serviteurs (ὑπηρέτης) des Luminaires
(φωστήρ) saints, et ils le reçurent dans ....] lumière de sa
paternité».[8]

On dégage des trois textes gnostiques les schémas suivants :

Authentikos Logos	*Exégèse de l'âme*	*Protennoia*
repas	ablution	participation aux
onction	onction	mystères
investiture	investiture	investiture
présentation	hiéros gamos	ablution
remontée	couronnement	intronisation
entrée dans le trésor	remontée	glorification
hiéros gamos	participation aux mystères	
participation aux mystères		

La comparaison des schémas tirés des textes de Nag Hammadi avec
celui de II *Hénoch* et du *Testament de Lévi* suggère quelques observations. Notons d'abord que dans les textes gnostiques l'ordre des phases
du rituel a été bouleversé, certaines étapes manquent, d'autres ont été
ajoutées. Le rituel que les textes gnostiques nous proposent est un
rituel morcelé et désintégré. Il y a plus. Ce qui était dans les deux
Pseudépigraphes juifs un rituel céleste est devenu, dans l'*Exégèse de
l'âme* et dans l'*Authentikos Logos*, un rituel de la remontée. L'ascension au ciel, condition première et nécessaire du déroulement rituel,
devient ici sa conséquence ultime. Les étapes conservées du rituel
prennent une signification nouvelle : la présentation aux anges de II
Hénoch, reprise par l'*Authentikos Logos*, devient la parousie glorieuse[9]
de l'âme regagnant le ciel devant ses ennemis. Onction, repas, ablution
et investiture sont tous relégués dans l'*Authentikos* comme dans l'*Exégèse*, dans le κένωμα gnostique. Remarquons au passage la valeur
symbolique qui affecte ces étapes du rituel : le repas de pain et de
vin de *Lévi* 8.5 et l'onction avec l'huile (*Lévi* 8.4; II *Hénoch* 9.20)
deviennent dans l'*Authentikos Logos* (22.24-27; 35.12-14) des substances

---

[8] On retrouve au pr. 45 de la *Protennoia* un doublet du rituel d'intronisation :
on y note l'absence des anges ministres du rituel, la disposition différente des étapes
rituelles et une autre attribution (les gnostiques remplaçant le Fils du Sauveur). Des
parties fragmentaires du rituel apparaissent dans la *Protennoia* XIII.37.31 et 38.19.

[9] Il y a probablement ici un rappel des cultes hellénistiques des souverains, où la
παρουσία est l'entrée glorieuse du roi prenant possession d'une ville. Cf. A. Deissmann,
Licht vom Osten[4], Tübingen, 1923, pp. 314-320 et B. Rigaux, *L'Épître aux Théssaloni-
ciens*, Paris, 1956, p. 199.

spirituelles. L'ablution est un changement intérieur (*Exégèse de l'âme* 131.20-31). L'investiture, enfin, et le couronnement mettent en œuvre des éléments spirituels (*Exégèse de l'âme* 134.19-24; *Authentikos Logos* 32.4-8).

La tentative de donner une reponse à la question de toute Gnose, — où étions-nous, où allons-nous —, selon la formule fameuse de l'*Extrait de Théodote* 78,[10] a sans doute amené l'insertion du rituel d'intronisation dans ces deux textes de Nag Hammadi. La royauté de l'âme, en effet, est chargée dans ces deux textes d'une double signification, étant à la fois prise de conscience de ses origines et de sa destinée.[11] L'addition du hiéros gamos se situe bien dans la relecture gnostique du rituel d'intronisation. Le rituel culmine dans le mariage sacré : le retablissement royal de l'âme coïncide avec son union au Noûs.

On retrouve une fusion analogue entre idéologie royale et réunion de l'âme à son Noûs dans un autre texte gnostique, le *Chant de la Perle*,[12] ce qui nous permet d'affirmer que ce rituel d'intronisation avait fait l'objet dans un milieu gnostique d'une réinterprétation attentive. Rappelons toutefois que l'insertion de l'étape du hiéros gamos se relie, par ailleurs, au rituel d'intronisation mésopotamien, où l'union du roi avec la déesse constitue le sommet du rituel, donnant accès à la connaissance des mystères.[13]

La *Protennoia* appelle quelques observations.

Apparemment, le cadre du rituel proposé par ce texte recoupe celui de *Lévi* et de II *Hénoch*. Le rituel se déroule en effet dans les cieux, "dans la lumière parfaite, d'en haut" (*Protennoia* 49). Il concerne, comme dans le rituel mésopotamien et les Pseudépigraphes, une entité masculine; il est administré par des anges aux fonctions fixées.[14] Enfin, la terminologie stéréotypée avec laquelle on décrit le rituel ne peut pas ne pas

---

[10] Ed. F. Sagnard, *Extraits de Théodote*[2], Paris, 1970, pp. 200-202.

[11] Il est bien dit dans l'*Authentikos Logos* VI.22.28-34.

[12] Dans les *Actes de Thomas* 108-113, éd. R. Lipsius, M. Bonnet, *Acta Apostolorum Apocrypha*, II, Leipzig, reimpr. 1959, pp. 219-224.

[13] Cf. G. Widengren, *Religionsphänomenologie*, Berlin, 1969, pp. 390-392.

[14] Nous retrouvons ailleurs quelques-uns des anges de la *Protennoia* chargés des mêmes fonctions : Micheus, Michar, Mnesinous sont associés au baptême et à l'eau de vie dans l'*Évangile des Égyptiens* IV.64.20, l'*Apocalypse d'Adam* V.84.5, *Zostrianos* VIII.6.10,15 (Michar et Mich[eu]), et le *Codex Bruce* 51.19-21. Bariel est, comme dans la *Protennoia*, un ange du trône selon un exorcisme juif de contenu gnostique (in E. R. Goodenough, *Jewish symbols in greco-roman period*, II, New York, 1953, p. 181. Gamaliel et Samblo sont les ὑπηρέται dans l'*Évangile des Égyptiens* IV.64.15-19, l'*Apocalypse d'Adam* V.76.20 et le *Codex Bruce* 18.34. Dans *Zostrianos* VIII.47.1-4 on retrouve Gamaliel et Mnesinous, gardiens de l'âme. Pour Samblo, cf. *Zostrianos* VIII. 47.24; pour Gamaliel, cf. *Marsanes* X.64.19.

rappeler le milieu d'où sortirent le *Testament de Lévi* et le II *Henoch*.[15]

Neanmoins, bien que le cadre externe ait été fidèlement respecté, la perspective dans laquelle on voit le rituel est fort différente de celle des Pseudépigraphes. Notons en premier lieu que la succession des étapes du rituel a été radicalement bouleversée : la connaissance des mystères, point final de tout développement rituel, est ici placée en tête du rituel. L'investiture précède l'ablution, la prise en charge de l'initié par les anges ministres du rituel clôt le rituel au lieu de l'ouvrir. Bref, le rituel échappe à toute logique de célébration : c'est que l'auteur de la *Protennoia* ne se soucie guère de la suite logique des événements, mais qu'il se situe sur un plan totalement spéculatif et en même temps totalement gnostique. Son attention porte en effet sur un plan atemporel, où tout mouvement et toute évolution sont supprimés dans l'ἀνάπαυσις du plérôme.

Le témoignage de la *Protennoia* fait clairement ressortir le processus d'idéalisation auquel le rituel d'intronisation fut soumis en milieu gnostique. Le rituel, déjà idéal dans les Pseudépigraphes, faisait toutefois référence à des liturgies précises.[16] Cela n'est plus qu'un écho dans l'*Exégèse* et l'*Authentikos*, où certains des étapes du rituel peuvent renvoyer à des cérémonies attestées en milieu gnostique, pour disparaître dans la présentation du rituel faite par la *Protennoia*.

A l'idéalisation du rituel se joint un processus d'intériorisation : le rituel dans les trois textes de Nag Hammadi ne se déroule que dans l'âme du gnostique. Cela nous amène à une dernière remarque : en milieu gnostique le rituel d'intronisation a été l'objet d'une certaine démocratisation. Il n'est plus reservé au roi et aux patriarches, mais à tous les πνευματικοί de la secte.

La parenté de ces textes de Nag Hammadi et des écrits intertestamentaires révèle l'influence que le judaïsme a eu sur certains milieux gnostiques. Alexandrie doit avoir été l'un des lieux privilégiés de ces rencontres.[17]

---

[15] La robe est une robe de lumière, la source, la source de l'eau de vie, le trône, un trône de gloire. Pour la robe de lumière, cf. III *Hénoch* 12.1-2; pour la source de l'eau de vie, I *Hénoch* 96.6 et *Odes de Salomon* 11 et 30; pour le trône de gloire, *Testament de Lévi* 5.1; III *Hénoch* 10; 15; 24 et passim.

[16] Cf. M. Philonenko, Un mystère juif? in : *Mystères et syncrétisme*, Paris, 1975, pp. 65-70.

[17] Cf. M. Philonenko, Une allusion de l'Asclepius au livre d'Hénoch, in *Christianity, Judaism and other greco-roman cults*, éd. J. Neusner, II, Leiden, 1975, pp. 161-163 et du même auteur, La plainte des âmes dans la Kore Kosmou in *Proceedings of the International Colloquium on Gnosticism*, Stockholm, 1977, pp. 153-156.

THE LETTER OF PETER TO PHILIP
AND THE NEW TESTAMENT

by

G. P. LUTTIKHUIZEN

Prof. Krause, Prof. Baumeister and I are jointly preparing an edition of Codex VIII, tractate 2: The Letter of Peter to Philip, with a German translation and a commentary. We began our work on this edition approximately 4 years ago, but due to other commitments this work has been delayed. It is presently planned that the edition will appear in the course of 1978.

In this brief report I will be able to present only some main results of our discussions so far. I myself am especially interested in the relation of this text to the NT and shall emphasize this aspect here. Also I shall call attention to some literary-critical problems.

The title, which is not integral to the work, is literally: ⲧⲉⲡⲓⲥⲧⲟⲗⲏ ⲙ̄ⲡⲉⲧⲣⲟⲥ ⲉⲧⲁϥϫⲟⲟⲩⲥ ⲙ̄ⲫⲓⲗⲓⲡⲡⲟⲥ, "The Letter of Peter, which he sent to Philip". However this work is not written in the literary form of a letter; it merely opens with a letter of Peter to Philip. The main body is a narrative, containing a revelation on the Mount of Olives, followed by a conversation between the apostles on their way to Jerusalem, and then a sermon by Peter in the temple and new appearances of the Lord to his assembled disciples. All these events precede the dispersion of the apostles to proclaim the Gospel in the world.

Many elements of the story, including some specific expressions, remind us of the conclusion of the Gospel of Luke and the first chapters of the canonical Acts of the Apostles.[1] Moreover the narrative of the Letter contains reminiscences of Matthew's story of the appearance of the risen Lord and his missionary commandment also. The last words of Jesus in the Gospel of Matthew are paraphrased twice. In 134, 17f. Jesus says: "I am Jesus Christ, who is with you in eternity"; in 140, 21f.: "Lo, I am with you in eternity".

The author of our text was thoroughly acquainted with these relevant passages of the NT Gospels and Acts and made free use of them; he does not quote literally.

In the introductory letter Peter writes that Philip, his ⲱⲃⲏⲣⲁⲡⲟⲥⲧⲟⲗⲟⲥ, has separated himself from the other apostles and did not want

---

[1] For details I refer to the commentary in the forthcoming edition.

THE LETTER OF PETER TO PHILIP

to join them. It appears that the apostle Philip is here identified with the evangelist Philip, one of the seven.[2] Thus Philip would have been on the way to preach the Gospel, while the other apostles were together and received the teachings of the Lord.[3] Peter calls him "to come according to the commandments (ἐντολή) of our God Jesus".

When Philip has received and read the letter, he goes to Peter joyfully. The letter of Peter and the reaction of Philip prepare the way for a new meeting of the apostles on the Mount of Olives. There they fall upon their knees and pray first to the Father and then to the Son. They ask the Father to hear them and pray to the Son: "Give us strength, for men seek after us to kill us". Here we come upon an important feature of our text.

Why do the apostles ask for strength? As we shall see, the revealer does not directly answer this prayer. Supposedly the author intends to say that the proclamation of the gnostic teaching, as it is summarized in the revelatory words which follow, is dangerous.

The teaching of the apostles in the cosmos is conceived in 137,22ff. as a struggle with the archons. The discussion about the suffering of Jesus and his followers and Peter's sermon about the same issue in the second part of our text must be seen together with the prayer for strength.

It is difficult to see these issues, as they appear here, merely as a literary or theological motif. The prayer for strength ("for men seek after us to kill us"), the conception of the teaching in the world as a struggle with the archons and the concern for the problem of the suffering of Jesus and his followers reveal something of the situation of the author.

Another characteristic feature of our text is the idea that the gnostic teaching, as enunciated by the σωτήρ in his revelation message, is a repetition of the words of the earthly Jesus.

When the revealer has identified himself as Jesus Christ and the apostles have asked some typically gnostic questions,[4] the Lord intro-

---

[2] Cf. Acts 6:5; 8:5ff. and 21:8. This identification of the apostle Philip with Philip the evangelist also in Eusebius' Ecclesiastical History III, ch. 31, in the Martyrium Andreae and the Acts of Philip. See Henn.-Schneem. II, pp. 29 and 404.

[3] Cf. Acts 1:2-4: before his ascension Jesus delivered commandments to his apostles, he appeared to them during forty days and spoke about the kingdom of God and commanded them not to leave Jerusalem, but to wait for the promise of the Father.

[4] Viz. questions about "the defectiveness of the aeons"; about "your (their?) pleroma"; "how are we detained in this dwelling-place"; "how have we come in this place"; "in what way shall we go"; "how do we have the ἐξουσία of the confidence (παρρησία)"; "why do the powers fight with us".

duces his answers to these questions with the words : "You yourselves are witnesses that I have told you all this earlier, but because of your unbelief I will say it once more".

The continuity between the teachings of the gnostic revealer and those of the earthly Jesus is often emphasized. We see this first when the Mount of Olives is designated as "the mountain, on which they (the apostles) used to come together with the ΜΑΚΑΡΙΟC N̄Χ̄C, when he was in the body (ϨΟΤΑΝ ΕϤϨΝ̄ CΩΜΑ)".[5]

This same reference to the somatic, the earthly Jesus is repeated twice. In 138,1-3 Jesus says : "Be not fainthearted (here follows unfortunately a corrupted passage, then :) as I said, when I was in the body (ϨΟΤΑΝ ΕΕΙϨΜ̄ ΠCΩΜΑ)". In 139, 10f. Peter says : "Our Lord Jesus, when he was in the body (ϨΟΤΑΝ ΕϤϨΝ̄ CΩΜΑ), has instructed us about everything". Compare also 138, 22ff, where the voice of Jesus says : "I have often told you, that it is necessary for you to suffer".

These texts are not directly dependent upon the New Testament, but rather point toward the earthly Jesus and more specifically toward the teaching of the earthly Jesus. The canonical gospels speak about this teaching of Jesus, but in the view of our author obviously in an insufficient and superficial way.

The gnostic teachings of the revealer are announced as a repetition of the words of the earthly Jesus. Because the apostles (and by implication the gospel-writers as well) were unbelieving, they have not understood Jesus' message. The gnostic teaching, as expounded in the revelation, is considered as the authentic and full teaching of Jesus. The writer thus makes no distinction between the teaching of the earthly and that of the risen Lord. But the apostles have not comprehended that the earthly Jesus was a gnostic revealer. Because of their unbelief a repetition is necessary.

In the revelation the gnostic questions of the apostles are answered. The cause of the ϢΩΩΤ N̄ΕΩΝ (the defectiveness of the aeons) is explained by the disobedience and the thoughtlessness of the Mother and by the appearance of the Αὐθάδης. The revealer says that he himself is the pleroma and that he is sent in the σῶμα (the dead πλάσμα) to teach the one who belongs to him (the fallen σπέρμα). The listeners are exhorted to conduct themselves as lights (φωστήρ) in the midst

---

[5] Cf. Lk 22:39 : ἐπορεύθη κατὰ τὸ ἔθος εἰς τὸ ὄρος τῶν ἐλαιῶν and 24:44 : οἱ λόγοι μου οὓς ἐλάλησα πρὸς ὑμᾶς ἔτι ὢν σὺν ὑμῖν.

of dead people and the Lord speaks briefly about the struggle with the powers (ΝΙϬΟΜ).[6]

It is important to make it clear that in this revelation [7] we find that there are no references to the New Testament or Christian ideas. However we do notice some conceptions and expressions which could come as easily from the New Testament as from gnostic sources : [8] the pleroma, the struggle with the powers, [9] the sending of the saviour, [10] etc. In this respect there is a striking discrepancy between this revelation and its context. It would appear that the author here has made use of a gnostic source (a composition of gnostic questions and answers).

As witnesses of Jesus in the world (a Lucan conception) the apostles are commissioned to proclaim this teaching in the world. The writer considered this, possibly from his own experience, a perilous task.

It is often stated in our text that the apostles come together or must come together. This is a third characteristic of the Letter of Peter to Philip. When they meet, they will be told how they must proclaim the Gospel, and then they will receive the power of the Father or of Jesus to preach the salvation in the cosmos.

I mention only the more important passages.

Already in the introductory letter Peter writes to Philip :

"We have received commandments from our Lord and the saviour of the whole world, [11] that we come together and teach and that we preach in (or on) the salvation that is promised [12] to us by our

---

[6] The last gnostic question ("why do the powers fight with us") is answered by the revealer as follows : "concerning this, that you shall fight with the powers : they do not have rest as you do, because they do not want (...) that you be saved".

[7] Which in fact is a concatenation of different gnostic tenets : cosmological, soteriological, paraenetic.

[8] Here we touch the larger problem of the relation between NT texts and gnosis. Cf. van Unnik, "The 'Gospel of Truth' and the New Testament", in : *The Jung Codex* (ed. F. L. Cross), London 1955, p. 108 : "Obviously we must exclude from consideration expressions showing agreement with New Testament texts in passages where certain scholars have held that they could establish an influence of Gnosis on the New Testament itself".

[9] Cf. Eph 6:12.

[10] *i.e.* his being sent in the σῶμα; the New Testament texts speak of the coming of Jesus Christ in the σάρξ, cf. Rom 8:3; I Tim 3:16; Jn 1:14; I Jn 4:2; II Jn 7.

[11] This is clearly not a gnostic conception. Cf. Jn 3:16f.; 4:42; I Jn 4:9; 4:14.

[12] ϨΡΑΪ ϨΜ ΠΙΟΥΧΑΪ ΕΤΑΥϬΡΗΤ ΜΜΟϤ, cf. 137, 24f.: †ϹΒⲰ ϨΜ ΠΚΟϹΜΟϹ ΜΠΙΟΥΧΑΪ ϨΝ ΟΥϬΡΗΤ.

Lord Jesus Christ[13] ... But you did not want us to come together in a place[14] and us to learn how we are called to preach the Gospel".

When the revealer has delivered his answer to the last gnostic question,[15] the apostles ask a new question. The terminology and the whole issue indicate that not only the redactional connection, but also the new question and its answer by the revealer are formulated by the author himself. This addition is apparently inspired by the last answer of the Lord. The rendering here is partially in my own words:

Then the apostles worshipped him once again and said: "Lord, tell us in what way[16] shall we struggle with the archons,[17] for the archons are superior to us". The voice of the revealer said to them *inter alia*, that they must assemble at a place and that they must gird themselves with the power of the Father. The assembling at a place and the teaching in the world of the salvation in a promise[18] are, as noted before, conceived as a struggle with the archons. The Lord gives assurance that the Father will help them. "Be not fainthearted (...) as I already said, when I was in the body".

After these words the revealer is carried off into heaven. The apostles return to Jerusalem.[19] On the way they speak "about the Lord", in fact about his suffering and in connection with this about their own suffering.

The ideas expressed here concerning the suffering of Jesus and his followers are not essentially different from those in the New Testament. The apostles say: "Since our Lord has suffered, how much more so should we". Peter answers and says: "He has suffered, because of us (ετвннт̄ν)", which is in entire agreement with the apostolic confession.[20] Peter continues: "It is also necessary for us, that we suffer, because of our littleness (τενмν̄ткоγει)". мν̄ткоγει has a negative sense here, whereas e.g. in the Gospel of Thomas and in the Gospel

---

[13] The salvation, in other words, is not a present reality; it is promised for the future.

[14] пιτρεнει εγмλ.

[15] Cf. n. 6.

[16] λω τε θε, not ετвε оγ, as in the last gnostic question.

[17] нιλρχωн instead of нιбом.

[18] Cf. notes 12 and 13.

[19] Cf. Lk 24:52f. and Acts 1:12.

[20] While περί is used in the NT in this sense, the more normal preposition is ὑπέρ (e.g. Christ has died ὑπὲρ ἡμῶν, ὑπὲρ τῶν ἁμαρτιῶν ἡμῶν). In the Sahidic NT ϩλ renders ὑπέρ and ετвε περί or διά *c.acc.* Cf. Rom 4:25 (пλï ν̄ταqτλλq ετвε нενновε); I Thess 5:10 (пλï ν̄ταqмоγ ετвннтν) and I Jn 2:2.

of Truth it has a positive meaning. Then a voice addresses them, saying: "I have often told you that it is necessary for you to suffer. It is necessary for you to be brought into synagogues and before governors (ἡγεμών),[21] in order that you suffer". The necessity of suffering for the disciples is more strongly emphasized than in the New Testament. The words οὐχὶ ταῦτα ἔδει παθεῖν τὸν χριστόν, spoken by the risen Lord to the disciples travelling to Emmaus, are applied here to the followers of Jesus (cf. Acts 14:22).

The apostles rejoice in these words of Jesus; they enter Jerusalem and come into the temple and heal many people.

Then begins a sermon of Peter on the same theme: the suffering of Jesus and his followers. But the content is different.
Peter does not speak to his ϢΒΗΡΑΠΟϹΤΟΛΟϹ, as the context requires, but to his disciples (ΝΕϥΜΑΘΗΤΗϹ).
The sermon consists of a short christological credo, followed by a gnostic interpretation.

This credo:

> our φωστήρ Jesus came down
> and he was hanged on a tree
> and he was buried in a tomb
> and he rose from the dead

is rather unskilfully interpolated with the sentence[22]: "and he carried (φορεῖν)[23] a crown of thorns and put on a purple robe (στολή)".[24]

Peter interprets this confession as follows: "My brothers, for Jesus this suffering is strange, but we have suffered because of the transgression (παράβασις) of the Mother" (a reference to the Sophia-myth or one of its variants, such as is mentioned in the revelation in the first section of the text). "And therefore", Peter continues, "he has done everything according to an image (or a likeness) in us (or among us)".[25]

It is unlikely that this gnostic sermon of Peter is formulated by the author of our text. He must have used and superficially adapted

---

[21] Cf. Mt. 10:17f. and parallels. Mt has ἀχθήσεσθε, which could explain the form ΤΡΕΥΝΤΗΥΤΝ̄.

[22] This interpolation focuses the attention on the passion of Jesus. The present order of the sentences is curious: "and he was hanged and he carried a crown of thorns and put on a purple robe and he was hanged on a tree" (cf. Acts 5:30 and 10:39).

[23] Cf. Jn 19:5: φορῶν τὸν ἀκάνθινον στέφανον.

[24] Here Jesus takes the initiative. This differs from what is told in the gospel-narratives.

[25] ΚΑΤΑ ΟΥΕΙΝΕ ϨΡΑΪ Ν̄ϨΗΤΝ̄.

a gnostic source. This also would explain certain doublets in the narrative.[26] But can we make clear then why he inserted this Christian-gnostic sermon of Peter?

I propose the following solution :

a) In our text a Christian who has been converted to the gnostic doctrine of salvation is speaking. When he chooses his own words, he still uses the vocabulary of catholic Christianity. This is especially apparent in his christological ideas : Jesus is the σωτήρ of the whole κόσμος, he has really suffered and has suffered because of us. He was convinced that in the gnostic teaching the deeper and fuller message of Jesus was revealed. He saw no substantial conflict between the catholic and the gnostic doctrine and therefore did not need to abandon his former views.

b) It is possible that the author of this work has been guided by the first letter of Peter in the New Testament. No other writing in the New Testament considers so fully the problem of the suffering of Christians. On the basis of I Peter he could have expected from Peter an answer to the problem of the significance of the suffering of Jesus' followers. The author has included then a gnostic-Christian sermon precisely because he came across a text in which Peter as a gnostic speaks about the suffering of Jesus and his followers. However because there are no specific allusions to I Peter, this last suggestion must remain conjectural.

---

[26] In 139, 7f. (before Peter's sermon) it is said that the apostles healed many people. In 140, 4ff. Peter asks the Lord : "Give us a πνεῦμα ἐπιστήμης, in order that we too may perform miracles (ϩⲉⲛϭⲟⲙ)"; 140, 9f. : "And each of them performed healings". That the apostles saw Jesus and that they separated to proclaim (ⲧⲁϣⲉ ⲟⲉⲓϣ) is told twice on p. 140.

LA LETTRE DE PIERRE À PHILIPPE : SA STRUCTURE

par

JACQUES É. MÉNARD

Plusieurs traités de la Bibliothèque de Nag Hammadi sont constitués de fragments ou de gloses. Nous pouvons citer l'exemple du *Livre de Thomas l'Athlète* du Codex II, des *Actes de Pierre et des Douze Apôtres* du Codex VI et du *Deuxième Traité du Grand Seth* du Codex VII.

Le *Livre de Thomas l'Athlète* renferme une première partie (p. 138, 4-142, 21) dans laquelle Jésus s'entretient avec Thomas et où ce dernier, comme dans l'*Évangile selon Thomas*, est le type du parfait, le jumeau de Jésus qui s'est identifié au Maître. La deuxième partie de l'opuscule (p. 142, 21-145, 16) n'a plus pour personnage central que l'Apôtre Thomas, mais elle est faite de bénédictions et de malédictions qui reflètent une doctrine ascétique qui aurait été celle de milieux se réclamant de Matthias. Ces différences ont porté J. D. Turner [1] à voir dans la première partie du traité, un dialogue de Jésus avec le spirituel représenté par Thomas, et cette partie remonterait à une tradition de Thomas ; la deuxième partie, elle, serait une homélie où se refléterait une tradition de Matthias, au nom duquel l'Antiquité chrétienne rattachait certains logia du Christ.

Un autre exemple d'écrit constitué de fragments est celui des *Actes de Pierre et des Douze Apôtres*, comme l'a montré M. Krause.[2] Après une Introduction qui raconte l'arrivée de Pierre dans la ville (p. 1, 3-29), un fragment non chrétien décrit la rencontre de Pierre avec Lithargoël (p. 1, 29-7, 23), et un autre fragment, cette fois chrétien, reprend le même thème, en identifiant Lithargoël à Jésus (p. 8, 13-12, 19). A l'intérieur même du premier récit de la rencontre de Pierre et de Lithargoël, deux fragments à la p. 4 traitent du don de la perle aux

---

[1] Cf. J. D. Turner, A New Link in the Syrian Judas Thomas Tradition, in : *Essays on the Nag Hammadi Texts in Honour of Alexander Böhlig*, éd. M. Krause (Nag Hammadi Studies, 3), Leiden, 1972, p. 109-119 ; *The Book of Thomas the Contender* (SBL Dissertation Series, 23), Missoula, 1975, p. 215-225.

[2] Cf. M. Krause, Die Petrusakten in Codex VI von Nag Hammadi, in : *Essays on the Nag Hammadi Texts in Honour of Alexander Böhlig*, p. 36-58.

mendiants : ce sont plutôt deux recensions, la première, brève, la seconde, longue.

Notre troisième exemple, nous l'empruntons au *Deuxième Traité du Grand Seth*. Ce traité comporte une première partie où sont juxtaposés deux mythes de descente du Sauveur (p. 49, 10 – 54, 14 ; 54, 14 - 59, 9) : à la chute de Sophia du premier mythe (p. 50, 30 - 51, 11) correspond la chute de la Petite Pensée (p. 54, 23-24). Ces deux mythes d'un Sauveur non chrétien sont tous deux émaillés de gloses chrétiennes sur la Passion et la Résurrection du Christ docétiste (p. 53, 24-27 ; 55, 9 - 59, 9). La deuxième partie est parénétique (p. 59, 9 - 70, 12) ; c'est une exhortation du Sauveur aux siens. Elle parle de son union avec eux, elle renferme une charge contre les grands personnages de l'Ancien Testament, pour mettre en valeur la supériorité des gnostiques sur eux, et elle insiste sur le mariage céleste. Elle est de la main du rédacteur.

Rien d'étonnant alors que la *Lettre de Pierre à Philippe* du Codex VIII soit elle aussi constituée de deux fragments. Un premier renferme un reste d'une Lettre de Pierre à Philippe et le second est une explication gnostique de la situation de l'homme ici-bas.

I. *La Lettre de Pierre à Philippe : un fragment de Lettre*

A la lecture de l'opuscule, on a la nette impression d'être en présence d'un traité ou d'un manuel dogmatique gnostique beaucoup plus que d'une Lettre. En effet, les p. 135 à 137 renferment différents points de la doctrine gnostique présentés sous forme schématique : la Déficience des Éons ou des Puissances qui, sous la direction de la Mère-Sophia et du Démiurge appelé Authadès, comme dans l'*Apocryphon de Jean* (ApocrJn) (cf. BG, p. 46, 1 Till) ou l'*Hypostase des Archontes* (Hyp Arch) (p. 90, 29 ; 92, 27 ; 94, 17 Bullard), ont construit un monde matériel qui n'est qu'une contrefaçon du monde céleste ; au contraire, le Plérôme, c'est le Christ qui en est descendu pour sauver la semence spirituelle tombée dans le monde dominé par les Archontes ; dans leur combat contre ces derniers, les disciples ou les pneumatiques doivent répandre la promesse du salut et souffrir la persécution (p. 138-139). Ce sont eux qui sont appelés à souffrir à cause de la Déficience (p. 138, 19) et de la transgression (p. 139, 23) de Sophia, car ce n'est qu'en apparence que le Christ-Illuminateur a souffert (p. 139, 15).

Et ces différents points de doctrine sont exposés à l'occasion de questions fictives des disciples. Le genre littéraire de *quaestiones*, posées par les Apôtres, et de *responsiones* données par le Christ, est particulièrement bien illustré, par exemple, dans la littérature apocryphe par l'*Epistula Apostolorum*, mais c'est aussi un genre littéraire répandu dans l'Antiquité.[3]

L'opuscule paraît être si peu une Lettre qu'on serait porté à croire qu'il s'agit plutôt d'un fragment d'une Lettre de Pierre à Philippe dont on n'aurait conservé que le début avec la mention de l'expéditeur et du destinataire, avec la salutation habituelle et la description de la situation de Philippe séparé des autres disciples (p. 132, 10-133, 8).

La Lettre ne prend à peine qu'une page d'un traité qui en compte neuf et qui est fait essentiellement de questions et de réponses, à la manière d'un traité dogmatique. Notre opuscule appartiendrait à des Actes apocryphes des Apôtres dont ne nous aurait été conservé au début qu'un fragment de Lettre suivi d'un traité dogmatique. On pourrait alors donner comme titre à l'ensemble :

Fragment apocryphe des Actes des Apôtres

dans lequel aurait été intégré le début d'une Lettre de Pierre à Philippe jusqu'à la p. 133, 8a. Et au v.8b de cette même page, commencerait à proprement dit le traité.

Mais cette explication ne demeure qu'une hypothèse de travail, et même le terme "fragment" peut porter à faux. Il ne saurait s'agir tout au plus que d'un Extrait de Lettre dont se serait servi le rédacteur pour introduire son traité dogmatique. Qui plus est, il serait quelque peu téméraire de modifier pour autant le titre déjà reçu de l'écrit. Le titre de *Lettre de Pierre à Philippe* donné à l'opuscule, malgré le peu de place que la Lettre y occupe, n'est pas une exception dans la bibliothèque de Nag Hammadi. On a donné par exemple à la *Paraphrase de Sem* ce titre, même si Sem n'intervient qu'en quelques endroits et que le reste de l'écrit traite de thèmes qui n'ont rien à voir avec Sem et qui peuvent être séthiens.[4] Et il n'est pas inouï que le titre de l'ouvrage soit renfermé dans l'*incipit*, en l'absence de colophon. On l'a vu pour l'*Évangile de Vérité*. Quelque grec que soit ce dernier, on a le droit de retrouver son titre dans son *incipit*, à l'exemple de certains

---

[3] Cf. K. Rudolph, Der gnostische Dialog als literarischer Genus, in : *Probleme der koptischen Literatur* (Wissenschaftliche Beiträge, 1[1968], K2), Martin-Luther Universität, Halle-Wittenberg, p. 85-107.

[4] Cf D. A. Bertrand, Paraphrase de Sem et Paraphrase de Seth, in : *Les Textes de Nag Hammadi* [Colloque du Centre de Recherches d'Histoire des Religions, Strasbourg, 23-25 octobre 1974], éd. J. É. Ménard (Nag Hammadi Studies, 7), Leiden, 1975, p. 146-157 ; J.-M. Sevrin, A propos de la Paraphrase de Sem, *Le Muséon* LXXXVIII, 1-2 (1975) 69-96.

manuscrits grecs, ainsi que nous l'avons nous-même souligné dans notre dernier commentaire de l'*Évangile de Vérité*.[5] Et même pour ce qui est de notre Lettre, les mots "Lettre de Pierre à Philippe" sont en retrait par rapport au reste du texte du papyrus. Ne serait-ce pas un indice que tel était bien le titre dans l'esprit du rédacteur?

II. *La Lettre de Pierre à Philippe : un manuel gnostique*

A compter de la p. 135,4 jusqu'à la p. 137,13 le Seigneur apporte une réponse gnostique aux questions des disciples sur la condition de l'homme :

a) de la p. 135,8 à la p. 136,15 il répond à la question sur la Déficience des Éons. C'est la désobéissance et la déraison de la Mère qui se sont manifestées : la Sophia, sans la puissance et la grandeur du Père, a voulu se susciter des Éons. Grâce à sa parole est né l'Authadès qui s'est emparé de la partie qui restait d'elle et cette portion est devenue la Déficience des Eons. Il a établi des Puissances et des Autorités qui se sont réjouies d'avoir été créées : parce qu'elles n'ont pas connu Celui qui préexiste, elles louent l'Authadès qui est vaniteux et jaloux;

b) de la p. 136,16 à la p. 137,4 Jésus répond à la question sur le Plérôme : le Plérôme, c'est lui, et il a été envoyé dans un corps à cause de la semence déchue. Il est venu dans la contrefaçon matérielle et terrestre fabriquée par les Archontes, mais ils ne le reconnurent pas, ils le prirent pour un homme mort. Il a parlé avec ceux qui lui appartiennent, qui lui sont propres, et il leur a concédé le droit d'entrer dans l'héritage de leur Père;

c) la p. 137,4-9 renferme la réponse du Christ à la question de l'emprisonnement des siens par les Puissances : "Si vous vous dépouillez de la corruption, alors vous deviendrez des luminaires au milieu des hommes morts";

d) à la question du combat mené par les spirituels contre les Puissances (p. 137,10-13) le Christ répond qu'elles n'ont pas de repos et qu'elles ne veulent pas qu'ils soient sauvés.

C'est alors que les Apôtres posent une cinquième question complémentaire : "Seigneur, enseigne-nous comment combattre les Archontes, puisque les Archontes sont au-dessus de nous" (p. 137,13-17). La

---

[5] Cf. J. É. Ménard, *L'Évangile de Vérité* (Nag Hammadi Studies, 2), Leiden, 1972, Introduction, p. 11-12.

réponse va jusqu'à la p. 138, 3 : les Archontes sont opposés à l'homme intérieur. Aussi les disciples doivent-ils les combattre : ils doivent se rassembler en un endroit et annoncer le salut dans le monde, se ceindre de la puissance de leur Père et adresser à ce dernier leur prière. Et celui-ci continuera de les aider. Jésus fait appel à sa promesse antérieure, alors qu'il était présent corporellement au milieu des siens.

Un thème qui pourrait réunir ces deux fragments de la Lettre serait celui du rassemblement, de la σύλλεξις gnostique. C'est aussi bien dans le rassemblement que les Apôtres peuvent annoncer la Bonne Nouvelle, que c'est grâce à lui qu'ils seront réunis dans le Sauveur pour remonter à travers les sphères des Archontes jusqu'au Plérôme.

LA BIBLIOTHÈQUE COPTE DE NAG HAMMADI

JACQUES-É. MÉNARD

En septembre 1974, Le Conseil des Arts du Canada accordait une subvention au *Laboratoire d'Histoire Religieuse* de l'Université Laval, suite à l'élaboration d'un projet d'édition française intégrale des textes de Nag Hammadi présenté par les Professeurs Hervé Gagné et Michel Roberge de la Faculté de Théologie de l'Université Laval et par moi-même. L'objectif du projet est la traduction française de chacun des traités avec, en regard, le texte copte collationné au Caire; cette traduction est précédée d'une Introduction et accompagnée de notes de collation et de traduction, d'un Commentaire et d'Index grec et copte.

Le groupe de l'Université Laval est composé de jeunes chercheurs qui travaillent sous la direction du Professeur Michel Roberge de la Faculté de Théologie et chercheur principal du projet. Chacun des chercheurs traduit un ou deux traités, mais chaque traité fait l'objet de recherches communes lors de "séminaires permanents" animés successivement par des spécialistes invités. Pour donner, en effet, au groupe de recherches une assistance formelle et efficace à cause des difficultés intrinsèques à l'œuvre et pour garantir à ce projet canadien un aspect de francophonie internationale, nous nous sommes assurés l'expertise d'agrégés, d'égyptologues, d'hébraïsants et de syriacisants : ils sont belges, français, suisses. Regroupés à l'Université des Sciences Humaines de Strasbourg, ils ont pour tâche de traduire et de commenter chacun un traité de la Bibliothèque de Nag Hammadi, de conseiller les chercheurs comme experts et spécialistes et d'animer respectivement les sessions intensives du groupe de l'Université Laval suivant un programme bien établi.

Pour ne pas retarder la publication des travaux en cours, nous publions chaque traité sous forme de fascicule dans la Collection "Bibliothèque copte de Nag Hammadi». La *Lettre de Pierre à Philippe* du Codex VIII et l'*Authentikos Logos* du Codex VI sont déjà sous presse à l'Imprimerie Orientaliste de Louvain; les traités hermétiques du Codex VI et la *Prôtennoia Trimorphe* du Codex XIII sont à la composition. Les autres traités qui sont en préparation sont :

— *L'Évangile selon Thomas*,
— *L'Évangile selon Philippe*,
— *L'Hypostase des Archontes*,
— *L'Écrit sans titre*,
— *Le Livre de Thomas l'Athlète* du Codex II ;
— *Les Actes de Pierre et des Douze Apôtres*,
— *La Brontè* du Codex VI ;
— *La Paraphrase de Sem*,
— *Le Deuxième Traité du Grand Seth*,
— *L'Apocalypse de Pierre*,
— *Les Leçons de Silvanos* et
— *Les trois Stèles de Seth* du Codex VII.

Nous ajouterons à cette édition des textes de Nag Hammadi celle des textes gnostiques du Papyrus de Berlin 8502. *L'Évangile de Marie* du Papyrus de Berlin est en préparation, ainsi que la *Sophia de Jésus-Christ* de ce même Papyrus et du Codex III de Nag Hammadi, qui est la version chrétienne d'*Eugnoste le Bienheureux* du Codex III et V.

L'Introduction qui précède chaque traité renferme des données de date, d'auteurs et surtout de doctrine.

Pour l'établissement du texte, nous avons sans doute à notre disposition l'édition fac-similé publiée par le comité international de l'UNESCO, mais cela n'est pas suffisant. Lors d'un colloque organisé par le Centre de Recherches d'Histoire des Religions de Strasbourg en 1974, nous nous sommes vite rendus compte de la nécessité de collationner les textes ici-même au Caire, la lecture du papyrus devant s'effectuer à l'aide de lampes ultra-violettes. Nous avons commencé à le faire en décembre 1974 et janvier 1975 et aux mois d'août 1975 et 1976 pour les traités qui sont sous presse ou à la composition et pour l'*Évangile selon Philippe*, l'*Hypostase des Archontes*, les *Actes de Pierre et des Douze Apôtres*, la *Brontè*.

Il suffirait de comparer l'édition qu'une de nos collaboratrices, Mlle Janssens, a fait paraître de la *Prôtennoia Trimorphe* dans le *Muséon LXXXVII,3-4* (1974) 341-412 et qui est basée sur les seules planches photographiques et celle, appuyée par une collation du texte sur le papyrus lui-même, qu'elle fait maintenant paraître dans notre collection. En effet, la très grande majorité des papyrus étant plus ou moins lacuneux, ce n'est qu'à l'aide des rayons ultra-violets que l'on peut déceler en marge des lacunes, des lettres effacées dont il reste toutefois des traits encore bien lisibles. Et, très souvent, ces lettres permettent au lecteur averti de se livrer à des conjectures qui viennent combler la lacune, une fois que l'on a bien mesuré, selon l'écriture du scribe, le nombre de lettres manquantes.

Notre méthode dans la traduction des textes est basée sur la méthode philologique de la rétroversion. La rétroversion n'est certes pas à retenir dans sa totalité, mais à tout le moins dans la signification des termes. Les textes de Nag Hammadi sont des traductions d'originaux grecs. On sait, par exemple, que la chute de l'homme ici-bas est comparée dans certains textes gnostiques à une prostitution, une πορνεία. Dans la *Paraphrase de Sem* du Codex VII, la τριβή (21), c'est la caresse sexuelle des membres inférieurs déchus qui dépeint l'union des eaux avec la φύσις comparée à la matrice retournée vers l'extérieur (p. 34, 16 comme dans l'*Exégèse de l'âme* du Codex II, p. 131, 27-33) et le πρόσθεμα mentionné aux p. 22 et 23 ne comporte pas l'idée de multiplication, mais il s'agit du membre viril (πόσθη) qui s'unit aux démons tout comme les Ténèbres avaient caressé la matrice. A cet égard, si la *Paraphrase de Sem* peut présenter des analogies avec la *Paraphrase de Seth* connue de l'*Élenchos* d'Hippolyte, c'est que l'une comme l'autre décrivent l'acte d'un Sauveur raffinant sans cesse le monde, en séparant les éléments du feu et de la lumière de ceux des eaux. Seul le retour au grec peut permettre, en les décomposant, de saisir aussi la signification de termes comme Saphaïna (la "Vérité pleine", p. 31, 28) et Molychtha, la "terre souillée" (p. 32, 2) ou, encore mieux, le fameux $\overline{\text{ANACCHC}}$ $\overline{\text{AYCHC}}$ de la p. 11, 22 qui signifie ἀνάστασις-δύσις, le lever et le coucher du soleil, le commencement et la fin. L'expression $\overline{\text{200KM}}$ à la p. 38, 10 ne signifie pas non plus "devenir faible", mais son équivalent grec est μαραίνειν, qui signifie "liquéfier" : l'Intellect ne doit pas être liquéfié au contact de l'eau, il ne doit pas se laisser tarir par l'eau et devenir un poisson (p. 19, 2.13). Le vêtement de la p. 39, 2 n'est pas enfin celui qui est unique, mais celui qui n'a pas de double ($\overline{\text{MMNTEC}}$ CAEIϢ), c'est-à-dire qui n'a pas de ζεῦγος, de jumeau, à l'exemple du vêtement terrestre. Il est fait mention à la p. 62 du *Deuxième Traité du Grand Seth*, de la communion entre les parfaits qui doit être une communion de nature, de totalité et non de partialité. La mystérieuse expression des l. 22-23 ΟΥΚϢ ΕϨΡΑΪ pourrait faire allusion, sans doute, à la position d'une note de musique ou d'une voyelle à l'intérieur d'un mot, qui est en bonne ou en mauvaise position, mais le terme copte traduit le grec παράθεσις qui signifie juxtaposition et est à l'opposé de cette σύνθεσις qu'est la gnose (cf. Liddell-Scott, p. 1309).

Le commentaire a pour but essentiel d'expliquer le texte en et par lui-même, puis de l'éclairer à l'aide des textes gnostiques qui lui sont proches.

Et c'est l'Index particulier à chaque traité et l'Index général de tous les traités qui peuvent aider à déceler les passages où le même terme copte revient. Cet Index, grec et copte, est d'ailleurs un outil indispensable pour mieux saisir le sens de chaque terme dans son contexte immédiat et médiat. A cet effet, nous avons trois fichiers, l'un à Nancy où l'index est établi, un à Strasbourg et un à l'Université Laval.

Ce projet d'Index est conçu comme un complément à l'édition de la "Bibliothèque Copte de Nag Hammadi". Dans un premier temps, est prévue la constitution d'un fichier général du vocabulaire des textes de Nag Hammadi réalisé à partir des Index particuliers qui accompagnent l'édition de chaque texte du Corpus. Une fois ce travail de collation terminé, une édition de l'Index général sera faite.

L'élaboration du fichier et la réalisation de l'édition finale ont été confiées à Bernard Barc, maître-assistant à l'Université de Nancy, et à Louis Painchaud, chercheur au laboratoire d'Histoire Religieuse de l'Université Laval. La réalisation du fichier a été planifiée sur une période de 7 ans, et prévoit un rythme d'indexation de 17000 mots-occurrences environ par an. Compte tenu du fait que certains textes du corpus dont l'édition n'est prévue qu'à la fin du projet, ont déjà été étudiés par d'autres équipes de recherches, il est possible d'envisager, si les moyens en sont donnés, de restreindre le délai prévu pour la réalisation du fichier.

La deuxième étape, la préparation de l'édition définitive, sera précédée d'une large consultation des spécialistes intéressés par cet instrument de travail. Cette consultation devrait permettre de créer un instrument qui réponde au mieux aux besoins des chercheurs de toutes disciplines qui s'intéressent au corpus copte de Nag Hammadi. Cette consultation pourrait commencer en 1979.

Mais, dès maintenant, le fichier général en voie de constitution (qui portera sur 8 traités en Juin 1977) sert d'instrument de travail aux chercheurs des équipes de l'Université Laval et de l'Université de Strasbourg.

Nous ne saurions terminer cette brève présentation du projet sans adresser nos remerciements les plus sincères au Conseil des Arts du Canada pour sa compréhension des problèmes humains et religieux que soulève la nouvelle découverte de Haute-Égypte et pour ses non moins généreuses subventions. Son Excellence Gamal Mokhtar, président de l'*Egyptian Organization of Antiquities*, nous a soutenus de sa

considération personnelle et nous a permis l'accès au Musée copte
du Vieux-Caire, où MM. les Professeurs Victor Girgis et Pahor Labib,
actuel et ancien directeurs du Musée, M. Maher Salib, actuel conser-
vateur et Mme Samiha Abd El Shaheed, chargée du Département
des papyrus, nous ont si chaleureusement accueillis. Si cette édition
française des textes de Nag Hammadi commence à voir le jour, nous
le devons tout particulièrement à la collaboration de l'équipe améri-
caine de la *Coptic Gnostic Library*, qui a mis à notre disposition
tous les textes et les traductions existantes aussi bien que son matériel,
et à une bienveillance particulière dont nous nous honorons, celle de
M. le Professeur et de Mme James Robinson.

KOPTISCH-GNOSTISCHE SCHRIFTEN, VOLUMES 2 AND 3

by

HANS-MARTIN SCHENKE

A German translation of the complete collection of gnostic texts in the Coptic language contained in the twelve or thirteen codices which were found near Nag Hammadi is one of the projects of the Berlin study-group for coptic gnostic texts (Berliner Arbeitskreis für Koptisch-gnostische Schriften). It is to come out in the series "Die Griechischen Christlichen Schriftsteller der ersten Jahrhunderte" of the Academy of Sciences of the German Democratic Republic (Akademie der Wissenschaften der Deutschen Demokratischen Republik) as "Koptisch-Gnostische Schriften" volumes 2 and 3. It is obvious that this project has been planned in analogy with and as a kind of continuation of the famous book of Carl Schmidt containing the translations of the texts of the codex Askewianus and the codex Brucianus.[1]

But that very project is only our third one, planned on a long term basis, and in a sense it is the last aim of all our efforts concerning directly the Nag Hammadi texts. In other words, it is not at all our intention to provide the German speaking public with the *first* complete translation of the Nag Hammadi library, rather (and that too in a certain analogy to the book of C. Schmidt mentioned above) with the *last* one. We are not in haste. We are prepared to wait patiently, first of all for the completion of the Facsimile Edition, and also eventually to see other German translations coming out earlier. In that case we might have the chance to avoid and correct any mistakes which they may make.

---

[1] *Koptisch-Gnostische Schriften*, Erster Band : Die Pistis Sophia — Die beiden Bücher des Jeû — Unbekanntes altgnostisches Werk, herausgegeben von Carl Schmidt (= *Die Griechischen Christlichen Schriftsteller der ersten drei Jahrhunderte*, Band 13), Leipzig 1905; 2. Auflage bearbeitet im Auftrage der Kommission für Spätantike Religionsgeschichte der Deutschen Akademie der Wissenschaften zu Berlin von Walter Till (= *Die Griechischen Christlichen Schriftsteller der ersten Jahrhunderte*, Band 45), Berlin 1954; 3. Auflage 1959; unchanged reprint of the 3rd edition 1962; 4th edition in preparation.*

We have actually not yet decided so far about the arrangement
of the material, whether simply to give the translations in the sequence
of the Codices from I to XIII and within each codex according to the
order the texts have in it, or to rearrange the texts on a systematic
basis, placing the related works together, e.g. the groups of Sethian
texts, of Valentinian texts, etc. But in that case, the best *principium
divisionis* is difficult to find, because there is more than one principle
and the respective principles are intersecting (cf. also Christian/pagan;
or the purely formal principle). Nevertheless, a systematic arrangement, whichever is selected, seems more appropriate to our general
ideas than to retain the given order which has come down to us only
by chance.

While our ideas in that area are not yet fixed, we have already
decided upon certain policies regarding the *kind* of translation we want
to give and the principles according to which they have to be worked
out. And here I am touching upon a general issue at which I should
particularly like to stop for a moment, and which might be not without
some use for all of us. According to similar movements in other
sections of Oriental Science we must not translate Coptic texts as our
Coptological grandfathers did and in their time were in a sense
allowed to. It should be possible for a reader who does not know Coptic
to comprehend the meaning of the translated text. We should refuse
and abstain from the often used manner of so-called translations that
are in truth only "concordant transpositions" (konkordante Über-
tragungen). We should strive for a true translation in which the
structure of the language aimed at, on the lexical and semantic level
as well as on the grammatical and syntactic one, is taken as seriously
as the structure of the language from which we begin, and in which
the difference of structure in both languages is fully taken into account.
That does not mean anything like a so-called "*free* translation", but
simply a completely *normal* one. The terms "literal(ly)" and "literal-
ness" and the conceptions for which they stand play a misleading rôle
in the present process of translating Coptic texts.

"Das Kriterium der 'Wörtlichkeit' kann überhaupt nur zur Aus-
übung einer Kontrollfunktion im Prozeß der Übersetzung selbst bzw.
als heuristisches Mittel sinnvoll sein, niemals aber als Gradmesser für
die Qualität einer fertigen Übersetzung. Wenn die Übersetzung sich
nicht wirklich — unter Berücksichtigung der stets vorhandenen Struk-
turunterschiede auf lexikalisch-semantischer Ebene ebenso wie auf
grammatisch-syntaktischer Ebene — desjenigen Idioms bedient, das

der vorausgesetzte Leser (auch der Nicht-Koptologe!) versteht, so kann sie auch unterbleiben". (W.-P. Funk, Die zweite Apokalypse des Jakobus, 7f.).

What kind of translation we recommend and intend to give can in principle already be seen in the selected texts the translation of which we published in the "Theologische Literaturzeitung". Cf. the following list

Hans-Martin Schenke (federführend), "Die Taten des Petrus und der zwölf Apostel" — Die erste Schrift aus Nag-Hammadi-Codex VI, *ThLZ* 98, 1973, 13-19.

Hans-Gebhard Bethge (federführend), "Nebront" — Die zweite Schrift aus Nag-Hammadi-Codex VI, *ThLZ* 98, 1973, 97-104.

Karl Martin Fischer (federführend), Der Gedanke unserer großen Kraft (Noēma) — Die vierte Schrift aus Nag-Hammadi-Codex VI, *ThLZ* 98, 1973, 169-176.

Wolf-Peter Funk (federführend), "Authentikos Logos" — Die dritte Schrift aus Nag-Hammadi-Codex VI, *ThLZ* 98, 1973, 251-259.

Karl-Wolfgang Tröger (federführend), Die sechste und siebte Schrift aus Nag-Hammadi-Codex VI, *ThLZ* 98, 1973, 495-503.

Andreas Werner (federführend), Die Apokalypse des Petrus — Die dritte Schrift aus Nag-Hammadi-Codex VII, *ThLZ* 99, 1974, 575-584.

Gesine Schenke (federführend), "Die dreigestaltige Protennoia" — Eine gnostische Offenbarungsrede in koptischer Sprache aus dem Fund von Nag Hammadi, *ThLZ* 99, 1974, 731-746.

Wolf-Peter Funk (federführend), "Die Lehren des Silvanus" — Die vierte Schrift aus Nag-Hammadi-Codex VII, *ThLZ* 100, 1975, 7-23.

Hans-Gebhard Bethge (federführend), "Zweiter Logos des großen Seth" — Die zweite Schrift aus Nag-Hammadi-Codex VII, *ThLZ* 100, 1975, 97-110.

Konrad Wekel (federführend), "Die drei Stelen des Seth" — Die fünfte Schrift aus Nag-Hammadi-Codex VII, *ThLZ* 100, 1975, 571-580.

Hedda Bethge (federführend), "Die Exegese über die Seele" — Die sechste Schrift aus Nag-Hammadi-Codex II, *ThLZ* 101, 1976, 93-104.

Dankwart Kirchner (federführend), "Das Buch des Thomas" — Die siebte Schrift aus Nag-Hammadi-Codex II, *ThLZ* 102, 1977, 793-804.

(In the press :)

Hans-Gebhard Bethge (federführend), Der Brief des Petrus an Philippus, *ThLZ*.

(Planned :)

Karl Martin Fischer (federführend), Die Paraphrase des Sēem.
Hans-Martin Schenke (federführend), Allogenes.

These are the texts in question and the members of our group who were in each case responsible for the external and final shape of our articles.

By the way, to publish the most important texts in this periodical, especially if they were unknown so far and provided their state of preservation is good enough, in order to make them available as soon as possible for further research in the general field of History of Religions and New Testament studies — that is just the first project of our group, which in connection with the second one enables us to avoid hastiness regarding the third and last one.

May I be allowed to include here immediately another remark concerning the group itself. It was not built up for these purposes, but has grown around me little by little, while the original common interest may have been the relevance of the Nag Hammadi texts for the interpretation of the New Testament and Early Christianity in terms of History of Religions. And this interest is still alive, of course, beyond the limitations of our present and concrete three projects, as is shown by other products of our group or of individual members of it. That our work became more specialized is a history of its own, but is basically connected with our getting in contact and even in cooperation with J. M. Robinson's Claremont team, which resulted on our side in well considered and distinct plans in accordance with what is possible for us and in relation to their larger Coptic Gnostic Library Project.

Finally I would like to say something further about our second and in a sense intermediate project. That is the monographical treatment of single texts of the Nag Hammadi library, their improved reedition and specific interpretation, mostly in the way of doctoral dissertations. The following results are already in hand :

Wolf-Peter Funk, Die zweite Apokalypse des Jakobus aus Nag-Hammadi-Codex V neu herausgegeben, übersetzt und erklärt, Texte und Untersuchungen zur Geschichte der altchristlichen Literatur, Bd. 119, Berlin 1976.

Walter Beltz, Die Adam-Apokalypse aus Codex V von Nag Hammadi — Jüdische Bausteine in gnostischen Systemen, Theol. Habil. Schr. Berlin 1970.

Hans-Gebhard Bethge, "Vom Ursprung der Welt" — Die fünfte Schrift aus Nag-Hammadi-Codex II neu herausgegeben und unter bevorzugter Auswertung anderer Nag-Hammadi-Texte erklärt, Theol. Diss. A Berlin 1975.

Andreas Werner, Das Apokryphon des Johannes in seinen vier Versionen synoptisch betrachtet und unter besonderer Berücksichtigung anderer Nag-Hammadi-Schriften in Auswahl erläutert, Theol. Diss. A Berlin 1977.

Dankwart Kirchner, Epistula Jacobi Apocrypha — Die erste Schrift aus Nag-Hammadi-Codex I (Codex Jung) neu herausgegeben und kommentiert, Theol. Diss. A Berlin 1977.

Konrad Wekel, Die drei Stelen des Seth (NHC VII, 5) : Text — Übersetzung — Kommentar, Theol. Diss. A Berlin (1976 handed in).

Gesine Schenke, Die dreigestaltige Protennoia (NHC XIII) herausgegeben und kommentiert, Theol. Diss. A Rostock 1977.

(in preparation :)

Hedda Bethge, Die Exegese über die Seele.

Hans-Martin Schenke, Das Buch des Thomas;
　　　　　　　　　　 Das Evangelium nach Philippus;
　　　　　　　　　　 Das Evangelium der Wahrheit.

(Works on general Nag Hammadi problems which are in preparation :)

Karl-Wolfgang Tröger, Die Passion Jesu Christi in der Gnosis nach den Schriften von Nag Hammadi, Theol. Diss. B Berlin (handed in 1978).

Rudi Pahnke, Probleme gnostischer Anthropologie im Spiegel der Nag-Hammadi-Texte.

ON INVESTIGATING
THE HERMETIC DOCUMENTS CONTAINED
IN NAG HAMMADI CODEX VI
The Present State of Research

by

KARL-WOLFGANG TRÖGER

1. *Some general points on the history of research into Hermetism*

The discovery of the Coptic texts in 1946 in Upper Egypt aroused a general interest for Hermetism again.

Since the beginning of the 20th century Hermetism has played an important part in the study of the history of religion, and many distinguished scholars have paid attention to this matter, for instance R. Reitzenstein (1904), Th. Zielinski (1905/06), W. Kroll (1912), J. Kroll (1914), C. F. G. Heinrici and E. v. Dobschütz (1918), F. Bräuninger (1926), W. Scott (*Hermetica*, vol. I-III, A. S. Ferguson t. IV, 1924-36 : texts, translation, notes, commentary), A. D. Nock and A. J. Festugière (*Corpus Hermeticum*, vol. I-IV, 1945-54 : texts, translation, notes), A. J. Festugière (*La Révélation d'Hermès Trismégiste*, vol. I-IV, 1944-54, a profound research into Hermetism), M. J. Lagrange (1924ff.), G. van Moorsel (1955) and many others.[1]

2. *Hermetic texts in Codex VI*

In the first numeration by J. Doresse and T. Mina (1949) this codex, which includes some hermetic texts, was given the number IX, and in the numeration by H.-Ch. Puech (1950) the number XI. In a later numeration our Codex received the number VI (Doresse 1958; Krause 1962, Robinson 1968, 1970, 1972). This is the official number now used by the Coptic Museum and in all recent editions and publications, and also in Scholer's *Nag Hammadi Bibliography : 1948-1969* (Leiden 1971) and its supplements (*Nov. Test.* XIIIff., 1971ff.).

---

[1] See K.-W. Tröger, Die hermetische Gnosis, in : *Gnosis und Neues Testament*, Berlin 1973, notes 1-27. This article will also be published in : *Studia Religionawcze*, Warszawa (in preparation).

There are three tractates of undoubted hermetic nature : NHC
(= Nag Hammadi Codex) VI, 6-8. For these three texts the Berliner
Arbeitskreis für koptisch-gnostische Schriften now uses the abbrevia-
tions OgdEnn (De Ogdoade et Enneade = VI, 6), PrecHerm (Precatio
Hermetica = VI, 7)[2] and Askl (Asklepios = VI, 8).[3] M. Krause
described these three hermetic texts in 1967.[4]

3. Editions of Codex VI

The Editio princeps of Codex VI by M. Krause and P. Labib :
Gnostische und hermetische Schriften in Codex II und VI (ADAIK,
koptische Reihe, 2) Glückstadt 1971 — appeared in 1972. In the same
year the first volume of the Facsimile Edition was published by E. J.
Brill, Leiden, "under the auspices of the department of antiquities of
the Arab Republic of Egypt in conjunction with UNESCO" : Codex VI.

Already in 1972, C. Colpe published an extensive and instructive
review of the Facsimile Edition of Codex VI and Krause's Editio
princeps,[5] this was followed by further reviews of the Facsimile Edition
by M. Bouttier (1973),[6] K. M. Fischer (1973),[7] R. Haardt (1973),[8]
H.-M. Schenke (1974),[9] and J. D. Turner (1974).[10]

4. Translations of Codex VI, 6-8

After the translations of NHC VI, 6-8 had appeared in the Editio
princeps by M. Krause the Berliner Arbeitskreis, led by H.-M. Schenke,

---

[2] Formerly : Or (Oratio).

[3] See *Gnosis und Neues Testament* (ed. K.-W. Tröger), Berlin/Gütersloh 1973, 20
(the list of abbreviations). NHC X, 1 was changed to : Mar (formerly : Theor); supplements : NHC I,1 : PrecPl; I,5 : TractTrip; XI,2 : ExpVal; XI,3 : Allog; XI,4 : Hyps;
XII,1 : Sextus.

[4] Der Stand der Veröffentlichung der Nag Hammadi-Texte, in : *Le Origini dello
Gnosticismo* (Colloquio di Messina 1966), Leiden 1967 (1970[2]), 61-89; to NHC VI :
77-88. Cf. also M. Krause, Zur Bedeutung des gnostisch-hermetischen Handschriften-
fundes von Nag Hammadi, in : *Essays on the Nag Hammadi Texts. In Honour of
Pahor Labib* (Hag Hammadi Studies VI), Leiden 1975, 65-89; 87ff.; K. Rudolph,
Gnosis und Gnostizismus. Ein Forschungsbericht, *ThR* 34, 1969, 132-134; and the
former publications by J. Doresse and H.-Ch. Puech (for bibl. data see J. M. Robinson,
The Facsimile Edition of the Nag Hammadi Codices, Introduction, Leiden 1972, notes
1-7).

[5] Heidnische, jüdische und christliche Überlieferung in den Schriften aus Nag Hammadi I, in : *JAC* 15, 1972, 5-18.

[6] In : *Études Théologiques et Religieuses* 48, 1973, 221.

[7] In : *ThLZ* 98, 1973, 106-110.

[8] In : *Bibliotheca Orientalis* XXX, 1973, 428-430.

[9] In : *OLZ* LXIX, 1974, 229-243 (NHC VI, 6-8 see 241-243).

[10] In : *JAAR* 42, 1974, 355-356.

made a careful investigation into NHC VI, 6 and 7, based essentially on the Facsimile Edition and including, in comparison with Krause's edition, a lot of other and new suggestions for the reconstruction of lacunae and conjectural emendations. The German translations of OgdEnn and PrecHerm were published in 1973.[11]

A revised English translation of the important hermetic text NHC VI, 6 was already prepared by J. Brashler in 1973. It is due to be published, together with other tractates, in the international English-language edition of the Coptic Gnostic Library and also in a single-volume publication of English translations of all the Nag Hammadi writings by the Claremont team in 1977/78.

An English translation in connection with an interpretation of NHC VI, 6 entitled: "The Eighth Reveals the Ninth: A New Hermetic Initiation Discourse" was published in 1974 by L. S. Keizer.[12]

5. Linguistic problems

Since those suggestions underlying our translation of NHC VI, 6 and 7 have not yet been published,[13] some of them, i.e. the most important ones, may be given here:

NHC VI, 6:

p. 52, 29: ⟨ce⟩naaπτ; p. 52, 29: n̄xⲱⲱⲙⲉ here: generations ("Geschlechter") and not: books, also p. 53, 33; 54, 9. 16. 25. 32; p. 53, 16f.: "haben sie denn auch Mütter?" — either: m̄/ⲙⲁⲩ from ⲙⲁⲁⲩ, or originally: ... m̄ⲙⲁⲩ ⟨n̄ϩⲉnⲙⲁ(ⲁ)ⲩ⟩; p. 53, 31: n̄ϯⲱⲁⲭⲉ = n̄ⲧⲁⲱⲁⲭⲉ (n̄ϯ = conj. praefix); p. 56, 10f. — the new sentence begins with πnoⲩⲧⲉ; ⲉϥⲙⲉϩ belongs to the preceding sentence; p. 61, 17: ⲙn̄ⲧnoⲩⲧⲉ = piety (Frömmigkeit), not: divinity (Göttlichkeit), also p. 70, 14. 16; 71, 7. 33; p. 62, 6: ⲫⲏⲗⲓⲟⲥ is the deity "Helios"!; p. 62, 18: m̄n πⲣⲏ ϩn̄ π̄ⲟ̄ⲥ oⲩⲉⲓⲉ (oⲩⲉ, distance): "... together with the sun (and thus) in the half distance of the day ...";
p. 62, 19f. read: ⟨ⲉ⟩ⲁⲙn̄ⲧⲏ m̄ⲙoⲓⲣⲁ r̄ⲡⲁ/ⲣⲁⲅⲉ m̄ⲙoⲉⲓ: "after 15

---

[11] Die sechste und siebte Schrift aus Nag-Hammadi-Codex VI, eingeleitet und übersetzt vom Berliner Arbeitskreis für koptisch-gnostische Schriften, in: ThLZ 98, 1973, 495-503 (K.-W. Tröger in co-operation with H.-M. Schenke).

[12] In: Academy of Arts and Humanities Monograph Series, No. 1. Seaside/CA, 1974.
[13] Apart from several proposals made for the understanding of p. 61, 20: πⲣⲁn̄ⲱ; 61, 30; 62, 15: πⲣⲁⲉⲓⲱ: "Lebenshaus"; p. 62, 3-10 (the eight guards are the Eighth of Hermopolis), and the end of the tractate p. 63, 31f.: ⲡⲁⲓ̈ ⲡⲉ πⲧⲉⲗⲉⲓⲟⲥ ⟨n̄ⲗⲟⲅⲟⲥ⟩ ⲉⲧⲱⲟⲟⲡ ⟨...⟩ ⲱ πⲁⲱⲏⲣⲉ — see H.-M. Schenke, OLZ 69, 1974, 241f.

grades have passed me"; p. 63,3 : ⲛⲉⳋⲱⲗⲓⲁⲕⲟⲥ : probably from ἐξωπικός (here : external) — a misspelling?

NHC VI, 7 :

p. 64,6 read : ⲡⲟⲩⲱⳉ; probably dittography of ⲟⲩ; p. 64,25 read : ⲛ̅ⲁ⟨ⲡ⟩ⲟ.

Moreover we have reconstructed the beginnings of the pages 52-59 and 62.

A German translation of NHC VI, 8 has been prepared by the Berliner Arbeitskreis, but has not been published so far. This text involves quite a number of problems, and its translation in the Editio princeps of M. Krause is not always clear. p. 65, 8-14 does not belong to Askl but to NHC VI, 7.[14]

6. *The importance of the hermetic texts in Codex VI for Hermetism*[15]

A comparison between NHC VI, 6 and CorpHerm XIII yields interesting results. Both tractates show the impact of mystery-religions (or mystery-faith) especially on the dualistic-gnostic branch of Hermetism. The content of Ogd-Enn is not identical with that of CorpHerm XIII, but has much in common with this very interesting combination of gnostic and mystery elements.[16]

NHC VI, 8 (= lat. Ascl 21-29) is of great importance for the textual history of the latin Asclepius (especially for the apocalypse p. 70, 2-74, 17 = Ascl 24-26)[17] and, moreover, for the question of the origin of Hermetism in Egypt.[18] The occurrence of many typically Egyptian elements in NHC VI, 8 (and also in NHC VI, 6)[19] leads us in this direction.[20]

---

[14] Cf. on the contrary M. Krause in his *Editio princeps*, 25 and 187, and in : *Die Veröffentlichung der Nag Hammadi Texte*, 81.

[15] Cf. K.-W. Tröger, Die Bedeutung der Nag-Hammadi-Schriften für die Hermetik, in : *Studia coptica*, ed. P. Nagel, Berlin 1974, 175-190.

[16] See K.-W. Tröger, *Mysterienglaube und Gnosis in Corpus Hermeticum XIII* (TU 110), Berlin 1971; K. Rudolph, Gnosis und Gnostizismus, *ThR* 36, 1971, 23-28; on NHC VI, 6 see J.-P. Mahé, Le sens et la composition du traité hermétique "L'Ogdoade et l'Ennéade" conservé dans le codex VI de Nag Hammadi, in : *RevSR* 48, 1974, 54-65.

[17] See M. Krause, in : *Die Veröffentlichung der N.H.-Texte*, 80f. Cf. also J. Doresse, Hermès et la Gnose : A propos de L'Asclépius copte, in : *NovTest* 1, 1956, 54-69; J.-P. Mahé, Remarques d'un latiniste sur l'Asclepius copte de Nag Hammadi, in : *RevSR* 48, 1974, 136-155.

[18] Cf. K.-W. Tröger, *Die hermetische Gnosis*, 99-102.

[19] Cf. p. 61, 18ff. 25ff.; 62, 3ff.

[20] M. Krause, Ägyptisches Gedankengut in der Apokalypse des Asclepius, in : *ZDMG*, Suppl. I, Wiesbaden 1969, 48-57.

Last but not least the hermetic texts in Codex VI have brought us a considerable step forward in the discussion about the mode of organisation of the hermetists and their forms of worship. NHC VI, 6 OgdEnn contains a long prayer and glorification (p. 55, 23-57, 25) and further praises (p. 58, 28-59, 9; p. 60, 17-61, 17), and a remarkable oath (p. 63, 15-24; cf. p. 62, 22ff.; 63, 25-31); NHC VI, 7 PrecHerm is a well known prayer (cf. Ascl 41 and Pap. Mimaut);[21] p. 65, 3-7 makes mention of a ritual kiss of brotherhood and a holy cultic meal (cf. the end of Ascl 41). A kiss of brotherhood is also mentioned in OgdEnn p. 57, 26f.[22]

This allows us to consider, at least to a limited degree, the possibility of cultic practice in hermetic conventicles. The occurrence of cultic elements in some other gnostic texts of the Nag Hammadi Library is likewise remarkable in this connection (cf. for instance NHC VII, 5 StelSeth).

---

[21] Cf. J.-P. Mahé, La prière d'actions de grâces du codex VI de Nag Hammadi et le discours parfait, in : Zeitschr. f. Papyrologie und Epigraphik 13, 1974, 40-60. For the correspondence between the prayer included in NHC VI, 6 (request for ascent : p. 55, 23-57, 25) and the thanksgiving prayer in VI, 7 see W.-P. Funk, Die Zweite Apokalypse des Jakobus aus NHC V (TU 119), Berlin 1976, 218f. (211-220).

[22] Cf. Rom 16.16; 1 Peter 5.14; NHC II, 3 EvPhil p. 59, 2-4 (§ 31); NHC VIII, 2 EpPt p. 140, 14.

JACOB AS AN ANGEL IN GNOSTICISM AND MANICHEISM

by

ALEXANDER BÖHLIG

In the list of the bringers of salvation which the Nag Hammadi Gospel of the Egyptians presents as a sequel to the work of Seth,[1] there is in the second group of persons a divergence between Codex III and Codex IV. The text runs : "the great leaders (στρατηγός) Jakobos (so III, Jakob in IV) and Theopemptos and Isavel".[2] In their introduction[3] the editors have already drawn attention to the fact that in the New Testament the Greek ending was used only with the names of contemporary persons, while the name was not grecised "when it indicates an Old Testament person or when a New Testament person is named in a ceremonial tone".[4] Since, however, they saw no occasion for expecting the patriarch Jacob in the passage in question, they assumed that the enumeration in the list was intended to give a ceremonial tone to the name and that in consequence Jakob stood for Ἰάκωβος. The further difficulty that the reference is not to James the Righteous but to "the great Jakobos" could, it seemed, be explained by his elevation into the higher world, especially since in the New Testament there is mention also of a James the Less.[5] In view of the importance which James possesses in Gnosticism also, his elevation among the bringers of salvation would be no surprise. Indeed, it is he to whom the believing gnostic is to turn and who carries further the work of Jesus.[6] In that case Codex III would not have been sufficiently aware of the hieratic character of the list and would have inserted the

---

[1] Nag Hammadi Codex III 64, 9 - 65, 26 ∼ IV 75, 24 to 77 end (the last lines are damaged).

[2] NHC III 64, 12 - 14 ∼ IV 75, 27 - 76, 1.

[3] *The Gospel of the Egyptians* (The holy book of the great invisible Spirit) edited with translation and commentary by Alexander Böhlig and Frederik Wisse (Leiden 1975), 16.

[4] F. Blass-A. Debrunner, *Grammatik des neutestamentlichen Griechisch* (11th Edition, Göttingen 1961), § 53, 2.

[5] W. Bauer, *Wörterbuch zum Neuen Testament* (5th Edition, Berlin 1958), s.v.

[6] Cf. the references in the Gospel of Thomas, Logion 12, the two apocalypses of James and the apocryphal letter of James in the Nag Hammadi library.

normal form Ἰάκωβος. If, however, Codex III had put the New Testament James in the place of the Old Testament Jacob, that would be a change of some significance, which would provide evidence of a lack of understanding on the part of the scribe of Codex III. This would not be impossible, if we take into account other similar passages.[7] However, the version in Codex IV also, although in general it offers the better text, has some variants which destroy the sense.[8] External criteria of textual criticism are therefore not sufficient to determine which form of the text here is correct. However, there is in Manichean fragments a mention of Jacob as an angel which in association with a fresh examination of Jewish material casts new light on the passage in the Gospel of the Egyptians.

The view that Jacob was a great warrior and commander can be traced back to the Old Testament. Although he fled to the East alone, he nevertheless returned at the head of a considerable army, not indeed to wage war against Esau but to effect reconciliation with him. In the course of this journey there occurs the wrestling of Jacob with God at the river Jabbok.[9] Because of this he receives from God the name "Israel", because he has striven with God (שׂרה "strive"):[10] "You shall no longer be called Jacob but Israel, for you have striven with God and with men and have prevailed". Even though in the sayings of Balaam Jacob and Israel are used collectively, we can also read out of them an understanding of Jacob as a great ruler and war-like hero.[11] Reference is made to them also in Qumran.[12] This characterisation is presented in greater detail in the book of Jubilees. Admittedly, here too the reconciliation between Jacob and Esau is reported,[13] and Esau is at first portrayed as very willing to adhere to his oath.[14] His sons, however, finally persuade him to break the oath and to take the field at their head against Jacob.[15] Jacob is at first quite incredulous[16] but then strikes Esau down and conquers his

---

[7] Particularly striking is the interpretation of ⲡϯ as ⲡⲛⲟⲩⲧⲉ, cf. *The Gospel of the Egyptians*, 191.

[8] E.g. ⲥⲟⲟⲩⲛ as a translation of δόξα in the sense of ⲉⲟⲟⲩ; cf. *The Gospel of the Egyptians*, 172.

[9] Gen 32, 22-32.

[10] Gen 32, 28.

[11] Num 23, 7-10; 18-24; 24, 3-9; 15-24.

[12] 1 QM XI, 6f. 4Q test 9ff.

[13] Jub 29, 13.

[14] Jub 37, 1-11.

[15] Jub 37, 12ff.

[16] Jub 37, 16ff.

army.[17] In 4th Esdras likewise Esau and Jacob are set in opposition. Here the names are employed as types of political entities.[18] They represent the kingdoms which succeed one another at the end of the first and the transition to the second aeon : "the heel of the first aeon is Esau, the hand of the second is Jacob. The beginning of man is the hand, his end the heel." This means that with the end of Esau, i.e. the Roman Empire, begins the world dominance of Jacob, i.e. Israel. In Philo also Jacob is described as ἄρχων and ἡγεμών as well as δεσπότης, and to him Esau was subject even in their mother's womb.[19]

The examples presented would already be sufficient as evidence for Jacob as a military leader. Still lacking, however, is any reference to his transcendence, which may be characteristic for him as a being appearing in the list of the Gospel of the Egyptians and in the Manichaica. For this also there is a text in a document of the Greek-speaking Jewish Diaspora. This is the "Prayer of Joseph", of which fragments are still extant.[20] Here Jacob describes himself as an angel : "For I who speak to you, I Jacob-Israel — an angel of God am I and a ruling spirit[21] — and Abraham and Isaac were created before all things. But I Jacob, who am named Jacob by men, have also the name Israel 'the man who sees God', with which I was named by God, because I am the first-born of all living beings which were called into life by God".[22] According to these words Jacob is a pneumatic angelic figure in whom existence from primeval times and the power of sovereignty find expression. Jacob is also, as is often the case with Seth, projected into the higher world. His particularly high position in the angelic hierarchy is emphasised in a report which constitutes a transmutation of the struggle at the Jabbok : "But when I came from Mesopotamia in Syria there appeared Uriel the angel of God and he said that I had descended to the earth and had taken up dwelling among men and I was named by the name of Jacob. Full of passion he fought with me and wrestled with me, and said that his

---

[17] Jub 38,1 ff.

[18] 4 Esdr 6, 7-10.

[19] Leg. allegor. III 29 ed. L. Cohn I, p. 132.

[20] A.-M. Denis, *Fragmenta Pseudepigraphorum quae supersunt graeca* (Leiden 1970), p. 61-62. Cf. A.-M. Denis, *Introduction aux pseudépigraphes grecs* (Leiden 1970) 125 ff. and J. Z. Smith, The prayer of Joseph, in : *Religions in Antiquity, Essays in Memory of E. R. Goodenough* (Leiden 1968) 253-294.

[21] It is questionable whether ἀρχικόν here means in the first place "ruling" or "original". It is probable that as in gnostic texts there is a deliberate ambiguity.

[22] Fragment in Orig. in Joh. 2, 31, § 189 f.

name would have the precedence over my name and that of every other angel. Then I named my name to him and told him what was his rank among the sons of God : Are you not Uriel my eighth, but I Israel the arch-angel of the power of God and chief commander among the sons of God? Am I not Israel the first servant before the presence of God, and have I not called upon my God with the incorruptible name?"[23] Here Jacob occupies an established position in the angelic hierarchy. For Uriel who ranks as the highest ruler among the angels of the stars[24] confronts Jacob-Israel. When Jacob describes him as his "eighth", this is because Uriel is set as the eighth above another seven angels of the stars. He knows Jacob as an angel, but at the Jabbok he wishes to give effect to his own claims to sovereignty. On the other hand the author of this document demonstrates how exalted Jacob-Israel is as an arch-angel, and how powerful as a commander of the heavenly host. This may make it clear that the idea of a heavenly *strategos* Jacob derives from Judaism.

Both Judaism and Gnosticism have exercised an influence upon Manicheism and in particular with mythological ideas. This subject will be dealt with separately and in greater detail elsewhere. This influence is all the more understandable since Manicheism indeed belongs to Gnosticism in the wider sense, and the Jewish elements either as a whole or at least in part passed into Manicheism through Gnosticism.[25]

Jacob also found his way into Manicheism. In Mani's original work "τὰ τῶν μυστηρίων" there is a chapter : "of the testimony of ... against himself in Jacob's favour".[26] What content this chapter may have had can no longer be determined with any certainty. Could Esau perhaps have made a confession of guilt for Jacob's benefit?

Mythological statements about Jacob are also however to be found in hymns from Turfan. Two examples serve to make plain how the governing angel Jacob was taken up into pious thought, and indeed adduced in support of a feudalistic theory of society.

1. Jacob appears frequently in M 4b,[27] where we find an invocation

---

[23] Linked by Origen to the preceding quotation with καὶ ἐπιφέρει.

[24] Enoch 72 ff.

[25] Compare the case of the book of Enoch.

[26] There is a lacuna in the oldest manuscript. The interpretation of the name Jacob in Flugel, *Mani* (Reprint Osnabrück 1969) n. 310 seems to me false. It is not a case of a disciple of Mani. The context in which this chapter stands suggests personalities from the religious past : Juštasp, the Messiah, Jesus.

[27] F. W. K. Müller, *Handschriftenreste in Estrangelo-Schrift aus Turfan, Chinesisch*

of the angels (pēvahišn i frēstagān). Following on a strophe addressed to the archangels Raphael, Michael, Gabriel and Sariel, the angel Jacob is called upon.[28] That frēstag here does not mean "apostle",[29] and also does not refer to a disciple of Mani by the name of James, is clear from his position among heavenly heroes :

> We worship the Lord Jacob, the angel
> with the principalities, powers, the good spirits,
> that they may themselves protect us with strong power,
> themselves lead us in and out.

> We bow in joy before the strong power,
> Jacob the angel, the leader of the angels.
> Do thou receive from the whole holy Church
> ever new blessing and praise, thou strong One.[30]

In this hymn Jacob is not, as in the Prayer of Joseph, the rival of other angels. The position of the four archangels is here left unassailed, and Jacob is set alongside them as commander of the heavenly host. When he appears in association with principalities and the powers, that corresponds entirely to the royal household of gnosticising heavenly beings. The very idea of the mighty heavenly commander as a bringer of salvation is here present just as in the Gospel of the Egyptians. After a prayer for peace and salvation from Zervan, the highest God of light, for these principalities and spirits, the community turns in further verses once more to Jacob :

> May new power come from the angel Jacob,
> new bliss from all the angels.
> May it remain upon this district.
> May they themselves lead in peace ever new.[31]

In this strophe what is in question is the actualisation of the power bestowed by the angels. The land in which this hymn is used as a

---

Turkestan, II (Abhandl. d. Preuss. Akad. d. Wiss. Berlin 1904), p. 55ff. Cf. the analysis of M4 in M. Boyce, *A catalogue of the Iranian Manuscripts in Manichaean script in the German Turfan Collection*, Berlin 1960.

  [28] *Op. cit.*, 56.

  [29] So D. Weber, *Die Stellung der sog. Inchoativa im Mitteliranischen* (Diss. Göttingen 1970), p. 76.

  [30] Müller, *op. cit.* 56.

  [31] Weber, *op. cit.*, from whose translation I depart in reading "lead" instead of "travel" and "angel" in the place of "apostle". Cf. also Müller, *op. cit.* 57.

prayer is to stand under the perfect power of Jacob and his angels, and enjoy their guidance in peace.

In a fragment which belongs to the same manuscript this invocation of Jacob is taken up again. After a general prayer for the protection of the angels the community turns again to Jacob, who here appears in the framework of a divine triad :

> The emissary Rāymast yazd,[32] the loving, to be regarded as charming,[33]
>> the strong God with the noble name,
>> the King Frēdōn and Jakob Nariman,
>> may they themselves protect the church and us the children.
> Blessing and praise from us all
>> be accepted before the three princes,
>> that they may send power and strength,
>> on this day and in the time of joy.[34]

From the second strophe it is clear that a triad of gods or angels is being invoked. It consists of Mani, Frēdōn and Jacob. Mani in these hymns is regarded as an eschatological heavenly figure. We need only compare the identification with Buddha Maitreya and Christ in the Manichean book of prayer and penitence! As a lord coming from heaven he possesses power. When he is described as rāymast yazd, "the judicious God", this emphasises the element of the νοῦς which already took on special form in Jesus. Or is Jesus here being invoked? One should consider that Mani has already had prayers addressed to him in a preceding strophe. With this the attribute wryhr would also fit very well. Frēdōn and the epithet Nariman assigned to Jacob point to Iranian mythology. Frēdōn is the Middle Iranian form of the Old Iranian Thraetaona.[35] He is along with Keresaspa a king of the primaeval age. Both are slayers of dragons.[36] The function of Frēdōn as that of a god who protects in time of conflict comes to the fore in an

---

[32] Rāymast "intelligent, judicious" : cf. W. Henning, *Ein manichäisches Bet- und Beichtbuch* (Abhandl. d. Preuss. Akad. d. Wiss. 1936, Phil.-hist. Kl. Nr. 10, Berlin 1937), index s.v.

[33] I owe the translation of wryhr "nice, charming" to D. Weber, who also drew my attention to the parallels in M. 74 I R 13. There the word refers to Jesus. The abstract noun wryhryy (M 221) is translated by W. Henning as "charm" : The book of the Giants, *BSOAS* 11, 1 (1943) 52-74; cf. also p. 64, note 1.

[34] Müller, *op. cit.* 58 ff.

[35] Cf. G. Widengren, *Die Religionen Irans* (Stuttgart 1965), p. 23.

[36] Widengren, *op. cit.* 23.

earlier passage of the present hymn, in which he is invoked along with Mihryazd, the living spirit, who indeed in Middle Persian Manichean texts is represented as the victorious conquerer of the evil powers.[37] When Jacob receives the second name Nariman = the Old Iranian nairyō-manah, "the one with masculine disposition", he has taken over a second name which occurs as such in Middle Iranian mythology, but has also become a proper name. Both in the Iranian version of Mani's Book of the Giants[38] and also in the East Iranian burial ritual[39] Sam and Nariman appear as independent figures beside one another. In the latter they are the closest associates of Keresaspa, who elsewhere also bears Nariman as a second name. Jakob Nariman can thus, when he appears as a warrior alongside Frēdōn, have taken the place of Keresaspa Nariman. At the same time, however, he may also represent the Vahman Nariman of other Manichean texts, especially since Vahman = νοῦς also possesses the character of a ruler; indeed he is also called "Vahman Nariman, the ruler of the holy religion". So also Vahman appears as the third member of the triad Jesus, Virgin of Light, Vahman.[40]

Frēdōn however occurs not only as a form of expression in Iranian Manichaica, but also in Western Gnosticism. In the "anonymous early gnostic work" of the Codex Brucianus[41] he is built into the peculiar mythological metaphysic of this text. That through the addition of a prefixed vowel the form "Aphredon" has been produced should not occasion any surprise. As his nature ἀφρηδωνία is named. It presents similar characteristics to the properties of Frēdōn in Iranian, especially that of power. The association with the λόγος-δημιουργός recalls the association of Frēdōn with the Living Spirit:[42] "and then this λόγος-δημιουργός became a divine power and lord and saviour (σωτήρ) and χρηστός and king and ἀγαθός and father and mother; this it is whose work brought benefit; he was honoured and became father of those who have believed. He became law (νόμος) through the ἀφρηδωνία and powerful (δυνατός)". What an exalted being of the other

---

[37] M 4 : Müller, op. cit. 55. Cf. also the invocation in a Manichean magic text; W. B. Henning, Two Manichaean magical texts, BSOAS 12 (1947) 39-66.

[38] Henning, BSOAS 11.

[39] Cf. Widengren, op. cit. 340.

[40] Cf. the index to F. C. Andreas-W. B. Henning, Mitteliranische Manichaica aus Chinesisch-Turkestan II (Sitz.-Ber. d. Preuss. Akad. d. Wiss., Phil.-hist. Kl., Berlin 1933).

[41] Cf. C. Schmidt-W. Till, Koptisch-gnostische Schriften I (3rd ed. Berlin 1962), index of names and subjects.

[42] Schmidt-Till, op. cit. 351, 11.

world this Aphredon is is shown by the circumstance that in the creation of the divine man a part of his body is formed after the type of Aphredon.[43] Admittedly it remains a question what one should imagine as an "Aphredon-face".[44] Yet his localisation in the world of light appears to be possible. He is connected with a βάθος in which an only-begotten one is hidden, who reveals three powers and is mighty in all his powers : "When the idea comes forth from the βάθος, so Aphredon takes the thought (ἐπίνοια) and leads it to the only-begotten (μονογενής), and the only-begotten brings it to the child, and they bring it to all the aeons as far as the place of the τριδύναμις, and so on".[45] In another passage there is also an association with βάθος, but there Aphredon is surrounded by twelve χρηστοί and also stands in relation to a κανοῦν, a basket, which is located in immortality.[46]

2. The Sitz im Leben can very readily be determined in the case of another fragment which contains Jacob as an angelic commander.[47] It is a Middle Persian prayer for a Uigur khan. He is addressed as "occupant of the throne" and (in the Turkish language) as "our divine khan". Within the framework of a hymn of praise addressed to him protection and help are entreated on his behalf. The blessing which is to come upon him is to be sent to him by the heavenly host, the kirdagān "the mighty", farrahān "the principalities", wahšān "the spirits", at whose head Jacob stands. This strongly recalls the descriptions of heaven in the Gospel of the Egyptians. One is reminded in the same way when pāsbān "watchers" and pādār "protectors" stand beside the khan, and yazdān "gods", ba'ān "lords" and frēstagān "angels" are to prepare good fortune for him. The attributes preceding the name of Jacob, "the powerful God, the one praised with the voice, the commander in chief of the heroes, the battle-seeking, the valiant", must refer to Jacob, while predicates of glory appropriate to the sovereign precede his name : "glorious occupant of the throne, wearer of the diadem, divine Khan, Quyil bilga qān". Here then Jacob, the lord of the heavenly host, is described as the protector of the earthly ruler who as Khan of the Uigurs is the protector of the Manichean community. Such a prayer of the Manichees for the Khan is reported in a Persian historian of the eleventh

---

[43] Schmidt-Till, op. cit. 364, 25.
[44] Schmidt-Till, op. cit. 339, 7; 340, 33.
[45] Schmidt-Till, op. cit. 339, 9 ff.
[46] Schmidt-Till, op. cit. 338, 28 ff.; 349, 22 ff.
[47] M 43 : Müller, op. cit. 78-79.

century, Gardīzī; he reports that Manicheans every day gathered together at the governor's house ('āmil) and recited aloud from the books of Mani.[48] They seem in the course of this to have offered up prayers for the Khan of the Uigurs. This corresponds to the manner in which in Rome the clients appeared daily at the house of their patron to wish him every blessing.

One may see from this how the idea of Jacob as a commander among the angels, which Judaism had gradually developed beyond the Old Testament narrative, was taken over by Gnosticism and within Manicheism travelled through Babylonia as far as Chinese Turkestan.

Addendum :

I think that the Jacob found in the Chinese Hymnroll 215c is not a prince of the Church, as E. Waldschmidt-W. Lentz hold (*Die Stellung Jesu im Manichäismus*, p. 8 [Abhandl. d. Preuß. Akad. d. Wiss., Phil.-hist. Kl. Nr. 4, Berlin 1926]), but Jacob the prince of the angels. In the middle of the hymn (209-221), which praises all the emissaries of light who defend the law, Jacob is described as the chieftain, the great general who prepares arms and armour to shatter the opposing rebels. The reference (218a) to the general who conquers the Maras, i.e. the demonic powers, and by whom Jacob is probably meant, can also be interpreted of a metaphysical angelic being.

---

[48] Zajn al-Aẖbār, ed. Ḥabibi (Teheran 1968), p. 268.

REPORT ON THE COPTOLOGICAL WORK
Carried out in the context of the Tübingen research project

"The Hellenic and Hellenistic contribution to Syncretism in the Near East"

by

ALEXANDER BÖHLIG

Coptology no less than Egyptology has to face the historical problems of the Near East in general. From the time of Alexander the Great we can trace in the Eastern Mediterranean the rise of the so-called Hellenistic world, in which Greece and the Orient came to terms with one another and were associated in syncretism. It was precisely the cultural challenges which resulted from this that the Roman age also endeavoured to master; and therefore it is rightly assigned by many scholars to Hellenism in the wider sense. In this period Christianity assumed a very interesting and apparently contradictory role. On the one hand it disseminated its holy writings and its theological literature in the Greek language, and in so doing turned not only to the Greeks of the Orient but also to the natives who had accepted Greek culture. On the other hand, however, it stimulated the native Christians to develop their respective mother tongues into written and literary languages, so far as these did not already exist. To investigate to what extent the translation language was in a position to reproduce the fine and often philosophical nuances of the Greek models, or whether the language in the process perhaps altered various emphases because of its own conceptions and ideas, is a very wide ranging task which entails a working through not only of the documents translated into oriental languages but also of original oriental documents, and comparing them with Greek ideas. Here we have to consider to what extent Greek ideas were taken over in their original form or in a hellenistic transmutation. Such an investigation therefore cannot be carried through without a comparison also of the processes of hellenisation, preceding or parallel to the influence of Christianity, which penetrated Judaism as well as Greek pagan religion and its world of ideas. For the work done in Tübingen in this field I have, in the first place, to thank Professors Martin Hengel and Wolfgang Haase, and their collaborators.

The coptologists assembled here in Cairo will probably, however, be especially interested in that part of the Tübingen studies which is concerned with the hellenic or hellenistic influence on Coptic texts and here in particular the texts from Nag Hammadi. Since Gnosticism is a form of religious thought with which the infant church had to come to terms, it seemed to us appropriate to begin our work on the hellenisation of Coptic with the gnostic texts, or texts used by gnostics. So it came about that in the University of Tübingen, where once Ferdinand Christian Baur departed from an investigation of Gnosticism and Manicheism couched purely in terms of the history of dogma and substituted an approach from the point of view of the history of religions, today again work is being enthusiastically carried out on the gnostic sources, a task imposed by the unexpected discoveries of Medinet Madi and Nag Hammadi. That in the organisation of the work the library of Nag Hammadi is being dealt with first, and Manicheism only thereafter, is due to the fact that in the difficult situation facing our financial sponsors limited and not too far-reaching undertakings ought to be completed first and as soon as possible.

Before describing the special tasks, or the results which have already been gained, something should first be said of a more fundamental character. When we speak here of hellenic and hellenistic influence this does not mean that we intend by our researches to demonstrate the origin of Gnosticism from Greek thought. Our concern is far rather to work out what Greek material is present in Gnosticism. Here we have to investigate not only whether the relevant trains of thought, mythologumena or theologumena were active or indeed dominant in the formation of a gnostic conception, but equally whether they played a merely passive role as material already in existence which was worked up by the gnostics. In this way it will be possible to form a more objective judgment of the activity and the influence of other cultures; and not least it will be possible to do the fullest justice to the autonomous and independent character of gnosticism.

If at first it was our intention to handle our appointed theme in such a way that we grouped together the separate documents and assigned them to individual collaborators, we subsequently resolved to assign the various major problems of Gnosis to individuals and to let each investigate the Nag Hammadi discovery from these different aspects. The areas have accordingly been assigned as follows :

1. Metaphysics and cosmology are my own concern;
2. Anthropology is under the charge of Robert Timothy Updegraff, and
3. Ethics are the concern of Frederik Wisse

There is, of course, a certain amount of overlapping here, for example between metaphysics and anthropology in regard to the doctrine of the soul or between anthropology and ethics in regard to the doctrine of good and evil in man; but this leads only to a more intensive and fruitful collaboration on the part of those concerned, who are investigating the texts from different points of view.

Since the problems are being handled on the basis of the texts, we owe a special debt of gratitude to Professor James M. Robinson, who has very generously placed at our disposal the transcriptions from the Institute for Antiquity and Christianity. I would like at this point to take the opportunity of thanking him also for the energetic way in which he has pressed on with the final restoration of the originals in Cairo and with the facsimile edition. We are very happy that in this work we were able to provide some slight assistance through the participation of American colleagues who are working on our project. Since in the interpretation of the texts the work involves to some extent material still not published and the state of the preservation of the manuscripts also varies quite considerably, the restoration of the text frequently forms an important part of the work; through interchange with other scholars working on the text, this could be made very fruitful. Contributions could also be made to the grammatical inter-pretation of details and from this point of view also to the question of the original language. I myself consider all the documents as translations from Greek. In working through the texts further problems arose which were of fundamental importance for a fruitful evaluation of the material; in the first place the question had to be raised as to how the evidently Greek material came into these documents or into the traditions underlying them. I was able to demonstrate that for this we must take the Greek school system into account. Scattered through the documents we find the use of themes from Greek education, which were dealt with in all forms of the Greek educational system and at all its stages: the alphabet, reading and writing, introduction to the classics, the writing of essays. General education was further supplemented by various special disciplines, although in the hellenistic period a real mastery of these had become more and more a matter for the specialists.

Thus we find mathematics in an atrophied form in the shape of numerical speculation; yet none the less the idea of comprehending the world or its constituent parts by means of number is worthy of proper attention. Greek medicine also had made its contribution in the portrayal of the human body. But also the doctrines of the organisation of the human body through souls, the doctrine of the emotions and the description of the process of perception are taken from Greek tradition which we find in the Platonic, the Stoic and also the Peripatetic schools of philosophy. The schools of philosophy and also the schools of rhetoric have left clear traces in the texts of Nag Hammadi. From the latter derive, in general, the formal characteristics of the texts, but in particular probably also the use of certain Topoi and in particular the "wonderful phenomena"; thus, for example, Egypt is portrayed as a land of particularly wonderful animals. But for the gnostic it was naturally above all the schools of philosophy which afforded him the material with which he could construct an image of the world which would unite religious feeling and scientific knowledge.

Greek philosophy may also have provided the model for the mythical form of presentation so frequently used in Gnosticism. It is not a question simply of "ancient stories", but of a portrayal of world history in a literary form into which, of course, such "ancient stories" could be incorporated. The Tübingen school of Platonic research has in Konrad Gaiser a very penetrating and profound interpreter of the Platonic myths and this helpful start is one which we must follow up in our work.

The Nag Hammadi library shows quite clearly that the circles who read these texts and still more those who composed them were to a certain extent familiar with the educational material of the Greek school. The social stratum in which Gnosticism was able to blossom into real life and to develop both in religious and in intellectual terms was an upper middle class, which in Egypt consisted not only of Greeks but also of so-called Greco-Egyptians.

Frederik Wisse has prefaced his work on ethics with a chapter in which he examines the new-found library in regard to its uniformity and internal consistency. Here he opposes the thesis of Torgny Säve-Söderbergh, who saw in the texts a source of information for the monks in their discussion with the heretics and believed that these texts had thereafter been discarded as no longer necessary. Wisse believes on the other hand that they could have been used as edifying religious material in the monasteries and only removed from the monasteries as a result of the Festal Letter of 367. I would assume that during the rapid development of Pachomian monasticism Pachomius himself could hardly have tested the orthodoxy of his monks to the last detail, and that therefore statements to that effect in his Life are retrospective. The most important result for Wisse is that we cannot speak of a library from Nag Hammadi, but that it may be a question only of a more or less accidental collection of volumes removed during the purging of the monastery library. J. M. Robinson also had already attempted to classify various groups of texts on the basis of the bindings of the codices. I myself, in a contribution to the volume "Aufstieg und Niedergang der römischen Welt", dedicated to Josef Vogt, on the importance of the discoveries of Medinet Madi and Nag Hammadi for the investigation of gnosticism, have discussed the problems further, following on Wisse, Säve-Söderbergh and Robinson; in particular I have endeavoured to differentiate various "Sitze im Leben" : (1) the "Sitz im Leben" of the different stages of the Coptic text, (2) that of the Greek models, and (3) that of the Aramaic elements which are present in the texts.

In connection with the problems of introduction Wisse has also produced an essay on the cryptograms in the Nag Hammadi documents.

In regard to the work on the major problems themselves the present situation is as follows :

(1) for metaphysics and cosmology (i.e. that part with which I am concerned) a starting-point is provided first of all by the works of Jan Zandee in the gnoseological field, my own observations and also from the side of classical philology the great work of the Tübingen philologist and philosopher Hans Joachim Krämer, "Der Ursprung der Geistmetaphysik". The theme of metaphysics is particularly important for the gnostic; for indeed he can construct no soteriology at all if he does not possess knowledge about the metaphysical and cosmological background of his own self which has been flung down into the world of darkness. The documents from Nag Hammadi themselves give us a glimpse of the authors' efforts to form a complete and rounded picture. Here they have the same end in view as the Greeks. In particular the Greek problem of the ἀρχή, the νοῦς and the world soul was of concern also to the gnostics. Their portrayal of the heavenly world and their idea of God must also be understood

against the background of Platonic and Neopythagorean philosophy. But in the interpretation of the individual texts we must make precise distinctions. The God who can only be described by negative predicates corresponds to the conception of Plotinus, but could already be present in the ἐπ᾽ ἐκεῖνα of Plato. I have dealt with the gnostic idea of God, their doctrine of the indescribable God, the God of light, of God as ἀρχή and ἕν, as well as the activity of this God, in an essay in the volume "Der Name Gottes" (Düsseldorf 1975) pp. 131-155. In all this, however, we must always pay attention to the peculiar character of gnostic thought and its special elaboration of Greek ideas. Of particular importance is the treatment of the Trinity, concerning which a study relating to their occurrence in Nag Hammadi is in preparation to assist the investigations carried on in the Sonderforschungsbereich 13 in Göttingen. One of the most interesting phenomena is the appearance side by side in these texts of the triads Father-Mother-Son and Father-Son-Spirit.

The bringing together of νοῦς and ψυχή in redemption points to their metaphysical pre-existence. But λόγος and πνεῦμα also, and ἔννοια and πρόνοια, as well as the doctrine of Heimarmene, are Greek elements, although of course the gnostic evaluation of them must in each case be precisely determined.

(2) In the course of the work on anthropology R.T. Updegraff, after collecting the material relating to the soul, has attempted to find in the texts different models of the gnostic conception. However, in order to present the material to the reader in as objective a form as possible he is at the present engaged in setting out the anthropological conceptions of each text separately; thereafter a final assignment to the models will follow. From this it will then be possible to determine the nature and the extent of the Greek influence. Anthropology, however, will take into account not only the origin of man but especially his bodily and psychic constitution.

(3) Ethics were the concern of F. Wisse, and here about half of the manuscript is already in being. The introduction already mentioned is followed by a discussion of the several documents. Here the following groups are included :

(a) the texts of hellenistic popular ethics, as they are presented by the Teachings of Silvanus and the Sentences of Sextus;

(b) the Hermetic texts;

(c) the heterodox christian documents; to these Wisse assigns the texts which are not absolutely gnostic but as apocrypha stand between orthodoxy and Gnosticism with a leaning more or less to one side or the other;

(d) the christian-gnostic tractates; these texts are likewise a hetero-geneous group, in which the mythological basis of gnostic ethics emerges very prominently;

(e) the texts of mythological Gnosis; in these the theoretical founda-tion of ethics is brought more strongly to expression than the practice.

In the discussion of the several documents possible hellenistic in-fluences are indicated so far as may be feasible, and then the final chapter will set out the results which could be worked out from the investigation of the relation between Nag Hammadi and hellenistic ethics. One particularly important result is, as Wisse has already shown in an essay on the Sentences of Sextus, the complete absence of liber-tine tendencies in Nag Hammadi. Wisse, who in the interval has withdrawn from the Tübingen project and taken up a teaching post in the Netherlands, will nonetheless carry the monograph to its con-clusion alongside his present concerns.

In Tübingen, Folker Siegert has taken his place, with the task of drawing up a catalogue of concepts for the Nag Hammadi collection. This task had already been fulfilled by Wisse for some texts. In this way the project is performing preliminary work for the great plan of a "Satzlexikon" of Hellenism and Gnosticism which Carsten Colpe has outlined. Since Colpe's project, owing to inadequate financial support, will however need a long time before its completion we shall in the first place publish independently the lexicon of concepts which we have worked out and this will be completed in two years.

The work of Gertrud Bauer may be regarded as a kind of auxiliary project which is both in tune with the essential point of our project, the investigation of the hellenisation process, but will also form a lexical aid which is intended to show also the development on the basis of examples. Frau Bauer is working on the uninflected words which Coptic has taken over from Greek, i.e. the conjunctive and subjunctive particles and the prepositions. As an incidental product of her researches she has already published a concordance of these words in the Bohairic version of the New Testament. The material for the main work is in all important respects already collected, so that this also can be completed within a short time. For the moment, however, Frau Bauer is pre-occupied with the urgent task of setting up at the library of the Oriental Institute of the German Oriental Society in Beirut a section for the Christian Orient.

This report is intended to show you how in Tübingen it has been possible to collaborate fruitfully in a wider context and, we hope, how it will also be possible to work in the future. We should be grateful to all of you if you could either continue to support us or begin to support us through your interest and by scholarly exchanges of information.

UN DOUBLE SYMBOLE DE FOI GNOSTIQUE
DANS LE *KEPHALAION UN* DE MÉDÎNET MÂDI

par

J. RIES

Le *Kephalaion 1* de Médînet Mâdi, intitulé *Au sujet de la venue de l'Apôtre*, se présente à nos yeux comme un document important pour l'intelligence des doctrines de Mani.[1] Une première section de cette catéchèse émet des considérations générales sur la mission apostolique.[2] Malgré les nombreuses lacunes du manuscrit, plusieurs indications précieuses se dégagent clairement de ces pages. Dans le contexte du calendrier égyptien des travaux et des jours, le rédacteur développe l'allégorie de l'agriculteur et en déduit le principe de tout apostolat : les semailles sont toujours suivies d'une récolte.[3] Ensuite, il souligne à gros traits gnostiques l'exposé du principe de la permanence des Envoyés depuis la création de l'humanité.[4] Nous y trouvons notamment une forte insistance sur le choix d'élus et de catéchumènes, sur le caractère éphémère de la mission de chaque Envoyé et sur la permanence du salut au milieu des hommes. La deuxième section du *Kephalaion* donne d'abord un bref aperçu de l'histoire du salut depuis Adam jusqu'à Mani, puis elle expose les croyances de l'Église manichéenne. C'est cette deuxième section du *Kephalaion* qui constitue l'objet de la présente recherche.[5] Enfin, dans une troisième section, Mani évoque les routes de son activité missionnaire depuis la fin du règne d'Ardashîr.[6] Le *Kephalaion* se termine par une doxologie : les disciples remercient leur Maître qui vient de leur communiquer la synthèse de sa doctrine, résumant ainsi ses propres *Écritures*. Ils le proclament à la fois "Paraclet venu du Père et Révélateur de tous les mystères".[7]

---

[1] C. Schmidt-H. J. Polotsky-A. Böhlig, *Kephalaia*, I, 1, Stuttgart, 1940, 9-16.
[2] *Kephalaion 1*, 9, 24-34; 10, 1-34; 11, 1-35; 12, 1-9.
[3] *Kephalaion 1*, 9, 24-34; 10, 1-7.
[4] *Kephalaion 1*, 10, 31-34; 11, 1-35; 12, 1-9a.
[5] *Kephalaion 1*, 12, 9b-34; 13, 1-35; 14, 1-32; 15, 1-24a.
[6] *Kephalaion 1*, 15, 24b-34; 16, 1-21a.
[7] *Kephalaion 1*, 16, 21b-23a.

I. *Une présentation gnostique de l'histoire du salut*

Mani a conscience d'être le sceau des Messagers du salut. Évoquant les grandes étapes du déroulement historique de la libération de l'homme, il cite quelques Envoyés : Sethel fils d'Adam, Enosch, Hénoch, Sem fils de Noé, le Bouddha et Zarathoustra.[8]

1. *Le venue de Jésus*

Après ces quelques lignes qui résument l'histoire religieuse de l'humanité depuis Adam jusqu'à Jésus le Fils de la Grandeur, Mani s'arrête plus longuement à la venue de "Jésus-Christ notre Seigneur" (12, 21). La relation de la vie de Jésus depuis sa venue jusqu'à son ascension regroupe huit événements.[9] La venue de Jésus est d'abord présentée selon une double perspective. La perspective gnostique — au sujet de laquelle Mani a entretenu ses disciples en d'autres occasions — insiste sur le corps spirituel de Jésus et n'hésite pas à parler d'une "venue sans corps" (12, 22-24a). Le rédacteur présente ensuite la perspective christologique des Apôtres qui ont parlé de la forme d'un esclave et d'une apparence humaine (12, 24b-26). Voici à présent une énumération des événements de sa vie. Jésus s'est manifesté au milieu du peuple juif. Il a choisi ses *Douze* et ses *Soixante-douze*. Il a accompli la volonté du Père (14, 26-29a). Satan est entré dans le cœur de Judas Iscariote, un des *Douze*. Ce dernier l'a dénoncé. Par un baiser il l'a livré aux Juifs et à la cohorte des soldats (12, 30b-34). Les Juifs se sont saisi du Fils de Dieu ; ils l'ont jugé contrairement à toute loi et ils l'ont condamné injustement, lui qui était sans péché. Ils l'ont suspendu au bois de la croix et l'ont crucifié en même temps que des brigands. Ils l'ont descendu de la croix et l'ont déposé dans le tombeau. Après trois jours, il est ressuscité d'entre les mots, il est venu vers ses disciples, il leur est apparu, il les a revêtus de force, leur a insufflé son Esprit Saint et les a envoyés dans le monde entier prêcher la Grandeur (13, 1-10a).

À la suite de ce document sur la vie de Jésus, le rédacteur relate quelques événements importants qui se sont déroulés entre l'ascension de Jésus et la mission de Mani. Malgré les lacunes du texte nous parvenons à saisir la trame du récit : le courage des Apôtres, la mission de Paul, la crise au lendemain de la prédication paulinienne. Deux Justes — probablement Marcion et Bardesane — ont tenté, mais sans

---

[8] *Kephalaion 1*, 12, 10-20.
[9] *Kephalaion 1*, 12, 22-34 ; 13, 1-10a.

succès, de redresser le monde. La véritable Église de Jésus était remontée dans le Pays de la Lumière. Ainsi, la terre est restée comme un arbre sans fruit. L'heure de Mani est arrivée.[10]

2. *La mission de Mani*

Afin de situer sa mission dans la lignée des grands Envoyés, Mani n'hésite pas à utiliser les paroles mêmes de Jésus : "Lorsque l'Église du Sauveur se fut élevée en haut, alors s'accomplit mon apostolat au sujet duquel vous m'avez interrogé. À partir de ce moment fut envoyé le Paraclet, l'Esprit de Vérité qui est venu auprès de vous en cette génération, comme le Sauveur l'a dit : "Quand je m'en irai, je vous enverrai le Paraclet et quand le Paraclet viendra, il blâmera le monde au sujet du péché et avec vous il parlera de la justice ... et du jugement'[11]". Présentée ainsi, l'œuvre de Mani est à la fois une restauration de l'Église de Jésus et la mission même du Paraclet annoncée par le Sauveur. Dans le texte johannique de l'annonce du Paraclet (*Joa.* 16, 8-11), le témoignage de l'Esprit qui vient sur les disciples porte sur le péché, sur la justice et sur le jugement. Le texte relatif à l'action du Paraclet cité par Mani garde les trois thèmes de Jean. Cependant, un phénomène analogue à celui que nous venons de relever dans la présentation de la venue de Jésus (12, 22-24a) se retrouve ici. L'insertion d'une perspective gnostique modifie profondément le sens du texte néotestamentaire. En effet, par l'introduction d'un dualisme radical dans le groupe des auditeurs du Paraclet, le rédacteur du *Kephalaion* parvient à changer le sens des paroles de Jésus au point d'en faire l'annonce de la mission de Mani. Alors que chez Jean, le Paraclet "blâmera le monde au sujet du péché, de la justice et du jugement",[12] selon Mani, Jésus a dit : "Le Paraclet blâmera le monde au sujet du péché, mais avec vous il parlera de la justice et du jugement".

Les lacunes du manuscrit nous empêchent de connaître le commentaire qu'a fait de ce texte le rédacteur du *Kephalaion* (14, 12-24a). Heureusement les détails historiques relatifs au début de l'apostolat de Mani sont bien conservés (14, 24b-32). Après avoir rappelé que la crise de l'Église prisonnière de la chair a marqué l'heure de la rédemption des âmes comme le mois de Pharmouti indique le temps de la

---

[10] *Kephalaion 1*, 13, 10b-35 ; 14, 1-2.

[11] *Kephalaion 1*, 14, 3-10 ; *Joa.*, 16, 8-11.

[12] Dans le texte copte de *Joa.*, 16, 8, ϥⲛⲁϫⲡⲓⲉ en sahidique et ⲉϥⲉⲥⲟϩⲓ en bohairique (texte de Horner). ϥⲛⲁϫⲡⲓⲁ dans le manuscrit Thompson, sahidique.

récolte, le Prophète évoque sa naissance sous le règne d'Artaban, roi des Parthes. Au passage il souligne que le Paraclet lui-même a formé son *eikôn*, c'est-à-dire son corps. Il s'agit d'une allusion manifeste à la préexistence de Mani qui est chargé de rendre présent sur terre le Paraclet céleste. Sous le règne d'Ardashîr, le roi des Perses, arrive la plénitude du temps. C'est l'heure de la rencontre avec le Paraclet vivant.

Les événements relatés ici de façon très sommaire nous sont mieux connus à présent grâce à la *Vita* de Mani du *Codex* de Cologne.[13] Formé dans la secte elkhasaïte depuis l'âge de quatre ans, Mani reçut le 1er avril 228 la visite d'un messager du Royaume de la Lumière, l'ange *at-taûm* (le jumeau) appelé *súzugos* (le compagnon) dans le *Codex*. Douze ans plus tard le même messager, appelé le Paraclet Vivant dans le *Kephalaion*, est venu révéler à Mani les mystères insondables et lui donner l'ordre de proclamer la vérité et le salut. Cet événement semble postérieur de quelques jours au couronnement de Shâpûr Ier comme co-régent d'Ardashîr, le 12 avril 240. Mani avait vingt-quatre ans.

Au terme de cette analyse nous saisissons mieux la structure de la présentation gnostique de l'histoire du salut. En deux parties articulées de la même manière le rédacteur décrit la mission de Jésus et celle de Mani. Après une introduction qui n'est qu'un rappel des noms des grands Envoyés venus depuis Adam, le texte groupe en huit articles les principaux événements de la vie de Jésus. Ensuite, dans le contexte d'une réforme permettant l'institution de la véritable Église, la mission de Mani est annoncée par Jésus lui-même. Elle se situe au lendemain de l'apostolat des Apôtres, de Paul et de deux Justes. Elle constitue l'œuvre du Paraclet annoncé par Jésus à ses Apôtres. La mission de Mani ne fait que continuer celle de Jésus. Nous sommes en présence du sceau de la révélation. Mani est le Paraclet annoncé par Jésus et chargé par lui de former la véritable Église.

II. *La révélation des mystères dualistes*

1. *Les douze mystères*

Après avoir situé clairement sa mission dans la lignée des Envoyés, après avoir montré que son œuvre continue l'œuvre de Jésus par la fondation de l'Église du Paraclet, Mani livre à ses disciples les mystères

---

[13] A. Henrichs-L. Koenen, Ein Griechischer Mani-Codex, (P. Colon. inv. n° 4780) dans : *Zeitschrift für Papyrologie und Epigraphik*, 5, Bonn, 1970, 97-216 et Der Kölner Mani-Codex, dans : *Z.P.E.*, 19, Bonn, 1975, 1-85.

révélés : "Le Paraclet Vivant est descendu sur moi et a parlé avec moi. Il m'a révélé le mystère caché qui fut caché aux mondes et aux générations, le mystère de la profondeur et de la hauteur. Il m'a révélé le mystère de la lumière et des ténèbres, le mystère de la lutte, de la guerre, de la grande guerre commencée par les ténèbres. Il m'a révélé aussi comment ... s'est fait le mélange de la lumière et des ténèbres et comment ce monde fut créé. Il m'a encore expliqué comment furent fixées les barques afin que les [...] de lumière puissent y prendre place en vue de la libération de la lumière ... Il m'a fait comprendre le mystère de la création d'Adam le premier homme et le mystère de l'arbre de la connaissance dont Adam a mangé, ce qui lui a ouvert les yeux. Il m'a enseigné le mystère des Apôtres envoyés dans le monde pour choisir les Églises, le mystère des élus et de leurs commandements, le mystère des pécheurs et de leurs œuvres et du châtiment qui les attend. Ainsi, tout ce qui est arrivé et tout ce qui arrivera encore m'a été révélé par le Paraclet".[14]

Ce texte énumère les douze mystères révélés à Mani par le Paraclet. Il s'agit d'une présentation des douze dogmes dualistes : les deux royaumes, la lumière et les ténèbres, leur combat, le mélange de la lumière aux ténèbres, la constitution du cosmos, la libération de la lumière ou mystère du salut, la création d'Adam, le mystère de la connaissance, la mission des Envoyés, les mystères des élus, des catéchumènes et des pécheurs. Dans ce symbole doctrinal s'imbriquent deux données fondamentales : d'une part, les mystères dualistes axés sur les deux principes lumière-ténèbres ; d'autre part, l'histoire gnostique du salut présentée non plus dans la perspective de la mission gnostique des Envoyés mais dans la perspective de la lutte des ténèbres contre la lumière. Cette histoire du salut s'articule en trois temps. Le premier temps est constitué par la séparation radicale des deux royaumes. Le deuxième temps englobe les événements cosmiques de leur affrontement : la chute d'une partie de la lumière dans la matière ténébreuse, la création du cosmos, la libération des parcelles lumineuses. Ce temps du mélange est le temps médian. Le troisième temps amènera le retour définitif à la situation originelle. En effet, par la libération de toute la lumière, le salut est assuré de manière irréversible.

2. *Les deux royaumes et les trois temps*

Les deux royaumes constituent le mystère fondamental de la révélation gnostique. Aux origines coexistent deux natures, la lumière et les

---

[14] *Kephalaion 1*, 15, 1-20.

ténèbres, principes éternels, inengendrés et constitutifs des deux royaumes. Le Royaume de la Lumière situé en haut est la maison du Père de la Grandeur. L'Esprit y fait vivre les cinq éléments qui se partagent ce domaine peuplé de douze esprits lumineux. En bas se trouve le Royaume des Ténèbres avec ses cinq gouffres. C'est le domaine de la matière et des cinq nuits : nuit de la matière, nuit de la mort, nuit de l'erreur et du mensonge, nuit de la chair et du désir. Ce dualisme radical caché au monde et aux générations est révélé par Mani. Il comporte deux éléments qui sous-tendent la cosmogonie et la sotériologie : les cinq domaines et les douze esprits. Le dualisme des origines forme le premier temps. Ce sont les deux premiers mystères.

Le temps médian va comporter trois moments. Le premier moment est celui de l'Homme Primordial qui avec ses cinq fils combat les ténèbres. Au cours de la lutte une partie de la substance lumineuse de Dieu est enchaînée à la matière. Ici commence l'impérieuse nécessité du salut, la libération de la lumière. L'Esprit Vivant descend avec ses cinq fils, tend sa droite à l'Homme Primordial et le fait remonter auprès du Père, où, sauveur sauvé, il reste le prototype des âmes à libérer. Vient alors le deuxième moment du temps médian. C'est la création, œuvre de l'Esprit Vivant qui châtie les archontes en créant le cosmos fait de leurs os, de leurs peaux, de leurs chairs, de leurs excréments. Le Troisième Envoyé continue l'œuvre du salut ce qui amène la création de la végétation, des arbres, des animaux de même que d'Adam dont la descendance porte en elle la majeure partie des parcelles lumineuses encore enchaînées. Le troisième moment du temps médian est celui des messagers gnostiques. Le Père fait sortir de lui Jésus la Splendeur, un être transcendant et cosmique, vie et salut des hommes qui commence par provoquer le réveil d'Adam puis met en place la Grande Pensée et ses deux diadoques, *Tôchme* et *Sôtme*, Appel-Écoute. Toute l'œuvre de Jésus la Splendeur porte un nom : c'est la Gnose, fille de la Grande Pensée. À présent vont se succéder les divers messagers de la Gnose depuis Sethel fils d'Adam jusqu'à Mani. Ainsi les trois moments du temps médian englobent les dix autres mystères révélés par Mani. Ils préparent le troisième temps, le retour aux origines avec la séparation définitive des deux royaumes. En présentant ses douze mystères dualistes Mani n'hésite pas à dire que le "Paraclet lui a révélé tout ce qui est arrivé et tout ce qui arrivera" (15, 19-20). Ainsi, il a pu révéler le commencement, le milieu et la fin.

III. *Deux symboles de foi gnostique*

Le titre du *Kephalaion 1* nous fait entrevoir un développement consacré à la venue de Mani. L'analyse du chapitre nous a montré qu'il s'agit d'une véritable introduction à un traité de catéchèse gnostique. Parmi les trois sections dont se compose le *Kephalaion*, la deuxième est la plus importante. En deux volets elle nous présente la doctrine fondamentale de la religion de Mani : la mission des Envoyés et la révélation des mystères. L'allusion répétée aux *Écritures* de Mani (12, 23 ; 16, 21-22) confère à notre document une valeur supplémentaire. Nous sommes en présence d'un abrégé de la doctrine manichéenne relative à l'histoire du salut et aux mystères dualistes.

1. *Jésus et Mani*

Dans l'ordonnance gnostique du salut, Jésus occupe une place centrale car il est le Fils de la Grandeur. En fait, les textes de Médînet Mâdi nous présentent Jésus sous trois figures différentes dans lesquelles les traits mythiques et historiques se mélangent curieusement. La première figure est Jésus la Splendeur, la cinquième grandeur lumineuse du Royaume, celle que le Père a chargé de la quatrième libération de la lumière.[15] Au cours de sa mission Jésus fait d'abord sortir Adam du sommeil. Ensuite, afin de conférer au message du salut une force et une valeur permanente, Jésus institue la Grande Pensée et ses deux diadoques, Appel-Écoute. La deuxième figure est l'âme du monde, le *Jesus patibilis* dont parle Augustin.[16] Dans les *Kephalaia*, ce Jésus souffrant constitué par l'ensemble des parcelles lumineuses prisonnières de la matière, porte le nom de Croix de Lumière.[17] Ces deux figures mythiques de Jésus ont de nombreux traits communs avec la figure iranienne du *salvator salvandus* et avec la figure du *Bodhisattva* dans le *Mahâyâna* bouddhique.

Un troisième personnage vient recouvrir les deux autres et ajouter à leur dimension mythique une dimension historique : c'est Jésus-Christ venu en ce monde au milieu du peuple juif. Dans le *Kephalaion 1* Mani insiste sur cette dimension historique. Elle lui est indispensable pour fonder et justifier sa mission. Aussi le voyons-nous relater huit événements de la vie de Jésus, manifestement repris à un document chrétien probablement à un symbole de foi dont il a modifié le sens par son

---

[15] *Kephalaion 1*, 49, 29-31 ; 53, 28-32 ; 54, 1-9a.
[16] *Cont. Faustum*, 20, 2.
[17] *Kephalaion 85*, 208-213.

insistance sur le corps spirituel de Jésus.[18] À ces huit faits de la vie
du Christ, il a ajouté trois articles sur l'activité des Apôtres, sur la
mission de Paul, sur l'essai de réforme tenté par deux Justes. Au
douzième article de ce credo de la mission gnostique, Mani se sert de
l'annonce du Paraclet faite par Jésus pour présenter sa propre mission
d'Envoyé et de sceau des Prophètes.[19] Le texte du symbole de la foi
manichéenne qui sert de base à la présentation de la mission gnostique
est une relecture gnostique des événements du salut depuis la venue
de Jésus jusqu'à l'avènement de Mani. Par le texte de *Joa*, 16, 8-11,
Mani met sa mission directement en relation avec la mission de Jésus
le Fils de la Grandeur. Son Église ne fait que continuer l'Église de
Jésus exactement comme Jésus l'avait prévu et annoncé.

2. *Mani et le Paraclet*

Le Paraclet Vivant est descendu sur Mani et lui a révélé "le mystère
caché aux mondes et aux générations, le mystère de la profondeur
et de la hauteur" (15, 1-3a). Ainsi, le mystère fondamental est le
dualisme universel et radical. L'action révélatrice du Paraclet est décrite
à l'aide du verbe *kjôleb abal*, le verbe spécifique de la révélation dans
les textes de *Médînet Mâdi*.[20] *Kjôleb abal* est aussi le mot technique
utilisé pour désigner les émanations gnostiques, à savoir la procession
des cinq Envoyés du Père chargés d'organiser la libération de la
lumière. Ainsi, dans une étape antérieure et cosmique, celle de l'émana-
tion des Éons sortis de l'essence du Père, la révélation a été une
véritable ontophanie gnostique située au début du premier moment
du deuxième temps. À la fin du déroulement du temps du salut, après la
venue de tous les Messagers, intervient le Paraclet afin de mettre un
terme à la révélation. Par Mani son jumeau il fait connaître l'essence
des mystères. "De cette manière tout ce qui est arrivé et tout ce qui
arrivera m'a été révélé par le Paraclet" (15, 19b-20). À la fin du *Kephalaion*, dans la doxologie adressée à leur Maître par les disciples,
ces derniers n'hésitent pas à proclamer leur foi: "Tu es le Paraclet
venu du Père, le Révélateur de tous les mystères".[21] Aux yeux de son
Église, Mani s'identifie au Paraclet.

---

[18] *Kephalaion 1*, 12, 21-34; 13, 1-10.
[19] F. Kattenbusch, *Das Apostolische Symbol, ein Beitrag zur Symbolik und Dogmen-
geschichte*, I, Leipzig, 1894, II, Leipzig, 1900.
[20] J. Ries, La révélation dans la gnose de Mani, dans : *Forma Futuri, Studi in onore
del Cardinale Michele Pellegrino*, Torino, 1975, 1085-1096.
[21] *Kephalaion 1*, 16, 29-31.

Dans la description de la mission gnostique nous avons pu reconnaître une présentation de douze événements majeurs, dont huit sont relatifs à Jésus et dont quatre sont consacrés à l'avènement de Mani. Dans l'abrégé de la révélation gnostique, l'articulation en douze mystères paraît vraiment évidente. Le nombre douze est un nombre gnostique. Sans parler des douze Apôtres que Mani a choisis à l'imitation de Jésus, nous découvrons à maintes reprises le nombre douze dans nos *Kephalaia* : les douze *zôdia* cosmiques,[22] les douze juges du Père,[23] les douze éléments.[24] Sans doute faut-il consacrer une mention spéciale aux douze Fils de lumière qui sont appelés les douze Éons du Père et qui se présentent de la manière suivante : les cinq Fils de l'Homme Primordial, les cinq Fils de l'Esprit Vivant, les deux diadoques mis en place par Jésus la Splendeur.[25] Dans pareil contexte est-il étonnant de voir présenter en douze articles, d'une part l'histoire de la mission gnostique, d'autre part la révélation des mystères?

3. *Mani et la foi des disciples*

L'analyse de la deuxième partie du *Kephalaion 1* de Médînet Mâdi nous invite à y trouver, chaque fois présenté en douze articles, un double résumé des doctrines de Mani : d'une part la mission gnostique, d'autre part les mystères dualistes. La facture de ces deux textes mise en évidence par notre analyse, suggère l'utilisation par le rédacteur du *Kephalaion*, des deux volets d'un symbole de foi gnostique. Ajoutons que la doxologie finale vient confirmer nos conclusions. Au terme de l'exposé catéchétique, les disciples s'adressent à leur Maître afin de lui exprimer leur gratitude pour l'initiation reçue : "Là-dessus, lorsque ses disciples eurent entendu (*sôtme*) tout cela de sa bouche, ils furent remplis de joie. Leur esprit (*noûs*) était illuminé et dans leur allégresse ils lui dirent : "Seigneur, nous te remercions d'avoir décrit pour nous, dans tes *Écritures*, ta venue. Nous avons accepté l'événement tel qu'il s'est déroulé et nous y avons cru. Mais voici que maintenant Tu nous a communiqué tout cela en une brève synthèse. Quant à nous, nous l'avons pleinement accepté et nous avons cru que Tu es, Toi, le Paraclet venu du Père, le Révélateur de tous les mystères".[26] Dans ces quelques lignes, les disciples font allusion aux

---

[22] *Kephalaion 69*, 166-169.
[23] *Kephalaion 28*, 79-81.
[24] *Kephalaion 71*, 175-176.
[25] Tout le *Kephalaion 16*, 49-55 est consacré à l'explication de cette doctrine.
[26] *Kephalaion 1*, 16, 23b-31.

deux documents par lesquels la venue de Mani leur est connue : le récit
conservé dans les *Écritures* et l'exposé inséré dans le *Kephalaion 1*.
Chacun de ces documents exige une double démarche de leur part :
l'acceptation de la mission du Prophète et l'adhésion aux mystères
dualistes. En parlant de l'exposé fait par Mani dans le *Kephalaion 1*,
le rédacteur souligne cette démarche avec plus d'insistance et montre
qu'elle est à l'origine de la croissance de la foi.[27] À la fin de la
doxologie, en une formule qui porte la frappe de la titulature gnostique, les disciples reportent sur la personne du Fondateur leur adhésion à l'histoire du salut et leur foi dans les mystères dualistes : "Tu
es, Toi, le Paraclet venu du Père, le Révélateur de tous les mystères".
Une conclusion semble s'imposer : le *Kephalaion 1* de Médînet Mâdi
nous a conservé les deux volets du *kanôn alètheias* de l'Église de Mani.

---

[27] *Kephalaion 1*, 16, 29. l'expression ϩⲛ̄ ⲟⲩⲁⲉⲓⲉⲩⲧⲉ (A) se trouve dans la version
bohairique de *Eph.* 4, 16, pour désigner la croissance du corps mystique du Christ.

EGYPTIAN SURVIVALS IN THE NAG HAMMADI LIBRARY

by

PAHOR LABIB

Jean Doresse,[1] Siegfried Morenz[2] and Martin Krause[3] have dealt with some of these Egyptian survivals in the Nag Hammadi Library. I shall speak to-day of only a few examples.

In Codex Jung, which in my book *Coptic Gnostic Papyri in the Coptic Museum*[4] I called Codex I of the Nag Hammadi Library, we find as a heading or a title of one of the treatises ΠΛΟΓΟC ΕΤΒΕ ΤΑΝΑCΤΑCΙC,[5] which has to do with resurrection. It is written in the form of a letter to a certain person named Rheginos, but the name of the sender is not given. The sender emphasizes the importance of resurrection.

We can trace the same belief of the importance of resurrection in the ancient Egyptian religion. The ancient Egyptian texts and the scenes of the private as well as the royal tombs deal on a large scale with this belief.[6]

In the texts of Nag Hammadi we find in Codex II a mention of paradise. Even Egypt is mentioned as the place of paradise.[7]

We all know that Egypt, the cradle of ancient civilization, has always had an idea about paradise. The ancient Egyptian texts often refer to this theme and also the representation of paradise has always been a

---

[1] J. Doresse, *The Secret Books of the Egyptian Gnostics*, London 1960, 272-275.

[2] S. Morenz, Fortwirken altägyptischer Elemente in christlicher Zeit in : *Koptische Kunst. Christentum am Nil*, Essen 1963, 55-56.

[3] M. Krause, Die Koptologie im Gefüge der Wissenschaften, in : *ZÄS* 100, 1974, 115 N. 45 and Ägyptisches Gedankengut in der Apokalypse des Asklepius, in : *Zeitschrift der Deutschen Morgenländischen Gesellschaft*, Supplementa I, Wiesbaden 1969, 48-57.

[4] Cairo 1956.

[5] I 50, 17-18. This treatise was published by M. Malinine, H.-Ch. Puech, G. Quispel, W. Till, adiuvantibus R. McL. Wilson, J. Zandee, *De resurrectione (Epistula ad Rheginum)* Codex Jung F. XXIIᵣ-F. XXVᵣ (p. 43-50), Zürich 1963.

[6] A. Erman, *Die Religion der Ägypter*, Berlin 1943, 207 ff.

[7] A. Böhlig u. P. Labib, *Die koptisch-gnostische Schrift ohne Titel aus Codex II von Nag Hammadi im Koptischen Museum zu Alt-Kairo*, Berlin 1962 (= Deutsche Akad. d. Wiss. zu Berlin, Inst. f. Orientforschung Nr. 58), 96 (= II 122 (= 170), 35 ff.).

subject of decoration in private tombs such as the tombs of Sn-n<u>d</u>m in Thebes.[8] We find that paradise is represented by the green fields of Jarw and also Shabties[9] were supposed to keep these fields green.

On the walls of the temples we find also representations of paradise, for example in the Medinet Habu temple we see king Ramses III ploughing and harvesting in the fields of paradise[10] according to the well known scenes represented in the Book of the Dead.[11]

Also in the tombs of the pharaohs in the valley of the kings at Luxor we find some scenes representing paradise, which are painted on the walls of the tomb of king Amenhotep II[12] and king Sety I.[13]

Again we can trace how ancient Egyptian deities survived in the Nag Hammadi Library, such as Seth,[14] Thot = Hermes Trismegistos[15] in Codex VI, the two bulls, that is to say the Apis bull of Memphis[16] and the Mnevis bull of Heliopolis,[17] in Codex II.[18] We can trace also typical ancient Egyptian sacred birds like the phoenix[19] or typical Egyptian animals like the crocodile.[20]

Again the idea of the triad (father, mother and son)[21] has its ancient Egyptian roots,[22] also the preference for the number three.[23]

---

[8] B. Porter and R. L. B. Moss, assisted by F. W. Burney, *Topographical Bibliography of Ancient Egyptian Hieroglyphic Texts, Reliefs, and Paintings. I. The Theban Necropolis.* Part 1. Private Tombs, Oxford ²1960, 1 ff.

[9] H. Bonnet, *Reallexikon der ägyptischen Religionsgeschichte*, ²1971 Berlin, 849 ff.

[10] Porter and Moss, *II. Theban Temples*, ² Oxford 1972, 481 ff.

[11] E. A. W. Budge, *The Book of the Dead. Papyrus of Ani*, London 1913.

[12] Porter-Moss, *Typographical Bibliography I*, Part 2, 554 ff.

[13] Porter-Moss, *l.c.* 535 ff.

[14] J. Doresse, *The Secret Books* 435 f. (Index); M. Tardieu, Les livres mis sous le nom de Seth et les Séthiens de l'hérésiologie, in : *Gnosis and Gnosticism* (Nag Hammadi Studies VIII), Leiden 1977, 204-210.

[15] M. Krause, *Ägyptisches Gedankengut* 49 N. 12.

[16] H. Bonnet, *Reallexikon* 46 ff.

[17] H. Bonnet, *Reallexikon* 468 ff.

[18] A. Böhlig and P. Labib, *Die koptisch-gnostische Schrift* 96 (= II 122 (= 170), 21 ff.).

[19] H. Bonnet, *Reallexikon* 594 ff., A. Böhlig and P. Labib, *Die koptisch-gnostische Schrift* 94 f. (= II 121 (= 169), 35 ff.).

[20] A. Böhlig and P. Labib, *Die koptisch-gnostische Schrift* 95 (= II 122 (= 170), 18 f.).

[21] AJ II 2, 14 f. par.

[22] S. Morenz, *Ägyptische Religion*, Stuttgart 1960, 150 ff., 270 ff.

[23] The *three* stelae of Seth : VII 118, 8 - 127, 32 in : *Christentum am Roten Meer*, 2. Bd. Berlin 1973, 180 ff.; three times : VII 120, 19; VII 120, 34-35 : ⲁⲕⲛⲟⲩϨⲙ ⲁⲕⲛⲟⲩϨⲙ ⲁⲕⲛⲁϨⲙⲛ; A. Böhlig, Urzeit und Endzeit in der titellosen Schrift des Codex II von Nag Hammadi, in : *BSAC* 16, 1962, 15.

God is often called male-female[24] like the Egyptian creator god.[25]

As in old Egyptian texts[26] there is a punishment in the Gnostic Texts : to go upside down.[27]

Here I stop. There are many other Egyptian survivals in the Nag Hammadi Library, a wide field of future research.

---

[24] ϨⲞⲞⲨⲦ-ⲤϨⲓⲙⲉ II 5,9; 6,8 and par.

[25] Morenz, *Ägyptische Religion* 27 and N. 52; E. Hornung, *Der Eine und die Vielen. Ägyptische Gottesvorstellungen*, Darmstadt 1971, 165 and N. 104.

[26] J. Zandee, *Death as an Enemy according to ancient Egyptian Conceptions*, Leiden 1960, 5 and N. 3.

[27] II 141,36; Krause, *Die Koptologie* 115 N. 45.

LITERARKRITISCHE PROBLEME
DER ZEPHANJA-APOKALYPSE [1]

von

BERND JÖRG DIEBNER

1. Antike und mittelalterliche Nachrichten über eine Zephanja-Apokalypse.

1.1 Ein Zephanja-Apokryphon in Kanonverzeichnissen.

Ein ψευδεπίγραφον,[2] eine προφητεία[3] oder eine ἀποκάλυψις[4] des Sophonias[5] bezeugen uns mehrere antike und mittelalterliche Verzeichnisse "apokrypher" Schriften zum Alten Testament.[6] Da diese Listen zT miteinander identisch sind, zT in wesentlichen Zügen über-

---

[1] Diese Arbeit ist die leicht veränderte Fassung des Referates, das ich in englischer Sprache am 13.12.1976 in Kairo während des First International Congress of Coptology gehalten hatte. — Im Blick auf die Edition der sog. Zephanja-Apokalypse in der Reihe JSHRZ musste ich die literarkritischen Probleme der betroffenen Texte durchdenken, da die Ergebnisse Steindorffs aus dem Jahre 1899 (vgl. Anm. 17) natürlich nicht einfach übernommen werden können. In die Einleitung zur Textausgabe können nur die Ergebnisse dieser Überlegungen aufgenommen werden. Vgl. DBAT 12 (1977), 30-45.

[2] Σοφονίου προφήτου ... ψευδεπίγραφα heisst es in der Σύνοψις des Pseudo-Athanasius (Th. Zahn, *Geschichte des Neutestamentlichen Kanons. II*, Erlangen und Leipzig, 1890, 317; vgl. zur Datierung dieser Kompilation *l.c.* 302-315 : 6. Jh. oder später); ähnlich die von Zahn zitierte Fassung der στιχομετρία des Nicephorus aus der Mitte des 9. Jh.s (vgl. Zahn II 300; zur Datierung : 295-297).

[3] Eine lateinische Variante der Stichometrie des Nicephorus liest prophetia (Zahn II 300, kritischer Apparat zu Zeile 58[A]); Σοφονίου προφητεία scheint auch die griechische Vorlage zu haben, auf der die von G. Steindorff (vgl. unten Anm. 17) 23 zitierte Ausgabe Dindorfs beruht.

[4] Von einer Σοφονίου ἀποκάλυψις spricht das in mehreren Handschriften überlieferte Verzeichnis Περὶ τῶν ξ' βιβλίων καὶ ὅσα τούτων ἐκτός (No. 12 der Bücher "ausserhalb" des Kanons; vgl. Zahn II 292; 289f. zu den MSS und ihren Datierungen; vgl. auch Steindorff, Anm. 17, 23).

[5] Gräzisierte Form des hebräischen Namens ṣ : panyāh = Zephanja. Von der "Zephanja-Apokalypse" (Abkürzung : ApcZeph) wird im folgenden gesprochen, wenn die deuterokanonische Schrift gemeint ist, ohne Berücksichtigung der Frage, welche der mit der ApcZeph in Zusammenhang gebrachten Texte diese nun tatsächlich repräsentieren. Diese Texte erhalten eindeutige Bezeichnungen.

[6] Vgl. hierzu die Angaben bei Steindorff (Anm. 17) 22f. und bei J.-M. Rosenstiehl, *L'Apocalypse d'Élie*. Introduction, traduction et notes (Textes et études pour servir à l'histoire du Judaisme Intertestamentaire T. I); Paris, 1972, 13f.

einstimmen oder doch viele gemeinsame Merkmale aufweisen, dürften sie literarisch voneinander abhängen oder doch traditionsgeschichtlich miteinander verwandt sein.[7] Deshalb werden die Listen trotz der verschiedenen Bezeichnungen vermutlich ein und dasselbe Sophonias-Buch im Auge haben. Diese Vermutung wird durch eine Beobachtung des Kontextes bekräftigt, in dem die Sophonias-Schrift erwähnt ist : soweit unsere Kenntnis der genannten Schriften überhaupt ein Urteil zulässt, können wir annehmen, dass es sich bei den verzeichneten Apokrypha zumeist um "apokalyptische" Bücher handelt. Die Listen werden also wohl unabhängig von der jeweils verwendeten Bezeichnung eine Sophonias-Schrift apokalyptischen Inhalts nennen.

Wegen der wahrscheinlichen Abhängigkeit der Listen voneinander wird man aber kaum oder nur mit Vorsicht von verschiedenen Bezeugungen eines in alter Zeit bekannten apokryphen Sophonias-Buches sprechen können. Es wird sich eher um mehrere Varianten einer Bezeugung handeln. Fraglich dürfte zumindest für die späteren unter den Kompilatoren der Kanonlisten sein, ob sie alle von ihnen verzeichneten Bücher noch aus eigener Anschauung kannten. Hier ist "methodischer Zweifel" besonders für solche Schriften geboten, die nicht von der Kirche[8] offiziell benutzt wurden (dh nicht im engeren Sinne "kanonisch" waren) und uns dazu nicht eindeutig überliefert sind. Hierzu gehört das in den Listen erwähnte apokryphe Sophonias-Buch. Der Wert seiner Bezeugung in den Verzeichnissen wird durch diese methodische Überlegung eingeschränkt. Man wird von einer indirekten oder mittelbaren Bezeugung sprechen müssen : Die Kanonlisten bewahren womöglich nur die "Tradition" von der (früheren) Existenz eines apokryphen Sophonias-Buches mit apokalyptischem Inhalt.

1.2   Ein Kirchenschriftsteller-Zitat.

Ein Zitat (im folgenden Z genannt), das möglicherweise aus einer

---

[7] Zu dieser komplizierten Frage vgl. Zahn II bes. 302ff. und Rosenstiehl, *L'Apocalypse d'Élie* 14. — Wie man das Problem traditionsgeschichtlicher Verwandtschaft derartiger Listen methodisch angeht, bedarf vielleicht noch einer Erörterung. Angesichts der Zufälligkeit, der wir die wenigen erhaltenen MSS verdanken, dürfte rein literarkritisches Vorgehen der Frage nicht gerecht werden. Hier bestimmt die Vorstellung von direkter Vorlage und Abschrift zu sehr die Denkstruktur.

[8] Die methodisch und geistesgeschichtlich schwierige Frage, inwieweit Kanonverzeichnisse Rückschlüsse auf die Kirchengemeinschaften erlauben, der die Verfasser oder Kompilatoren jeweils angehören, soll ausgeklammert werden.

mit Sophonias verbundenen Apokalypse stammt, ist uns in den Stromata des Clemens Alexandrinus erhalten :[9]

ἆρ᾽ οὐχ ὅμοια ταῦτα τοῖς ὑπὸ Σοφονία λεχθεῖσι τοῦ προφήτου; "καὶ ἀνέλαβέν με πνεῦμα καὶ ἤνεγκέν με εἰς οὐρανὸν πέμπτον καὶ ἐθεώρουν ἀγγέλους καλουμένους κυρίους, καὶ τὸ διάδημα αὐτῶν ἐπικείμενον ἐν πνεύματι ἁγίῳ καὶ ἦν ἑκάστου αὐτῶν ὁ θρόνος ἑπταπλασίων φωτὸς ἡλίου ἀνατέλλοντος, οἰκοῦντας ἐν ναοῖς σωτηρίας καὶ ὑμνοῦντας θεὸν ἄρρητον ὕψιστον."

In der wissenschaftlichen Literatur wird Z durchweg als ein Bruchstück der in den alten Verzeichnissen erwähnten Zephanja-Apokalypse betrachtet.[10]

Bis gegen Ende des 19. Jh.s war ausser den oben genannten Daten nichts über eine ApcZeph bekannt.

2.   Textfunde vom Ende des 19.Jh.s.

2.1   Die Manuskripte Copte 135 der Bibliothèque Nationale in Paris.

Ein grösseres Bündel koptischer Papyri mit achmimischen und sahidischen Texten konnte im Jahre 1883 vom dēr el-abyaḍ bei Sohag erworben werden.[11] Die Manuskripte befinden sich heute in der Pariser Nationalbibliothek. Vierzehn Folios aus diesem Konvolut in achmimischem und sieben Folios in sahidischem Dialekt mit einem dem achmimischen überwiegend parallelen Text veröffentlichte Urbain Bouriant im Jahre 1885[12] als ApcZeph, wobei er den Fragmenten der nicht durchlaufend erhaltenen MSS eine hypothetische Reihenfolge gab, die Ludwig Stern in seiner deutschen Ausgabe von 1886[13] etwas veränderte. Der Grund für Bouriants Identifikation der MSS mit der aus der Tradition bekannten ApcZeph ist die Erwähnung eines "Sophonias" auf einer Seite des sahidischen MSs.[14]

---

[9] Clemens Alexandrinus, Στρωματεῖς V, XI 77,2 (GCS Clem. Alex. II 377 Ed. O. Stählin-L. Früchtel).

[10] Vgl. zB A. Harnack, *Geschichte der altchristlichen Literatur I*, Leipzig, 1893, 854; Steindorff (Anm. 17) 20.

[11] Vgl. zum folgenden Steindorff (Anm. 17) 1-3.

[12] U. Bouriant, *Les papyrus d'Akhmim. Fragments de manuscrits en dialectes Bachmourique et Thébain* (Mémoires publiés par les membres de la Mission Archéologique française au Caire, I, 2), Paris, 1884 (erschienen 1885), 260-279.

[13] L. Stern, Die koptische Apokalypse des Sophonias, *ZÄS* 24 (1886), 115-129.

[14] Sa. 1,22-23 nach der Numerierung Steindorffs, die um der Eindeutigkeit willen beibehalten werden soll.

2.2 Das Manuskript P 1862 der Staatlichen Museen zu Berlin.

Im Jahre 1888 entdeckte man bei einem Antiquitätenhändler in Achmim weitere acht, oder genauer gesagt : neun Folios desselben achmimischen Papyrus, zu dem die 14 als ApcZeph veröffentlichten gehörten.[15] Dieser Teil des MSs gehört heute den Staatlichen Museen zu Berlin (Ost). Dieser Fund markiert einen neuen Abschnitt in unserer Kenntnis des antiken jüdischen und frühchristlichen Schrifttums im Umkreis der Bibel. Das Verso eines Blattes (vermutlich handelt es sich um die letzte Seite des MSs[16]) trägt die Unterschrift

†ΑΠΟΚΑΛΥΨΙΣ
Ν2ΗΛΕΙΑΣ

Diese Information regte Georg Steindorff dazu an, das Problem der Anordnung und der Identifikation der Textfragmente sowohl des achmimischen wie auch des sahidischen MSs neu zu durchdenken. In seiner Ausgabe der zuvor schon von Bouriant und Stern veröffentlichten Texte und der neuentdeckten Teile des achmimischen MSs, die im Jahre 1899 erschien und noch immer "demeure l'ouvrage de base",[17] weist Steindorff den grösseren Teil des achmimischen Textes (S. 19-44 in seiner Zählung) und den weitaus grössten Teil des sahidischen MSs (Sa. 3-14) der ebenfalls aus alten Kanonverzeichnissen und durch mehrere Erwähnungen im altkirchlichen Schrifttum bekannten[18] Apokalypse des Elias (ApcEl) zu. Die Bezeichnung ApcZeph behält nur ein Blatt : das sahidische Folio (Sa. 1-2), das "Sophonias" beim Namen nennt (im folgenden S [= Sophonias-Text] genannt). Neun Folios des achmimischen MSs (S. 1-18), deren Text offensichtlich S verwandt, wenngleich an keiner Stelle direkt parallel ist, die aber keinen Namen enthalten, mit dem die Schrift sich hypothetisch identifizieren liesse, erhalten von Steindorff die provisorische Bezeichnung "Anonyme Apokalypse" (im folgenden A [= anonymer Text] genannt). Bis heute ergaben sich noch keine Gesichtspunkte, die einen Falsifizierungsversuch der hypothetischen Unterscheidung zwischen einer achmimischen und einer sahidischen Fassung der ApcEl auf der einen Seite und den übrigen Texten der beiden MSS auf der anderen

---

[15] Vgl. zum folgenden Steindorff (Anm. 17) 3 ff.

[16] S. 44; vgl. auch Steindorff (Anm. 17) 4.

[17] Rosenstiehl, *L'Apocalypse d'Élie*, 21. — G. Steindorff, *Die Apokalypse des Elias, eine unbekannte Apokalypse und Bruchstücke der Sophonias-Apokalypse. Koptische Texte, Übersetzung, Glossar.* (TU 17, 3), Leipzig, 1899.

[18] Vgl. Rosenstiehl, *l.c.* 13-17.

Seite sinnvoll erscheinen liessen. Deshalb kann bei unserer Betrachtung von dieser Unterscheidung ausgegangen werden. Praktisch bedeutet das : die von Steindorff als ApcEl identifizierten Textpartien der beiden MSS bleiben bei einer Untersuchung des Komplexes "Zephanja-Apokalypse" ausser Betracht.

Paul Riessler unterscheidet in seiner deutschsprachigen Ausgabe altjüdischen Schrifttums im Umkreis der Bibel von 1928[19] S und A durch römische Ziffern. Er spricht von ApcZeph I. und II. — Herbert-Pierrepont Houghton fasst in seiner Ausgabe von 1959[20] S und die sahidische Fassung der ApcEl ohne jede Begründung "sous le titre inattendu"[21] "Sahidic Sophonias Apocalypse" zusammen.

Die hier beobachteten Differenzen zeigen, dass man sich nicht mit "der Zephanja-Apokalypse" befassen kann, ohne das Verhältnis der relevanten Texte zueinander durchdacht zu haben. Zu den "relevanten" Texten gehört auch Z. Ich hebe das hervor, weil Z bisher mehr oder weniger ausdrücklich, stets aber fraglos (dh ohne dass die Frage gestellt wurde, ob und unter welchen Bedingungen dies möglich sei) der ApcZeph zugerechnet wurde.

3.   Das literarische Verhältnis von S, A und Z zueinander.

3.0   Die Formulierung der die Untersuchung leitenden Fragen.

Literarkritische Probleme begegnen bei den traditionell zum Komplex "Zephanja-Apokalypse" gerechneten Texten auf zwei Ebenen. Eine Ebene ist das traditionsgeschichtliche und literarische Verhältnis der Texte S, A und Z zueinander. Die andere ist die Ebene der literarischen Produktionsvorgänge, denen die Texte S und besonders A ihre vorliegende Gestalt verdanken. Hier soll nur das in den Abschnitten 1 und 2 entwickelte Problem behandelt werden, also die zuerst genannte Ebene.

Zur Klärung des literarischen Verhältnisses der Texte S, A und Z zueinander sind folgende Fragen sinnvoll :

1. Gibt es Hinweise für die Annahme, dass es sich bei S und A um ein sahidisches bzw. um achmimische Fragmente e i n e s antiken Buches oder verschiedener Rezensionen dieses e i n e n Buches handelt?

---

[19] P. Riessler, *Altjüdisches Schrifttum ausserhalb der Bibel.* Heidelberg 1928. (2. Aufl. Reprographischer Nachdruck Heidelberg 1966), 168-177.
[20] H.-P. Houghton, The Coptic Apocalypse, *Aegyptus* 39 (1959), 40-91. 179-210; davon S und ApcEl(sah) : S. 41-67; A : S. 68-91.
[21] Rosenstiehl, *l.c.* 23 Anm. 27.

2. Gibt es Hinweise für die Annahme, dass es sich bei Z um das Bruchstück einer griechischen Fassung oder Rezension entweder von S oder von A oder von dem Buch handelt, das S und A womöglich gemeinsam bezeugen?

3. Gibt es Hinweise für eine hypothetische Identifikation von S, A und Z, oder von zweien oder einem dieser Texte mit der apokryphen Sophonias-Schrift, deren Name uns in den alten Kanonverzeichnissen überliefert ist und die diese Listen eventuell im Auge hatten?

Da die hypothetische Beantwortung einer vorausgehenden dieser Fragen den Horizont der jeweils folgenden eingrenzt, ist es sinnvoll, die Fragen in der genannten Reihenfolge zu behandeln.

3.1. Das Verhältnis der Texte S und A zueinander.

Einige Beobachtungen sprechen für die Annahme, S und A als sahidische bzw. achmimische Fassung oder Version eines apokalyptischen Buches zu betrachten.

1. S und A enthalten eine Reihe vergleichbarer Motive, die zT mit sehr ähnlichen Begriffen, Wendungen und Formulierungen geschildert werden. Man vergleiche hierzu S 1, 8-10[22]

ⲁⲓⲣϩⲟⲧⲉ ⲁⲓⲛⲟⲭ⸗
ⲧ ⲁ[ⲭ]ⲛ̄ⲡⲁϩⲟ ϩⲱⲥⲁⲉ ⲛ̄ⲧⲉ-
ⲛⲁⲃ̄ⲗ̄ⲗⲉ ⲛ̄ⲥⲉⲃⲱⲗ ⲉⲃⲟⲗ

mit A 5, 4-5

ⲧⲁⲣⲓⲛⲟⲁⲉ ⲁⲣⲁⲩ ⲁⲓⲣ̄ϩⲛⲱⲱ⸗
ϩⲉ

und mit A 7, 16-19

ⲁⲛⲁⲕ ⳓⲉ ⲧⲁⲣⲓⲛⲟ[23] ⲁⲉⲓⲡⲁϩⲧ ⲁϩⲣⲏ⸗
ⲓ̈ ⲁⲭⲛ̄ⲡⲁϩⲱ ⲙ̄ⲡϥⲙ̄ⲧⲟ ⲁⲃⲁⲗ
ⲭⲁⲉⲓⲛⲁⲟⲩⲱϣⲧ ⲛⲉϥ ⲁⲓ̈ⲣ̄ϩⲛⲱ⸗
ⲱϩⲉ ⲙ̄ⲡϣⲁ

---

[22] Die hier gegebenen Texte entstanden mit Hilfe neuer Photographien der Manuskripte in Paris und Berlin (Ost), die mir freundlicherweise für die geplante Edition überlassen wurden. Daraus erklären sich einige Abweichungen vom koptischen Text Steindorffs. Vgl. hierzu bes. unten Anm. 28.

[23] Vielleicht ist hier im Blick auf den Sprachgebrauch an anderen Stellen der Schrift (8, 14; 10, 2) ⲁⲡⲁϥ zu ergänzen; vgl. hierzu P. Lacau, Remarques sur le manuscrit achmimique des Apocalypses de Sophonie et d'Élie, *JA* 254 (1966), S. 184.

sowie schliesslich besonders mit A 8, 14-19

     ⲁⲛⲁⲕ ⲇⲉ ⲧⲁⲣⲓⲛⲟ ⲁⲣⲁϥ ⲁⲓ⸗
ⲣ̄ ϩⲛⲱⲱϩⲉ ϩⲏⲧϥ ϩ̇ⲱⲥⲧⲉ ⲁⲧⲉ-
ⲛⲁⲙⲉⲗⲟⲥ ⲧⲏⲣⲟⲩ ⲙⲡⲁⲥⲱⲙⲁ ⲃ⸗
ⲱⲗ ⲁⲃⲁⲗ ⲁⲓⲡⲁϩⲧ ⲁϩⲣⲏⲓ̈ ⲁⲭⲙ̄-
ⲡⲁϩⲱ ⲙ̄ⲡⲓⲃ̄ⲛⲃⲁⲙ ⲛ̄ϩⲱϩⲉ ²⁴ ⲁⲣ⸗
ⲉⲉⲧ

Ferner vergleiche man S 1, 10-15

                    ⲁϥϯ-
ⲧⲟⲟⲧ ⲛ̄ϭⲓⲡⲁⲅⲅⲉⲗⲟⲥ ⲡⲉⲭⲁϥ
ⲛ̣ⲁ̣ⲓ̈ ⲭⲉ ⲉⲣⲟ ⲡⲉⲕⲛⲁⲭⲣⲟ ²⁵ ⲁ̣ⲩⲱ
ϭ]ⲙ̄ϭⲟⲙ ⲡⲉⲕⲛⲁⲭⲣⲟ ⲁⲡⲕⲁⲧ⸗
ⲧ̣ⲏⲅⲟⲣⲟⲥ ⲁⲩⲱ ⲕⲛⲏⲟⲩⲉ⸗
ϩⲣⲁ̣ⲓ̈ ϩⲛ̄ⲁⲙⲛ̄[ⲧ]ⲉ

mit A 12, 10-15

         ⲁⲛⲁ ϭⲉ ⲁⲓ̈ⲧⲱⲛⲉ ⲁⲓ̈ⲱϩⲉ
ⲁ]ⲣⲉⲉⲧ ⲁⲓ̈ⲛⲟ ⲁⲩⲛⲁϭ ⲛ̄ⲁⲅⲅⲉⲗⲟⲥ ⲙ̄ⲡⲁ⸗
ⲙ̣ⲧⲟ ⲁⲃⲁⲗ ⲉϥⲭⲟⲩⲙ̄ⲙⲁⲥ ⲛⲉⲓ̈ ⲭⲉⲭⲣⲟ
ϭ]ⲛ̄ⲃⲁⲙ ⲭⲉ ⲁⲕϭ̄ⲛⲃⲁⲙ ⲁⲕϭⲣⲟ ⲁⲡⲕⲁ⸗
        ⲧⲏⲅⲟⲣⲟⲥ ⲁⲕⲉⲓ ⲁϩⲣⲏⲓ̈ ²⁶ ϩ̄ⲛ-
ⲁⲙⲛ̄ⲧⲉ ⲙⲛ̄ⲡⲛⲟⲩⲛ

und mit A 13, 19 - 14, 3

     ⲭⲣⲟ ⲙ̄ⲙⲁⲕ ⲡⲉⲓ̈ ⲉⲧⲁϥⲭⲣⲟ ϭ̄ⲛ-
ⲃⲁⲙ ⲡⲉⲓ̈ ⲉⲧⲁϥϭ̄ⲛⲃⲁⲙ ⲛⲧⲁⲕ ⲅⲁⲣ
ⲁϭⲃⲣⲟ ²⁷ ⲁⲡⲕⲁⲧⲏⲅⲟⲣⲟⲥ ⲁⲕⲣ̄ ⲁⲃⲁⲗ ⲛ̄⸗
ⲧⲟⲟⲧϥ ⲛ̄ⲡⲛⲟⲩⲛ ⲙⲛ̄ ⲁⲙⲛ̄ⲧⲉ

Man vergleiche schliesslich noch S 1, 23-33

           ⲁⲩⲱ
ⲛⲁϥⲙⲟⲟϣⲉ [ⲛ]ⲙ̣ⲁⲉⲓ ⲛ̄ϭⲓⲡⲁⲅ⸗
ⲅⲉⲗⲟⲥ ⲙ̄ⲡⲭ[ⲟ]ⲉⲓⲥ ⲁⲓ̈ⲛⲁⲩ ⲉⲩ⸗
ⲛⲟϭ ⲙ̄ⲙⲁ ⲉ[ϥⲟ]ⲩⲟϣ̄ⲥ ⲉⲃⲟⲗ
ⲉⲩⲕⲱⲧⲉ ⲉⲣ[ⲟϥ] ⲛ̄ϭⲓ̣ ϩⲛ̄ϣⲟ ϣⲟ

---

²⁴ Statt ⲛ̄ϩⲱϩⲉ 1 ⲛ̄ⲱϩⲉ; vgl. Steindorff 49 Anm. 4 und Lacau, *JA* 254, 184.
²⁵ Vgl. hierzu Steindorff 111 Anm. 4.
²⁶ Vgl. hierzu Steindorff 55 Anm. 2.
²⁷ Vgl. zu der Form Lacau, *JA* 254, 186.

ⲛⲥⲁ ϩⲃⲟⲟⲩⲣ[ⲙ⟨ⲙⲟ⟩]ϥ ⲁⲩⲱ ϩ[ⲛ⸗
ⲧⲃⲁ ⲛ̄ⲧⲃⲁ ⲛ̄[ⲥⲁ⟨ⲟⲩⲛ⟩]ⲉⲙ ⲙ̄ⲙ⸗
ⲙ̄ⲙⲟϥ ⲟⲩⲉⲧ ⲧⲙ̄[⟨ⲓⲛⲉ⟩] ⲙ̄ⲙ[ⲡⲟⲩⲁ
ⲡⲟⲩⲁ : ⲉⲣⲉ ⲛⲉⲩ[⟨ϥⲱⲉ ⲃⲏⲗ⟩ⲉⲃⲟⲗ
ⲛ̄ⲑⲉ ⲛ̄ⲛⲁⲛⲓϩⲓⲟⲙ̣[⟨ⲉ ⲉⲣⲉ⟩ⲛⲉⲩ⸗
ⲁⲃϩⲉ ⲟ ⲛ̄ⲛⲑⲉ [⟨ⲛⲛⲁⲃϩⲉ ⲛ̄⟩²⁸

mit A 8, 8-12

ⲉⲡ̄ϥϥⲟⲩⲉ
ⲡⲁⲣϩ ⲁⲃⲁⲗ ⲛ̄ⲧϩⲉ ⲛ̄ⲛⲓⲗⲁⲃⲁⲓ̈ ⲉⲛⲉϥ⸗
ⲛⲉⲉⲝⲉ ⲙ̄ⲡⲃⲗ̄ ⲛ̄ⲣⲱϥ ⲛ̄ⲧϩⲉ ⲛⲟⲩ⸗
ⲁⲣⲕⲟⲥ ⲉⲡ̄ϥϥⲟⲩⲉ ⲡⲁⲣϩ ⲁⲃⲁⲗ ⲛ̄⸗
ⲧϩⲉ ⲛ̄ⲛϩⲓⲁⲁⲙⲉ

und besonders mit A 4, 13 - 5, 4

ⲁⲛⲁⲕ ϭⲉ ⲛⲁⲉⲓⲙⲁϩⲉ ⲙⲛ̄⸗
ⲡ]ⲁ̣ⲅⲅⲉⲗⲟⲥ ⲙ̄ⲡⲭⲁⲉⲓⲥ ⲁⲉⲓⲥⲱⲛⲧ
ⲙ̄]ⲡⲁⲙⲧⲟ ⲁⲃⲁⲗ ⲁⲓ̈ⲛⲟ ⲁⲩⲙⲁ ⲙⲟ
ⲙⲛ̄ ϩⲉ]ⲛ̣ϩⲟ ⲙⲛ̄ ϩⲉⲛⲧⲃⲁ ⲛ̄ⲧⲃⲁ ⲛ̄ⲁⲅ⸗
ⲅⲉⲗⲟⲥ] ⲉⲩⲙⲁⲁϩⲉ ⲁϩ[ⲟ]ⲩⲛ ϩⲓⲧⲟⲟⲧ⸗
ϥ ⲉⲡⲟ]ⲩ̣ϩⲱ ⲉ ⲛ̄ⲧϩⲉ ⲛ̣ⲟⲩⲡⲁⲣⲁⲁ⸗
ⲗⲓⲥ ⲉ]ⲛⲟⲩϩⲁⲗ ⲙ̄ⲡⲃⲗ̄ ⲛ̄ⲣⲱⲟⲩ ⲛ̄⸗
ⲧϩⲉ ⲛ̄]ⲛⲓϣⲁϩⲉⲩⲧ ⲉⲛⲟⲩⲃⲉⲗ
ⲧⲏϩ ϩⲓⲥⲛⲁϥ ⲉ ⲡⲟⲩϥⲟⲩⲉ ⲃⲏⲗ ⲁⲃⲁ⸗
ⲗ ⲛ̄ⲧϩⲉ ⲙ̄ⲡϥⲟⲩⲉ ⲛ̄ⲛϩⲓⲁⲙⲉ ⲉⲩ⸗
ⲛ̄ ϩⲉⲛⲫⲣⲁⲅⲉⲗⲓⲟⲛ ⲛ̄ⲕⲱϩⲧ ϩ̄ⲛⲛⲟ⸗
ⲩϭⲓⲝ

Diese sowohl in S wie auch in A begegnenden Motive machen 50
Prozent der lesbaren Textmenge von S aus. Deshalb möchte man zum
mindesten an eine traditionsgeschichtliche Verwandtschaft zwischen
S und A denken.

2. Text A weist drei grössere Lücken auf²⁹ : am Anfang, zwischen
den Seiten 12 und 13, sowie am Schluss (nach S. 18). Vom Umfang her
geurteilt hätte ein S entsprechender achmimischer Abschnitt in jeder
dieser Lücken Platz gefunden.

---

²⁸ Die Winkelklammern < ... > geben an, welche Textteile Steindorff wohl noch
lesen konnte, die aber inzwischen offenbar verloren gingen.
²⁹ Vgl. Steindorff 9.10f.

Einige Beobachtungen sprechen gegen die oben geäusserte Annahme :

1. Motivfolge und Gedankengang von S begegnen nicht in A.

2. Geht man aus von Steindorffs Überlegungen zur Konzeption von A und von seinen daraus folgenden Vermutungen über den Inhalt der verloren gegangenen Teile dieses Textes,[30] so kommt eigentlich keine der Lücken für eine S entsprechende Passage infrage.

3. Bei dem Versuch, das literarische Verhältnis zweier Texte zu bestimmen, ist eine methodische Voraussetzung zu beachten, die mE gerade bei so "typisch geprägter" Literatur wie der apokalyptischen berücksichtigt werden muss : Für die Annahme, zwei — zudem nur fragmentarisch erhaltene — Texte seien literarisch voneinander abhängig oder seien gar Teile zweier verschiedener Fassungen oder Rezensionen eines und desselben Buches genügt nicht eine Übereinstimmung in allgemeinen Zügen oder in geprägten Wendungen, Formeln und Motiven, die "typisch" sind für einen bestimmten Texttyp ("Gattung"), es sei denn, diese allgemeinen Züge begegneten in beiden Texten in einer bestimmten, in anderen Texten so nicht üblichen Reihenfolge. In diesem Falle können auch generelle Merkmale für einen Text "charakteristisch" sein.[31] Sichereres Kriterium für literarische Verwandtschaft im oben beschriebenen Sinne ist die Entsprechung oder Übereinstimmung in möglichst "individuellen", besonderen Merkmalen, die nicht für den Texttyp als solchen charakteristisch sind. Unter dieser methodischen Voraussetzungen muss man die Entsprechungen zwischen S und A differenziert betrachten :

a) S 1,8-10 (die Furcht des Sehers angesichts einer "schrecklichen" Offenbarung), 23-26 (geleitet vom angelus interpres wechselt der Seher von einem Ort apokalyptischer Offenbarung zu einem andern über) und 27-29 (die "tausendmal tausend" und "zehntausendmal zehntausend" Engel) sind wohl die "gattungstypischsten" Elemente in S, die auch in A begegnen. Hierzu könnte man noch S 1,1.15-22 (der Seher schaut eine gepeinigte Seele und erfragt den Grund für ihre Qual) rechnen, ein Element, das so in A nicht bezeugt ist.

b) S 1,30-33 (die Beschreibung der Engel, die am Ort der Qual Dienst tun) ist ein Motiv, das weniger häufig in der apokalyptischen Literatur begegnet, das aber doch sprachlich stark "traditionell" geprägt und somit "typisch" wirkt. Ähnlich könnte man S 1,2-8 (Engel bewachen, entführen und schlagen die sündige Seele) beurteilen, ein Motiv, das in A nicht bezeugt ist.

---

[30] Vgl. Steindorff 10f.
[31] Vgl. aber hierzu im Blick auf unsere Texte, was bei 1. gesagt wurde.

c) Lediglich S 1, 10-15 (die Ermunterung des Engels an den Seher durchzuhalten) dürfte nicht im eigentlichen Sinne "typisch" sein für unsere apokalyptische Literatur, obgleich das zugrunde liegende Motiv (der Held muss allerlei Anfechtung und Gefahr auf sich nehmen, bevor er schliesslich die Mächte der Finsternis überwindet) in vielen Legenden und Märchen begegnet.

Nur die zuletzt erwähnte Passage aus S berechtigt dazu, eine nähere Verwandtschaft zwischen S und A anzunahmen. Damit soll aber noch keine Vorentscheidung über die Art dieser Verwandtschaft gefällt sein. Denn trotz aller Ähnlichkeit haben S 1, 10-15 und die entsprechenden Abschnitte in A (12, 10-15; 13, 19 - 14, 3) verschiedenen Funktionen. In A (12, 11; 13, 14 f.) ermuntert ογnaб naггελoc den Seher und bestätigt ihm, dass er den "Ankläger" und die Unterwelt überwunden habe (14, 1-4). In S ermutigt der angelus interpres den Propheten. Man vermisst in A keinen weiteren Appell dieser Art an den Seher, schon gar nicht aus dem Munde des Begleitengels. Man kann sich auch schwer vorstellen, wo eine solche Passage gestanden haben sollte: kaum in der Lücke zwischen den Seiten 12 und 13 und noch weniger wahrscheinlich am Beginn der Schrift. Der nicht erhaltene Schluss dürfte nach 13, 19 - 14, 4 gar nicht infrage kommen.[32]

S enthält hauptsächlich Elemente, die für einen bestimmten Typ apokalyptischer Literatur "typisch" sind. Diese Elemente können nur dann zur Stützung der Annahme verwendet werden, es handle sich bei S und A um zwei Fassungen oder Rezensionen eines bestimmten Buches, wenn sie in beiden Texten in einer in wesentlichen Zügen übereinstimmenden Reihenfolge vorkommen. Das ist nicht der Fall und kann auch nicht für die verlorenen Abschnitte von A postuliert werden. Selbst das "untypischste" Element in S (1, 10-15) erscheint in einem andern Verwendungszusammenhang als die entsprechenden Abschnitte von A.

In dieser Lage erhält ein eher zufälliger Tatbestand etwas argumentatives Gewicht: unglücklicherweise nennt A nicht den Namen des apokalyptischen Sehers.[33] Dieser dürfte zum mindesten am nicht erhaltenen Beginn des Buches erwähnt worden sein. Allerdings ist die Anonymität des Sehers von A für unsere Überlegungen methodisch nicht von grosser Bedeutung. Schriften im Umkreis der Bibel können unter verschiedenen Pseudonymen tradiert werden und doch literarisch

---

[32] Vgl. Steindorff 15 f.
[33] Vgl. Steindorff 13-16, bes. 14 f. Anm. 1; S. 11 erwägt Steindorff, ob der Seher in einer verloren gegangenen Unterschrift ähnlich Elia S. 44 hätte genannt sein können.

eng verwandt sein. Umgekehrt bedeutet dasselbe Pseudonym grund-
sätzlich noch keine literarische Verwandtschaft.

Mit allen nötigen Vorbehalten im Blick auf den Erhaltungszustand
der Texte lässt sich über das Verhältnis zwischen S und A sagen:
S und A gehören zu traditionsgeschichtlich nahe verwandten Büchern.
Eine literarische Abhängigkeit der Schriften voneinander ist nicht aus-
zuschliessen. S und A sind jedoch kaum Fragmente einer sahidischen
bzw. achmimischen Fassung eines und desselben apokalyptischen
Buches. Bestenfalls bezeugen sie zwei voneinander stark abweichende
Rezensionen einer Schrift.

3.2.   Das Verhältnis der Texte Z und S(/A) zueinander.

Einige Beobachtungen sprechen für die Neigung,[34] Z als Bruchstück einer griechischen (Original-)Fassung der ApcZeph zu betrachten,
dessen Entsprechung uns in einem koptischen Text nicht erhalten ist:

1. Vor der Entdeckung von S und A kannte man nur den Titel einer
Sophonias-Schrift mit apokalyptischem Inhalt und das Sophonias in
den Mund gelegte Zitat bei Clemens Alexandrinus.

2. Clemens zitiert ein apokalyptisches Wort des "Sophonias". In
S 1, 22-23 nennt sich der Seher selbst "coφωΝιΑc".

3. Z und S sind Bruchstücke apokalypher Literatur.

4. Bislang wurde von S nur ein Folio gefunden.[35] Nur eine Seite
dieses Folios ist lesbar. Z könnte gut zu dem uns nicht zugänglichen
grösseren Teil von S gehört haben.

5. Man darf annehmen, dass nicht viele apokalyptische Bücher innerhalb der antiken jüdisch-christlichen Literatur unter dem Namen
des alttestamentlichen Propheten Zephanja = Sophonias verfasst und
tradiert wurden. Bis zu einem gewissen Grade darf man daraus folgern,
dass zwei antike Fragmente apokalyptischer Schriften, die mit dem
Namen dieses Propheten verbunden sind, zusammengehören, auch
wenn sie in verschiedenen Sprachen abgefasst sind und auf recht unter-
schiedlichen Wegen uns zur Kenntnis kamen.

Einige Beobachtungen stehen dieser "Neigung" entgegen:

1. Trotz des zuletzt genannten Arguments für die Meinung, Z und S
gehörten zu der gleichen apokalyptischen Schrift, muss man mit der

---

[34] Weil diese generell vertretene Auffassung mW nie methodisch überprüft wurde,
vermeide ich es, sie als "Annahme" oder gar "Hypothese" zu bezeichnen.

[35] Der Fund von 1888 zeigt, dass die Entdeckung weiterer Blätter des sahidischen
Sophonias-Buches nicht auszuschliessen ist.

Möglichkeit rechnen, dass zu antiker Zeit mehr als ein ausserkanonisches, vielleicht sogar mehr als ein apokalyptisches Buch unter dem Pseudonym "Sophonias" tradiert wurde, gleichgültig ob diese Schriften traditionsgeschichtlich oder literarisch miteinander verwandt gewesen sein mögen oder nicht. Man vergleiche hierzu die verschiedenen Schriften, die zB unter den Pseudonymen "Esra", "Elia", "Jesaja", "Henoch", u.a.m. verbreitet waren.

2. In den meisten apokalyptischen Schriften, in denen ein menschlicher Offenbarungsempfänger, der in überweltliche Mysterien eingeweiht wird, von einem "Ort" zu einem andern weitergeht, wird er von einem oder mehreren Engeln geleitet. Man vergleiche hierzu ausser S und A zB: ApcAbr, ApcBar[gr], ApcEsr, Hen[äth], Hen[sl], TestIs, TestAbr. Dieser Engel steht dem Seher für Auskünfte zur Verfügung ("angelus interpres"). Vergleichsweise wenige Texte berichten wie Z, dass der Geist den Seher von einem Offenbarungsort zum andern transferiert (aber, nota bene, nicht eigentlich leitet oder als Interpret wirkt): etwa das kanonische Hesekielbuch oder die ApcEl(hb). Dass innerhalb einer Schrift einmal der Geist den Seher transferiert, dann aber wieder der angelus interpres ihn geleitet, wird man kaum erwarten dürfen. Es wäre natürlich vorstellbar, dass bei verschiedenen Rezensionen einer Schrift der Transfer einmal vom Geist, das andere Mal durch einen Engel besorgt wird. Wann immer aber die Funktion des Transfers mit der des ständigen Geleits und des Erklärens verbunden ist, wird ein angelus interpres benötigt. Mir sind kaum Texte bekannt, wo der Geist als angelus interpres fungiert.[36] Daher ist es nicht sehr wahrscheinlich, dass die von Clemens zitierte Apokalypse demselben Typ angehörte wie S, wo der angelus interpres vermutlich, wie auch in A, konstitutiv ist.

3. Mit einiger Wahrscheinlichkeit, wenngleich auch nicht aufgrund zwingender Argumente, darf man als verlorenen Kontext von Z eine apokalyptische Himmelsreise vom Typ der griechischen ApcBar oder des slavischen Henoch annehmen, wo der Seher in immer höhere Himmel gelangt.[37] Anderseits gibt es Beispiele dafür, dass der Seher auf Anhieb bis in den dritten Himmel emporgeführt wird.[38]

---

[36] Am ehesten vgl. Hes 11, 1 ff., weniger Hes 3, 24 ff.
[37] Die Verwandtschaft zwischen Z und der AscJes 7, 13 ff. (ed. A. Dillmann, Ascensio Isaiae Aethiopice et Latine, Leipzig, 1877, 31; vgl. Steindorff 20) soll hier angemerkt werden.
[38] Vgl. die ApcSedr 2, 4 (Riessler 157).

Der geringe Umfang von Z und der fragmentarische Zustand von S erlauben kaum weitere Aussagen. Ich glaube allerdings, das Gewicht der drei letzten Überlegungen spricht für die Annahme, dass Z und S zwei recht verschiedenen Sophonias-Apokalypsen angehören. Hierbei wird stillschweigend vorausgesetzt, dass Z überhaupt einer Schrift entnommen wurde, die zur Zeit des Clemens Alexandrinus unter dem Pseudonym "Sophonias" tradiert wurde.

Sollten Z und S, entgegen den hier angestellten Wahrscheinlich-keits-Überlegungen, die griechische bzw. sahidische Fassung oder Rezension einer und derselben Apokalypse repräsentieren, so wäre dies allerdings ein weiterer Grund gegen die Hypothese, dass S und A als verschiedene Rezensionen oder gar Fassungen eines Buches zu betrachten seien. Nicht nur dass eine Z entsprechende Passage in A nicht bezeugt ist, obwohl diese Schrift doch, Steindorffs begründeten Erwägungen zufolge,[39] zu drei Vierteln ihres vermutlichen Umfangs erhalten sein dürfte; die erhaltenen Teile von A geben keinen Hinweis dafür, zu welchem Teil des verlorenen Textes eine Z entsprechende Passage gehört haben könnte. Das gilt auch für den verlorenen Schluss von A, wo man eine derartige himmlische Vision noch am ehesten erwarten würde.

Alle diese Überlegungen vernachlässigen einen, methodisch allerdings kaum fassbaren Umstand: dass zumal in antiker apokalyptischer Literatur nahezu alles möglich ist.[40]

3.3 Das Verhältnis der Erwähnungen eines Sophonias-Buchs in alten Kanonverzeichnissen zu den Texten Z, S und A.

Oben (vgl. 1.1) wurde besprochen, dass die verschiedenen Listen apokrypher Literatur im Umkreis der Bibel vermutlich voneinander abhängen und so nur als ein "external evidence" für ein ausserkanonisches Sophonias-Buch gelten können. Zudem ergab sich, dass unabhängig von der jeweils verwendeten Bezeichnung des Sophonias-Apokryphons (ψευδεπίγραφον, προφητεία oder ἀποκάλυψις) stets ein

---

[39] Vgl. Steindorff 9-11.
[40] Ich möchte hier an W. Boussets im Blick auf die ApcEl geprägtes Wort von der apokalyptischen "Mosaikarbeit" (Beiträge zur Geschichte der Eschatologie. Die Apokalypse des Elias, *ZKG* 20 [1900], 104) erinnern, das gewiss auch für andere Schriften dieses Genres gilt. Oft scheint es, als gebe es ein Repertoire von Bausteinen, Bedeutungsträgern eines apokalyptischen "Geheimcodes", dessen Elemente sich in anscheinend unbegrenzter Variabilität kombinieren und auch ergänzen lassen — wenn es gilt, die Tradition neuen Situationen und Interessen anzupassen.

und dasselbe Buch, und zwar ein Buch apokalyptischen Charakters, gemeint sein dürfte.

Die Beantwortung der Frage dieses Abschnitts unserer Betrachtung wurde durch die Ergebnisse der Erwägungen in den Abschnitten 3.1 und 3.2 bereits vorgeklärt.

1. In Abschnitt 3.1 ergab sich wenig Wahrscheinlichkeit für die Annahme, dass S und A zwei Fassungen oder auch nur zwei verschiedenartige Rezensionen eines Buches bezeugen. Überlegungen im letzten Teil von Abschnitt 3.2 gingen in die gleiche Richtung. Daher möchte man kaum meinen, dass A in der Antike unter dem Pseudonym "Sophonias" tradiert wurde.[41] Das bedeutet: A ist kaum mit dem Sophonias-Buch identisch, das die Tradition der Kanonverzeichnisse im Auge hat.

2. Den Überlegungen in 3.2 zufolge sind Z und S kaum Fragmente einer griechischen bzw. sahidischen Fassung oder Rezension eines und desselben Buches. Allerdings gehören beide Texte zu apokalyptischen Schriften, und beide Schriften wurden vermutlich als Sophonias-Bücher betrachtet. Deshalb ist es wahrscheinlich, dass eines der beiden Bücher die ApcZeph ist, die die Tradition der Apokryphenlisten kennt.

Es ist mE zulässig, darüber zu spekulieren, welches der beiden infrage kommenden Bücher dies gewesen sein könnte. — In allen der genannten Kataloge finden wir ein Eliasbuch und ein Sophoniasbuch. Entweder folgt letzteres direkt auf das erstere, oder beide sind durch nur einen weiteren Titel, ein Jesaja-Buch, voneinander getrennt. Offenbar gehörten beide Schriften in der Tradition eng zusammen.[42] Eine derartige Zusammenstellung eines Elia- und eines Sophonias-Buchs begegnet ausserhalb der Listen in dem sahidischen MS, zu dem S gehört. Dieses MS enthält ja ausser dem Folio mit dem Namen "Sophonias" noch sechs weitere Blätter, deren Text mit dem Teil des achmimischen MSs parallel geht, zu dem die Unterschrift "Apokalypse des Elia" auf der vermutlich letzten MS-Seite gehört. Dh das sahidische MS

---

[41] Vgl. oben S. 161f. zum "methodischen Gewicht" von Namensgleichheit und Namensungleichheit bei der Erörterung der Frage, in welchem literarischen Verwandtschaftsverhältnis zwei (apokalyptische) Schriften aus dem Umkreis der Bibel stehen. Hier geht es indessen um die literarische "Identität" zweier Schriften, zu der dann auch wesentlich die Identität der (angeblichen) Person des Verfassers gehört.

[42] Hier muss daran erinnert werden, dass die Kataloge womöglich nur als ein einziger "external evidence", in diesem Fall für eine traditionelle Verbindung der beiden Apokalypsen betrachtet werden können; vgl. oben bei 1.1. (Gerade deshalb aber könnte das Nebeneinander der beiden Schriften in den Listen auch rein zufällig sein und gar keine Rückschlüsse erlauben.)

bezeugt ausser einem Sophonias-Buch noch eine Elia-Apokalypse. Nehmen wir an, dies sei nicht irgend eine denkbare andere ApcEl, sondern die von der Tradition der Kanonverzeichnisse gemeinte, dann können wir folgern, dass die in den Katalogen erwähnte ApcZeph eher mit S identisch ist als mit Z.

Daher ist es wahrscheinlich, dass uns mit dem kleinen Fragment S ein Teil jener ApcZeph in die Hände kam, über deren Existenz in alter Zeit wir durch die mittelalterlichen, auf antiker Tradition basierenden Kanonverzeichnisse seit langem unterrichtet waren.

4. Das Ergebnis.

Die sehr hypothetischen Resultate unserer Überlegungen sollen der Einfachheit halber thetisch formuliert werden. Für die nötigen Differenzierungen verweise ich auf die Teile 1-3 dieser Erwägungen.

1. Das sahidische Fragment S (Sa. 1-2 in Steindorffs Zählung; Teil der MSS Copte 135 der BN Paris) ist ein Bruchstück der aus antiker Tradition bekannten Zephanja-Apokalypse. Steindorffs Annahme konnte in diesem Punkte bestätigt werden.

2. Die nur wenig fragmentarische Schrift A (S. 1-18 in Steindorffs Zählung; Teil der MSS Copte der BN Paris [S. 1-12.17-18] und [von P 1862] der Staatlichen Museen zu Berlin [S. 13-16]) kann trotz inhaltlicher Verwandtschaft mit S nicht als achmimische Fassung oder Rezension der ApcZeph betrachtet werden.

3. Das Sophonias-Zitat bei Clemens Alexandrinus (Stromata V, XI 77, 2) kann einer pseudepigraphischen Sophonias-Apokalypse entstammen. Diese Schrift wäre aber keine griechische Fassung oder Rezension des Buches, das S bruchstückhaft bezeugt. Das Zitat kann nicht mehr unkritisch als zur gleichen ApcZeph wie S gehörig betrachtet werden.[43] (Abgeschlossen am 30.1.1977).

5. Ein Nachtrag.

Recht gute neuere Photographien der Pariser Bibliothèque Nationale erlauben die Entzifferung einer etwas grösseren Textmenge der Seite 2 des sahidischen Fragments, als dies Steindorff möglich war. Einige Worte und Wortsequenzen zeigen eine nahe Verwandtschaft mit einer Passage des achmimischen Textes. Es handelt sich um den Abschnitt

---

[43] Dr. Claudia Nauerth, Heidelberg, danke ich dafür, dass sie die hier behandelten Fragen im Rahmen einer Übung über die Zephanja-Apokalypse im Wintersemester 1976/77 kritisch mit durchdacht hat.

S 2, 25 ff im Vergleich mit A 1, 18 - 2, 1. Da eine weitere Säuberung des Steindorff zufolge verdreckten, aber zugleich sehr brüchigen sahidischen Fragments ohne Gefahr für das Papyrusblatt nach Auskunft der Bibliothèque Nationale nicht möglich ist, habe ich das Angebot der BN wahrgenommen, mir "un cliché sous rayons ultra-violets et un cliché sous lumière infra-rouge" anzufertigen. Das Ergebnis steht zZt noch aus. Vielleicht aber wird dadurch noch etwas mehr Text lesbar. Es ist durchaus denkbar, dass unter dieser Voraussetzung das Verhältnis von S zu A noch einmal überprüft werden muss.

INDEX

I. NAG HAMMADI CODICES

I, 2 *The Apocryphon of James*
(*Epistula Jacobi Apocrypha*) 34ff.,
116, 122

2:33,35	40
3:8ff	41
3:17	42
3:28	35,40,41,42
3:32	35,40,41,42
3:36-37	40
4:1-21	40
4:23-6:21	38
4:29-30	38
5:5,6	43
5:19	39
9:25-28	43
9:33	41
10:2	35
10:5-6	41
11:11-14	43
12:30	40
12:39	43
12:39f.	42

I, 3 *The Gospel of Truth*
(*Evangelium Veritatis*) 25, 35, 101,
105f., 116

18:21-25	39
20:11,25-30	39
43:2,22	42

I, 4 *The Treatise on Resurrection*
(*De Resurrectione*)

50:17-18	149

II, 1 *The Apocryphon of John* 1ff., 40,
42, 52, 87, 88, 116
See also III, 1; IV, 1; BG 8502,2

1:30-2:9	4
2:14f.	150
5:9	151
6:8	151
9:25-10:28	10
61:17-62:15	32
62:24-34	32

II, 2 *The Gospel of Thomas* 35, 42, 67,
68, 73, 74, 101, 103, 109

log. 1/2	68
log. 2/3	41
log. 12	122

II, 3 *The Gospel of Philip* 109, 116

59:2-4	121

II, 4 *The Hypostasis of the Archons* 7,
22, 64, 76, 87, 109

87 (135 Bullard):6-9	21
90 (138):29	104
92 (140):27	104
94 (142):5-19	21
94 (142):7-23	8
94 (142):17	104
95 (143):4-8	32

II. PAPYRUS BEROLINENSIS 8502   1, 2, 4, 9, 52

III. OTHER GNOSTIC LITERATURE
See also Hermetica; Hippolytus; Irenaeus

IV. MANICHAICA

V. OLD TESTAMENT

VI. APOCRYPHA AND PSEUDEPIGRAPHA

VII. NEW TESTAMENT

VIII. NEW TESTAMENT APOCRYPHA

IX. PAPYRI AND OTHER DOCUMENTS

X. ANCIENT AUTHORS AND OTHER SOURCES

XI. MODERN SCHOLARS